ISBN 978-1-332-34565-6
PIBN 10316886

Similar Books Are Available from
www.forgottenbooks.com

Gladys C. Welman

LORDS AND LADIES OF THE
ITALIAN LAKES

ANNA SFORZA (AS SAINT GIUSTINA)
AND ALFONSO D'ESTE

ALESSANDO MORETTO
IMPERIAL MUSEUM, VIENNA

[See page 242

BY

John EDGCUMBE STALEY

AUTHOR OF

"KING RENÉ D'ANJOU AND HIS SEVEN QUEENS," "GUILDS OF FLORENCE," "FAIR
WOMEN OF FLORENCE," "TRAGEDIES OF THE MEDICI," "DOGARESSAS
OF VENICE," "HEROINES OF GENOA AND THE RIVIERAS," ETC

WITH COLOURED FRONTISPIECE AND FORTY-FIVE
OTHER ILLUSTRATIONS

"On dansant tout le jour au soleil!"

LONDON
JOHN LONG, L
NORRIS STREET, HAYMARKET
MCMXII

ANNA SFORZA (AS SAINT GIUSTINA)
AND ALFONSO D'ESTE

ALESSANDRO MORETTO
IMPERIAL MUSEUM, VIENNA

BY

John EDGCUMBE STALEY

AUTHOR OF

KING RENÉ D'ANJOU AND HIS SEVEN QUEENS," "GUILDS OF FLORENCE," "FAIR
WOMEN OF FLORENCE," "TRAGEDIES OF THE MEDICI," "DOGARESSAS
OF VENICE," "HEROINES OF GENOA AND THE RIVIERAS," ETC.

WITH COLOURED FRONTISPIECE AND FORTY-FIVE
OTHER ILLUSTRATIONS

" On dansant tout le jour au soleil !"

LONDON

JOHN LONG, LIMITED

NORRIS STREET, HAYMARKET

MCMXII

TO

THE MEMORY OF MY PARENTS

THOMAS AND FINETTA STALEY

CONTENTS

LIST OF ILLUSTRATIONS

PREFACE

" LORDS and Ladies of the Italian Lakes !"—an author could not wish for a more delightful subject nor a more attractive title for his book. Few portions of this glorious old globe's surface are as lovely as the Lakeland of Lombardy. Nature and Art have gone revelling together there.

Charming as is my subject from every point of view, it has, alas ! narrow and jealous limitations. Lombardy is full from end to end of ancient castles and modern villas, each at one time or another the happy home or bustling world of famous Lords and Ladies. Around and about them all are woven webs, dark and light, of stories romantic and pathetic, humorous and tragic. To recount them all would require a good-sized library of books. I have, consequently, made choice of persons and places, great and small, fairly representative of the legions of my Lords and Ladies. Some of them are already known, but many are new aspirants for the admiration of English readers.

Fifty years ago (1861) my parents first visited the Italian Lakes ; their travellers' tales interested me vastly as a boy. Perhaps they gave me the "idea" of this volume. At all events, my own frequent saunterings in those beauty-spots and intercourse with some of my "Lords and Ladies" developed it.

In the compilation of my manuscript I have found very much useful matter in the following publications : "Ville e Castelli d' Italia-Lombardia e Laghi," published at Milan ; "Lombard Studies," by Countess Martinengo Cesaresco ; "Pallanza Antica e Pallanza Moderna," by Signore Agostino Viani · "The Lake of Como," by the Rev. T. W. M. Lund ; and frequent articles in "*Archivio Storico Lombardo.*" To the various authors I now offer my sincere acknowledgments and thanks.

With respect to the illustrations in this volume, I have had to content myself with likenesses of the more generally known and accessible Lords and Ladies. In every castle and villa are numerous family portraits, and other portraits, too ; but access to them for reproduction has not been granted by their owners.

I have given many quotations in Italian, some I have translated in footnotes : but I have left the quaint folklore dialect to speak for itself.

EDGCUMBE STALEY.

INTRODUCTION

READER fair and critic dubious, I beg to introduce to you my " Lords and Ladies of the Italian Lakes."

The North Italian Lakeland is beautifully illustrated by a strip of old rose point pillow-lace of Venice or Milan. The topmost border, worked in vandykes of twisted knots, stands very reasonably for the serrated ranges of the Southern Alps. The field of the *reticella*, or network, exhibits the plain of Lombardy, with its free rolling uplands. The open-work of the lace, artistically irregular in design, represents the lacustrine system, with its twenty lakes or more, of every conceivable shape and size. The more closely worked arabesques and scrolls are like ranges of hill and dale, where streams, rushing swiftly or gently purling, meander naturally. The little crowns or loops, in raised work, innumerable, are the thousand and one castles and villas of the " Lords and Ladies of the Lakes." The starlike or floral adornments in the network web of lace tell of Lombard towns and villages, scattered here and there. The coronals and wreaths of the imbricated edge are the great cities of the plain—Novara, Como, Milan, and Treviglio; Bergamo, Brescia, Mantua, and Verona!

This may be deemed an arbitrary and fanciful comparison; nevertheless, it is as worthy of acceptance as that better-known metaphor which likens Lombardy to an artichoke, the leaves of which were eaten off in turn by the valiant Lords of Piedmont. The root of the succulent vegetable is Milan, the chief capital of the territory with which this volume is concerned.

Whilst necessarily much that is topographical and artistic in interest and generally well known has been laid under contribution,—for this work is a sort of " Guide " to the Italian Lakes,—the aim in view has rather been to revivify those ravishing scenes and splendid villas, with the persons and doings of some of their most fascinating occupants. Two thousand years, from the times of the Greeks, Romans, and Lombards, to the days of the makers of Modern Italy, have rolled leisurely across the most famous pageant-ground in Europe. Go where you will in Lombardy, and you will not fail to note Grecian place-names, Roman inscriptions, and Lombard figures.

The Lombards made Pavia their first capital, but the Franks, two hundred years later, preferred Charlemagne's city of Milan, whose rulers and people sided with the Guelphs. Families came and families went,—the stronger and more unscrupulous always in the front,—until the Visconti discomfited all rivals, and became masters of all Lombardy. Their predominance lasted all but two centuries, and then the Sforzas ruled for one hundred years. France, Spain, and Austria fought for and gained the mastery in turn, each leaving characteristics of their dominion. Napoleon Buonparte created the first kingdom of Italy,—Lombardy, Venice, South Tirol, Istria, the Emilia, and the Marches,—with Milan for his capital. By the Peace of Zurich in 1859 Lombardy was ceded to Napoleon III., who transferred it to Sardinia in exchange for Savoy and Nice. Thus the cross of the House of Savoy rose triumphant over all the peninsula, and the Lords and Ladies of the Lakes became subjects of King Victor Emmanuel with the rest of the people of all Italy.

The itinerary of this book's pilgrimage through the Italian Lakeland opens upon the southern banks of Lake Maggiore with the blessing of San Carlo Borromeo at Arona. Including a brief visit to the idyllic lake of Orta, it carries us right up to Locarno, with time for meditation in the Church of the Madonna del Sasso. Thence to Lugano we fare, with her lake and guardian mountains, and to Varese and her chain of charming lakelets—

2

Biandrono, Monate, and Comabbio. Lake Como, the most beautiful of all, is the third stage of the progress; and then Lecco and the Brianza, with her cincture of lovely little lakes — Annone, Pusiano, Segrino, Alserio, and Montorfano—call us on our way to the Castle of Milan.

Fairy Lake Iseo and the captivating villages of the Bergamesque and Brescian Alps, and their rivers,—flowing through the plains of Lombardy,— lead into the last stage in the pilgrimage, the Lake of Garda, the grandest of all the lakes of Northern Italy. Upon the waters of these lakes, under the shady trees upon their banks, and in and out of the castles and villas, jotted sumptuously everywhere, " Lords and Ladies of the Lakes " from all the towns and cities of the Lombardy have foregathered, grimaced and postured, flirted, warred and died. Every village and hamlet has its story, every church and college its traditions, and the waters, mountains, and pastures have tales to tell of the romantic past.

The headings of the chapters of this volume are of classical nomenclature, and the names suggest a fantasy,—quaint and beautiful,—the ascription or dedication of each principal lake to the patronage of a resplendent goddess of mythology. Maggiore —" Verbano "—becomes the *studiolo* of Minerva ; Lugano—" Ceresio "—the harvest-home of Ceres ;

Varese—"Astræa"—the milky way of the Pleiades; Como—"Lario"—the boudoir of Venus; Lecco and the Brianza the hunting-glade of Diana; Iseo the dreamland of Psyche; and Garda—"Benaco"—the throne-room of Juno. This is not, after all, only a passing fancy; for, fortunately enough, in vindication of my fantasy, the environment of each lake exactly matches the attributes of each goddess in the cycle.

By way of further " Introduction " to the subject-matter of this book, and to expand a certain reference in the " Preface," the following quotations from " Autumn Rambles or Fireside Recollections," written by my mother, and published in 1863, are offered reverently :

" Entering the valley of the Maira, it appeared to be a marshy district. Lago di Riva, a picturesque little lake, surrounded by mountains, was soon in sight. At first we fancied this expanse of water must be a portion of Lake Como, but, passing under some tunnels excavated in the rock, we came upon an extensive plain or morass over which pestilence and malaria reign. Here the great road to the Stelvio branches off, and shortly we reached Colico, a small village, where we left the diligence; and, losing no time, made our way to the steamer, which was waiting at the pier-head to convey us to Como.

" On board we found a number of Sardinian troops in picturesque uniforms, and we were quite enlivened by the strains of their military band. . . . As we approached Bellagio, the hills bordering the lake were clothed with walnut and chestnut trees ; at their base nestled in profusion quaint villages with their tall white campanile churches. Many of the houses were most pictorial in external adornment, for the walls were covered with paintings of the gayest and grandest colouring, producing, however, in the distance a rich and novel effect. . . .

" At Bellagio, also, the rain descended in torrents. We were compelled to seek shelter in the cabin, and content ourselves with watching the deep blue waters from the small loophole windows ; and, by way of variety, we partook of a most wretched dinner. Truly there is only ' a step from the sublime to the ridiculous !' At Bellagio we heard of the arrest of Garibaldi, in whose movements (rash as they were) we could not help being deeply interested. Upon landing at Como, we made the best of our way to the Hotel del' Angelo, a comfortable building with balconies and terraces overlooking the lake ; but not waiting to explore the city in the unfavourable state of the weather, we determined to push on to Milan.

" In passing through the fertile plains of Lombardy, we noticed the luxuriant growth of the mulberry-trees, and how that beautiful villas, gardens, and cultivated fields gave a lifelike appearance to the scene. . . . Long before we arrived at Milan, the magnificent Duomo,—a mass of dazzling white marble,—appeared in the distance. . . . Driving to our hotel, we were charmed with the noble aspect of the city,—the streets spacious and the houses well built—all characteristic of wealth and comfort. . . . The Milanese ladies have much grace in their carriage, and wear black lace veils, arranged with taste, something in the Spanish mantilla style. . . . The Milanese are an excitable people, and one circumstance was a little symptomatic of their character. We saw written upon the walls of the principal thoroughfare : ' *A Morte Napoleone !*' . . .

" Having visited, examined, and admired the principal places of interest, we decided to return to Como. It is such a very quaint-looking town, and the natives are famed for their perseverance and industry. . . . The weather was glorious, and we were longing to feast upon the beauties of the exquisite scenery. . . . We seemed to be moving between banks clothed with olives, and vines, and orchards, embowered in trees, amongst which stood villas, with their gardens, fountains, and orange-trees. The sky above was a celestial blue, the water beneath clear as crystal. . . . As we approached Menaggio the sun beamed forth with delicious radiance, and, landing, we secured places in an open diligence for Porlezza. Before starting, we rambled about, and were interested with the manner in which the women were spinning. The flax is pulled to pieces without the aid of machinery, and the thread spun in the most primitive method. . . . Bellagio and the Lake of Lecco appeared in the distance, and the landscape seemed to be clothed with magical loveliness. . . . Embarking at Porlezza, we commenced our exploration of this exquisite sheet of water. Before landing at Lugano, we made arrangements with a coachman to drive us in an open carriage to Luino.

" Leaving Lugano, we made a considerable circuit, the views becoming very grand. . . . Vegetation here has attained a climax of richness and profusion, stamping upon the entire landscape a serenity and luxuriance perfectly bewitching. . . . Evening closing in, flashes of lightning and peals of thunder betokened the approach of a violent storm, but we were fortunate enough to reach the hotel at Luino without any rain . . . Lago Maggiore, the lake of renown, spreading its deep blue waters at our feet."

The year of my parents' visit to Italian Lake-

land was one of dire disaster for the United Kingdom, when all who could had to put their hands
in their pockets and open the instruments of aid
to assist the cotton operatives rendered destitute
by the lamentable civil war in the United States
of North America. In her "Preface" to "Autumn
Rambles," my mother, who was in delicate health,
says : " Being unable to join the devoted band of
ladies—true Sisters of Charity—an idea struck me
that I might turn to a charitable account a dis-
jointed diary I had kept during a recent visit to
the Continent " The book was published in due
course, and the proceeds vastly exceeded all ex-
pectation, for a sum of £50 was handed over to
the Cotton Operatives' Relief Fund.

*   *   *   *   *

Of each " Lady of the Lakes," Raffaelo Gual-
terotto's Tuscan poem of Nature and Love may
well be sung :

" Oh, ever pleasant and stately groves,
    Your scented foliage spread—cool and green,
      That our sweet Lady, 'neath your screen,
    On her couch of Love may safe repose.
      Link'd boughs of pine and beech, tall and fair,
    Green laurel, sweet myrtle, shady oak
      Shield from harm her golden locks of hair,
    Guard her form from noontide's fiery stroke."

LORDS AND LADIES OF THE ITALIAN LAKES

CHAPTER I

"VERBANO"

THE LAKE OF MAGGIORE

"Verbano,"—the classic style "*Lacus Verbanus*,"—has clung through all the ages to the chief of Lombardy's lordly lakes. Its shape is courtly—a bended knee: the token of worship, beauty, wisdom, and circumstance. In the Court of High Parnassus one divine personality has very specially all these attributes—Minerva, the goddess of the thew and wit of men. Upon her majestic head, upon her proud breast, and upon her supple hands, she wears the precious jewels of prudence, courage, and perseverance—Arbitress of mundane affairs, most wise of deities. Well may we see the derivation of " Verbano " in the classic name " Minerva ": Verbano, the watery domain of enterprise—the " *Studiolo* " of the Muses.

The aspect of the Goddess is enigmatic, and of

23

her inscrutable wisdom Dante Alighieri has spoken in " Il Paradiso " ·

> " Sanz esserimi profetta
> Da te la voglio lui discerno meglio,
> Che tu qualunque costa t' è più certa
> Perch' io la veggio vel verace speglio,
> Che fadi tè pareglio all' altre cosa
> E nulla face lui t' sè pareglio." *
>
> (Canto XXVI.).

Thus may we predicate of " Verbano " too, and her inexplicable charms which open and delight every sense. The Goddess of Maggiore is, however, no languorous mermaid—of such an one and her wiles Goethe wrote mysteriously :—

> " Half she drew him,
> Half sank he in,
> And never more was seen."

Minerva or " Verbano " enchants with words of wisdom and emboldens all who take heed.

" Maggiore " is quite a modern name— " Greater." Great she is in aqueous area, great in picturesque beauty, great in seductive charm, and great in historical romance.

* " No need thy will be told, which, I, unknown,
Better discern than thou, whatever thing
Thou holdst most certain : that will I see
In wisdom—Truth's mirror—comprehending,
By self-enlightenment all things enlightening,
All is open mind and heart."

Suga.

Vis Bruthie Ulecenus.

Scitia.

Intellegetia.

Circuipectio.

"BRUZIO VISCONTI" (ALLEGORICAL GROUP OF THE FOUNDERS OF THE FAMILY)

From a Coloured Print in "Famiglie Celebre Italiana," by P. G. Litta

To face page 24

Upon the opal-hued mirror of her wide expanse are reflected the lights and shadows of the sumptuous pageants of Lombardy and Milan. Her lovely features and her comely form are worthy, too, of the painter's canvas and the poet's song. She arrests the hurrying feet of travellers from afar, ever farther on their way by her lacustrine sisters—beauteous, like herself—whilst she tells her fascinating stories of the past.

Lepontini, Etruscans, Celts, and Romans, have all left marks ethnologically and archæologically in race and ruin. Ostrogoths and Lombards made the great reservoir of the Ticino their rendezvous in struggles for supremacy. Theodoric, Charlemagne and Alberic have, with their hosts, crossed and recrossed the ample water. Towers and castles sprang up on spur and spit, and feudal rule was absolute. Guelphs and Ghibellines struggled on lake and shore, and prolonged their feud when checked elsewhere; every town became a republic for the nonce, and rose in conflict with its neighbours. Dominating clans and families farmed the resources of the Lakeland, and fought with one another—Del Castello, Barbavara, Torriani, Visconti, Sforza, and Borromei. Good blood was shed plentifully, and crimsoned by it were the green-blue ripples, and dyed the shingles of the beach. The last-named family at length became champions and lords of Maggiore and its valley, and defenders of men's rights against the last desperadoes of the Dark Ages, the Mazzarditi of the Swiss frontier.´

The destinctive marks of Maggiore are her exquisite islets in the lake ; her splended range of mountain guardians, capped with snow ; and the pulsating movements of her ever-changing currents — these topographically ; economically the independent spirit of her peoples, their acute touch with modern movements, and their prosperity. " Maggiore," too, is the name the natives have for the most dreaded tempests which, in some years, lash the water to a maelstrom, and link earth and heaven in a consuming deluge, wherein things of man and man himself are annihilated.

I.

Pallanza is, from many points of view, the sovereign town of Lago Maggiore. Arona, Intra, and Locarno, across the Swiss border, may not grant her the distinction. Rivalries are inscrutable. Without wasting time in argument, it may be safely asserted that the life and soul of splendid " Verbano " are most vividly expressed at " *Pallanza la Graciosa.*"

On the fall of the Roman Empire, Pallanza was

conquered by the ubiquitous Lombards. Charlemagne made his North Italian home at the Castle
of Saint Angelo, on the fortified islet of San
Giovanni, and gave this desirable possession to
Bishop Luitardo, who was the travelling diocesan
of the Lakelands. He in time bequeathed the
castle, island, and the church, which he built, to
the Bishop of Novara in perpetuity. The good
Bishop's bequest, however, was annulled by
Frederic Barbarossa, who invested Giovanni del
Castello,—the commander of his Lombard contin-
gent of military rallies,—with the fief and freehold
rights. This ancient family was subsequently
divided into three principal branches—Barbavare,
Cavalcaselli, and Crollamonti. The Castle of
Pallanza, now a negligible ruin, within the grounds
of Villa Griffini, was built by the elder branch
for the defence of the rights of possession against
the claims of the Bishops of Novara. Meanwhile,
Pietro Cavalcasello, who had been chosen *Podestà*,
or mayor, of the rapidly growing town of Pallanza,
led the townfolk in an alliance with the inhabitants of Vercelli, and Lodi, and the valley of the
Ossola, in a league against clerical encroachment.
Times out of mind town, castle, churches, and
convents were sacked and burnt, and then for a
century the Barbavare held the Lord-Para-
mountcy of the commune. A still more powerful

family now came into conflict with the ruling race
—the Visconti of Milan—and drove them, men
and women, out, pacifying the people by a charter,
which constituted Pallanza a free town, in feu
neither to Pope nor Emperor. The last Visconto,
Duke Filippo Maria, in 1422 granted to his faithful
seneschal, Francesco Castiglione, the title and
rights of Count of Pallanza, and with these, quaint
powers—to legitimize children born in the commune out of marriage ; to grant degrees to doctors
and notaries ; and, as Captain-General, to levy
toll on all vessels passing up and down the lake.
The Castiglioni were an ancient Pallanza family.
Charles V., in 1541, named them the first family in
Lombardy, and created Pietro and Bartolommeo,
the two heads, Counts Palatine of the Roman
Empire. In the meantime the Sforzas of Milan
had succeeded to the possessions and honours of
the Visconti ; but their intrusion was resented by
the Borromei, and again the land and lake were
plunged in warfare, until Pallanza was again
acknowledged a sovereign - city under her own
Count and Captain-General of the Lake.

During all these commotions and vicissitudes,
many distinguished men made their marks upon
the " Roll of Fame," and many attractive women
graced the streets and houses—true " Lords and
Ladies of the Lake." Such were Francesco

Morizzia and Romerio Pozzoli, historians, Nicolò
Regna, Giovanni Morizzia, Giovannino Viani,
Gian Pietro Bianchini, and Gian Antonio Varnei,
champions of liberty; with Andrea Baglione,
Antonio Giacobino, Giacomo Ruffini, and Angelo
Cadolini — benefactors and administrators — the
last named preconized in the Cardinalate by
Pope Gregory XVI. The "Roll" may be ex-
ploited for two centuries more with profit and
instruction; indeed, Pallanza was recognized as
the nursery of literature and science. In 1603
she was called "a very ancient town, inhabited
by a goodly number of gentlemen, scholars, and
rich merchants." Bologna, Milan, Genoa, Venice,
Rome, and Naples, all felt the impress of talented
Pallanzaese. The fame of her schools, the renown
of her liberties, and the enterprise of her sons,
kept the flame and fame of the "fair city of
Verbano," as she was called, brightly illuminated
in every walk of human enterprise. Ascerbo Morizzia, writing his "Memorie" in 1603, says : "The
merchants of the noble town of Pallanza have now
to consider how best to hold a general fair to
accommodate the multitudes of peoples who con-
gregate in her marts, especially from distant
places, to buy and sell every conceivable thing
needful for human life, and, I may add," he very
quaintly says, "for eternity as well. . . " The

town is the granary of Lombardy, and of the
Swiss lords on the other side of the mountains. . . .
Cattle and horses are brought from the lands of
the Teuton, and with them come many crafty
dealers. . "

An amusing and perfectly characteristic anec-
dote of the time and dominion of Francesco
Sforza II. is quite apropos of the commercial
instinct of the Pallanzaese. It runs as follows :
"Battista Bertolotto, a member of a well-to-do
family and a leading citizen of Pallanza, was
one day in the cloth market of Milan, where he
boasted, not wisely, but perhaps truly, that he
could cover the Bay of Pallanza with scarlet noble
cloth ! The Duke heard of this rash statement,
and finding, by inquiry, that the man really was a
wealthy merchant, he sent for him. After asking
him about his business house and his business
methods, he naïvely proposed that he should, to
show his munificence and loyalty, undertake the
restoration of the Vercelli tower of the Castello
of Pallanza. Bertolotto never dreamt that the
Duke was in serious mood, but regarded the sug-
gestion as a compliment and a joke, and began
gracefully to deprecate the flattering proposal.
One look at Sforza's face was enough to disabuse
the merchant's mind of pleasantry ; for, with a
sardonic smile, and in a rasping voice, the Duke

repeated his proposal as a command. Kneeling, he kissed the Sovereign's ring, and professed himself honoured by the commission. Back he went with a sorrowful heart to his home on Verbano, and began to carry out Duke Francesco's order; but, as he progressed with the unwelcome work, more and more stringent were the orders from Milan. Certain architects were to be employed; their plans were to be approved by the ducal council, a certain kind of costly stone was indicated for use, and, to add to the poor man's perplexities, he was ordered to pay into the ducal exchequer a good round sum of money, by way of security that the work should be well done and finished to the Duke's satisfaction. Bertolotto resigned himself to fate; he made no more wild boastings, and to recoup his outlay he sagaciously advanced the retail prices of his goods, and raised the market against the ducal buyers. In the midst of his worries he put up on the fountain basin outside his palace a strange device—a human heart and a money-bag crowned with a ducal coronet, and under it the suggestive motto, 'I do not despair!'"

The tower which Bertolotto built,—called by the people of Pallanza "*Torrione il Pallanzotto*,"—stood well the test of the conditions of its construction, and four hundred years of fierce cold *tramontana* and burning hot *iverna* did it little damage. In 1848 frenzied hands of revolution demolished it, and not a stone remains to-day to mark the tower of Bertolotto's pride.

Spanish, French, and Austrian overlords of Lombardy have in turn traversed the piers and streets of Pallanza, robbing where they listed, and grinding down the inhabitants. To these scenes of tyranny, family feuds and religious rivalries have added categories of misfortunes ; but Pallanza has survived the hard knocks of the past, and still is " *Regina di Verbano* "—her people the proudest of all the lake - dwellers, lording themselves, as did their ancestors in the good old times long past.

One of Pallanza's most bitter inner squabbles still divides the population. In 1822 Cardinal Morozzo was called upon to arbitrate between the claims of Pallanza and the neighbouring town of Suna, to the sanctuary Church of La Madonna di Campania, situated between the two rival communities, at the foot of Monte Rosso. For generations each town claimed the privilege of the Sunday High Mass, and the celebration within the sacred building of their several religious anniversaries. No sooner were the Pallanzese comfortably upon their knees in devout contemplation, than the Sunese clamoured at the portals for their ejection—and *vice versa* ran the riot.

BATH IN THE GARDENS OF A VILLA

PICNIC IN THE FOREST (SEVENTEENTH CENTURY)

Assault and battery became the order of the day, and both sides claimed the victory. The worthy Cardinal devised a quixotic settlement : to Pallanza was alloted the grand Church of San Stefano,—to Suna that of Santa Lucia, whilst the Church of the Madonna was closed to both !

In the Church of San Leonardo is a tablet recording the virtues of one Bernardino Innocenti. The wildest of the wild in youthful days, he was sent as a student to the University of Padua, " to cure the devil in him '" Ringleader in all deeds of daring and turbulence, he was ultimately locked up with three other incorrigibles in the Castle guardhouse, and fed on spare food and daily whipped. Bernardino did not like this way of going on at all, and by some means or other he bribed his guardians, and made his escape to Bologna, where, apparently, he turned over a new leaf, for he took his degree of doctor within a twelvemonth, and was welcomed back at Pallanza by his doting parents and his old schoolmaster. In time the renegade became " the legal oracle of Lombardy," and King Philip IV. of Spain appointed him Fiscal Advocate for the entire Duchy of Milan.

Pallanza, from her administrative and military pre-eminence, no less than from the enterprise and opulence of her citizens, became the arbiter of fashion and the leader in refinement among the communes of the lake, and among the prosperous inhabitants of the adjacent valleys. Then, too, the distance from Milan and the other cities of Lombardy, and an inherent hatred and contempt of the Novarese, elevated the lacustrine capital to an autocratic position. To be sure, her travelled merchants brought home foreign ways and foreign things, but the Pallanzese looked askance on out-landish fashions, and stood by their own. In the architecture of her buildings and in the domestic arrangement of her households she held a uni-quity quite her own, and these are also traits of the native of to-day. The " *Spirito del Campanile* " was quite as rife in proud Pallanza as in fascinating Florence : it is so still !

Marriages were almost exclusively confined to youths and maidens native born. Brides and grooms were, as a general rule, baptized, con-firmed, and wedded in the selfsame churches. This had, to be sure, its disadvantages—first of all in the too intimate mixture of like blood, and then in the inconvenience of limited nomenclature. As a rule, every Pallanzese was known, not by his or her patronymic, but by a nickname. The law of primogeniture was very strictly observed, younger children taking, so to speak, pot-luck. Parents were accorded titles of nobility—" My

good Lord Father," and " My Lady Mother," were
in every child's mouth, rich and poor alike. Very
courtly manners were cultivated within the home
circle. Girls were required to curtsy lowly each
morning and evening to the parents, and to kiss
the wedding-ring of their mother. Boys obeyed
a still stricter rule of etiquette, for in addition to
reverential greetings, they were expected to bow
low to both their parents before and after common
meals and when they left the room.

With respect to sumptuary laws, the century
marked the vogue, not the year or month, and their
distinctive costumes became fixed fashions,—characteristic of the people of Pallanza,—when other
communities observed varieties of modes. Menfolk of all conditions had smooth-shaven faces and
well cut and powdered crops of hair. Three-
cornered hats, not round *berrette,* were rigorously
worn ; and tunics and hose were starched, embroidered, and adorned with parti-coloured ribbons.
Tall hats were not introduced till after the great
French Revolution .at the end of the eighteenth
century ; then, too, the fashion of heavy whiskers
and long hair came in, and big white cravats
muffled up the manly throat. The fair sex had
also their conventions in the laws of dress. They
wore, when under middle age, very little but thin
gauze fichus over their bare bosoms, but their

bodices were cut stiffly, and their skirts were fully
gathered and woven of stiff brocade of native manufacture or of stout woollen cloth. Jewels they
wore sparingly, but almost every woman weighed
down her ear-lobes with massive hoops of gold,
and a gold chain and pendant were added on
festivals and at receptions.

Religious observances were scrupulously celebrated. A son or daughter, or a dependant,
absent from Mass on Sunday was severely repri-
manded. The names of such citizens,—and there
was no respect of persons—who failed to hand to
the *Pievano*, or parish priest,—when he made his
yearly visit of domiciliary benediction on Ascension
Day,—their certificate of Communion at Easter,
were published from the pulpit and posted on the
church-doors. Members of Church fraternities
and guilds went up and down the streets with
stout staves in their hands before and during
Church services to hustle truants and loiterers of
all ages into church, and, when inside, sleepy wor-
shippers were aroused to devotional attention by
sound bumps upon their heads and backs ! All
worthy men competed at processions, in and out
of church, for the honour of bearing the poles of
the sacramental canopy and the crucifixes, and
banners of the festival. This custom is still observed in and about Pallanza. Places of business

and shops remained closed during Mass. Shoe-
makers only were allowed to work on Sundays,
and then with half-closed doors and for half the
day. This custom gained the designation of
Mezzanta (Half-and-Half !). Mondays were allotted
to slaves of the last for rest and prayer by way of
compensation.

The Pallanzese were great sticklers for the daily
siesta. Winter as well as summer found the menfolk, at least, sprawling indolently or cosily
chatting under the thick foliage of the chestnuts
and limes which had been planted for this express
purpose in a circle by the port, and called after
the Barbavara benefactor of the past. Gambling,
characteristically enough, formed the occupation
of the less sleepily inclined, and all games of
chance, — bar the gesticulatory *Mora*, — were
played craftily. Other games, too, of course,
were the fashion : bowls for the men and boys,
ninepins for the girls. These were enjoyed in the
courtyards around the esplanade. Whilst the men
on Sundays abstained from their sporting proclivities openly, the women of the town sauntered
to and fro displaying their best gowns, dyed by
preference in brilliant colours—scarlet, apple-
green, pistachio, and saffron. Blue was not in
favour ; it was the common colour of the coarse
linen cloth worn on week-days. Water-parties were

arranged to beauty-spots not far away—more frequently than not upon one of the Borromean Islands. The gondolas in use had gilded prows, and were covered with gay awnings and carried floating bannerets. These aquatic diversions were shared in by all the notables as well as by the ordinary citizens ; indeed, pride of family was displayed by " Lords and Ladies of the Lake," for each noble vied with his peer in the splendour of his craft, the costliness of its decoration, and the magnificence of his guests. Musicians, too, and entertainers of all kinds were afloat to amuse the company and gather in silver harvests. The proud Borromei in particular made brave shows on Sundays and festivals. Their high-decked gondola was, in fact, a *bucintoro,* or state barge, very beautifully carved in dark wood veneers, and thickly gilded. It was propelled by twenty oarsmen arrayed in the family colours and bearing the family badge upon their breasts and backs. The canopies were of silk with gold and silver fringes, and heraldic ensigns were borne aloft on gilded poles. The aim of all these gay water-parties was, of course, alfresco refreshment and amusement, and here citizen rivalled citizen in the gorgeousness of the display. It was little trouble to carry upon the festive craft silver and gold cups and brilliant crystal beakers. Flowers, too, formed delightful accessories to the feasts, placed among the viands and worn by the company.

One game there was—the game of games—*Pallone*, played by every sort of man. In this the woman's part was as spectator only. The pitch was the piazza by the harbour. Each festival the *Podestà* or *Sindaco* sent early intimation to all inhabitants in the square at what hour, before or after Vespers, the game would begin. Windows and architectural ornaments were ordered to be netted, or if the windows opened into rooms, to set them well back, as no claim was allowed for broken glass. The young men of the highest families were usually the players, arrayed in short tight drawers, bare-legged, with well-laced shoes. Their tunics were also tight to the body, and particoloured ; their heads were bare. The best-developed figures always, of course, gained the approbation of the fair sex, and the nimbler they were so much greater was the applause. Drawn games were inadmissible : the players played to a finish, sometimes after dusk,—when not infrequently they came to blows. If anybody got an unwelcome knock with the hard wooden ball, he was an object of derision, and had to rub the bruise in as he felt inclined !

The Pallanzese were fond, like other folk, of theatrical displays—not merely the well stage-

managed spectacle-plays and mysteries, but scenes
of humour, tragedy, and burlesque. At the end
of the sixteenth century a modest little theatre
was erected in Via Ruga, wherein gentlemen
visitors at the great houses within reach—and
sometimes the ladies, too,—gave attractive performances. The building had no boxes ; it had a
pit and gallery. The families of Innocenti and
Azari in particular were famous for their theatrical
displays, which were entitled "*Le Gelosie di
Zelinda e Lindoro*"—The Rivals, or Zelinda and
Lindoro—"*Il Laccio Amoroso*"—The Snare of
Love—and so forth. These performances and
concerts were generally given in behalf of local
charities. At the end of Via Ruga was a building
called "*Il Campidoglio*," a sort of Club House,
where, on winter evenings, the "Lords and Ladies,"
and the chief citizens, met for social intercourse,
gaming, dancing and other indoor recreations.
Within the entrance, on the ground-floor, was what
we now call a "restaurant,"—backed by a commodious kitchen,—where, beyond the long tables
spread with cleanest napery and furnished with
every adjunct of a comfortable meal, crackled and
blazed the great open fire, with its revolving spits
of roasting dainties. At the principal table in the
centre were high-backed chairs of circumstance
for the *Podestà* and magistrates and other men of

THE GAME OF SCARTINO

eminence. Disputes were frequent and abrupt; sometimes they turned upon the important question as to whose duty it was to poke the embers and put on more wood! The talk among the seniors was of politics and commerce; the young fellows girded at one another for success or failure in love-affairs and game records. Madonnas, with their daughters strictly under charge, were welcomed to postprandial conversation, and whilst the elder men entertained one another's wives, the maidens were drawn on one side by the young gallants. The older ladies favoured quiet games at cards, but the marriageable girls preferred the more suitable pastime of forfeits for kisses. Sometimes the curfew sounded whilst all were merry in their cups or absorbed in love passages, and then there was general commotion. Sometimes, too, of course, the evening's entertainments ended in quarrels and challenges to fight,—the turbulent spirit of the old Pallanzese was never laid.

In summer-time the *Campidoglio* was still the rendezvous for town amusement, but the company disposed themselves on benches outside and in the street. The ladies of the town in particular were habituées of these social gatherings. Sometimes their pique was excited by the jokes and gibes of mischievous youths looking out for pretty girls. There the elders sat and sat till past the bell of the *Ave Maria*, chatting and disputing, with stocking, garment, or fancy-work in hand. Quite the most ancient dames dropped their rosary beads when the gossip became too acrimonious or indelicate! The younger men and maids, behind their betters' backs, strummed and hummed love-ditties and flung chestnut-cobs at one another on the sly. On fine evenings the rasping by a violin or guitar of a dance measure made nimble toes move in unison, and round dances were seen on every side. The waltz, however, was taboo in public, but danced it was no less, and with other idylls made life pass merrily. In September, when the hemp was ingathering, the lads had a very favourite pastime. Pulling out the strands of the plant and twisting them into a lengthy rope, they lighted one end and trailed it blazing across the street, compelling all whom they met to leap well over, Many good-natured spills were the consequence, and high jumps for the girls were special features of the sport!

Amid all this licence and merriment some unwary souls were sure to transgress the rules of good behaviour, but for such there was in waiting the worthy *Travaligno*, or sheriff's officer. If a serenader became too noisy and too constant, or a wine-bibber forgot to check his voice and guide his steps, a dark cell awaited him. The next morning he was released, with a paternal warning, a wiser and a cooler man. Carnival, however, was a season of relaxation from legal obligations, and then all the world ran riot. At Pallanza the masquerades most in vogue were of the nature of satires on local topics and mimicry of local magnates. Sometimes the masqueraders came to blows; indeed, in 1792,—when a party from Intra met a similar company of Pallanzese,—local rivalries led to blows, and many a ruffian youth came by his death in consequence. The last day of the Carnival witnessed scenes of indiscriminate merriment and wild frolic. Every man twisted his girl, and others too, around the *"Albero della Libertà,"* The Tree of Liberty,—as it was called, a giant chestnut by the quay, and kisses were free for the taking. Men and maids who would not join the fun were chased up steps and yards and beaten. Class distinction disappeared in Carnival. The patrician families of Dognani, Cavallotti, Melzi, Biffi, Cadolino, and the rest, opened wide their doors and welcomed all the world to pot and pan. Fashionable ladies displayed their graces in elegant *minuetti* and *perigordini,*—danced and posed in gorgeous attire,—to all who came to view in the courtyards and at the portals of their palaces; and, be it said quite on the sly, no good-looking youth went away unkissed !

Verily the light-heartedness of most mortals is in exact ratio to their environment. The champagne atmosphere of the Lakeland, the translucency of the air, the beauty of the landscape, and the generous warmth of the red-gold sun, make life to be all joy and beauty, with very little time for grumbling and disquietude. The light-hearted Pallanzese called their place of public revelry " *Cuccagna* "—Land of Delights. It was their Paradise, and they were well content. Happy, playful Pallanzaese '

II.

Arona is the base-rock of the romance of Lago Maggiore. She is the leaping-off spot, so to speak, for all who would know the story of "Verbano." With lofty Angera opposite, she is the portal, too, through which all the " Lords and Ladies of the Lake " have come and gone. Before exploring these two fortressed towns on the way from Milan to the lake, we pass Somma Lombardo, on the right bank of the Ticino, with its enormous and venerable cypress nearly one hundred feet in height —perhaps the loftiest tree in Europe. It has witnessed many stirring events, and has cast its shadow over many a deed of love and war. Castello Visconti, fifteen miles from Arona, was built in 1448 by the brothers Francesco and Guido Vis-

conti. The workmen they employed were members of a bodyguard of twenty adherents who were
as well able to give a good account of themselves
in defence of their masters as they were to labour
for them in peaceful projects. Francesco, at the
end of the century, laid out the spacious gardens
which are still the glory of the estate. The old
church of Sant' Agnese has a fresco record of the
marriage of Ermo Visconti and Maria Bianca
Scapardona. Fourteen years of happy wedded
life were vouchsafed this notable couple—a span
far longer than the wont in those times of intrigue
and frenzy. Richly dowered by her consort, she,
however, promptly forgot his love, and within a
year of Ermo's death wantonly married Count de
Challant, a Savoyard gallant, who took her off to
his castle in the Val d' Avola, far from her friends
and home. The freedom to which Ermo Visconti
had accustomed her was curtailed, and de Challant
guarded his fascinating spouse so closely that she
was little better than prisoner at his will. This
life of captivity was not a bit to the liking of the
Countess, and within a year she fled to Pavia,
where were many old friends, and where she had
inherited a considerable property. Among her
intimates were Ardizzione Valperga di Masimo,
Pietro Cardona, and Count Roberto Sansovino.
Not tiring of married life, although it had brought

many sorrows as well as joys, the impressionable
fugitive was sought once more in marriage by
Valperga, whilst Cardona undertook to make
things agreeable with de Challant. Never was
there a worse bargain struck, for *bravi* in de Challant's pay seized the well-meaning go-between,
and instead of despatching him with their knives,
—as they were pledged to do,—they popped the
captive into guard to await their patron's torture-
pleasure. Cardona refused to disclose the where-
abouts of the errant couple, and for his faithfulness
to his friend he lost his life, for de Challant conveyed him to Milan, and there had him beheaded.
What happened to Bianca and her husband
number three, chroniclers have failed to record.
Perhaps their course of true love was rosy ; had it
been thorny, probably we should not have lacked
information !

Not very far away from Castello Visconti, and
west of Milan, was another Visconti mansion,—the
Castello di Benguardo,—built by Filippo Maria
Visconti, near Abbiategrosso, where the Duke
enclosed a deer-park and erected a garden-
pavilion for the entertainment of his mistress,
Agnese del Majne, and there he spent much of
his time divided between devotions to St. Hubert
and to " St. " Cupid. It was ever so among
" Lords and Ladies." All field-sports were Love's

favourite opportunities ! Francesco Sforza rather
brusquely turned out the charmer Agnese, and
gave the castle to Matteo Bolognini, who passed
it on to the family of his wife, the Tolontini.   The
Leyraldi bought it in 1490, and then the Tolontini
reacquired it in 1648.   Many such vicissitudes fell
to the lot of lordly pleasaunces in those times of
change and barter.   The Melzi family had among
their many estates a villa at Somma Lombardo.
It had been originally a religious house of Franciscan friars, founded by Francesco Maria Visconti,
who on his deathbed made a bequest of twelve
hundred *scudi* " for the good of his soul."   One
hundred years later the cloister and the chapel
were destroyed, and the Religious dispersed,
and then Giuseppe Giusti bought the estate on
behalf of the Melzi d' Eril family.   Succeeding
generations of lordly owners were apparently both
secular and given up to frivolities, and regular
and devoted to Church functions.   Well, in life
the evil and the good are blended and inter-
changeable,—and thus this sublunary existence
is a pageantry of humour and pathos, and interesting beyond the dreams and realms of trashy
fiction.

We must not, however, suffer ourselves to par-
ticipate in any more diversions by the way, for
Arona and Angera have opened their gates to

admit us to their joint and severed stories. The former is the most ancient township on Lake Maggiore. Its name is Roman, but its fame Dominican. Then came the warring Visconti and Duke Gian Galeazzo II.; both destroyed and built anew the castle. In 1439 the Borromei became possessed of Arona, its castle and its port, and bore bravely and judicially their title of Counts of Arona. The most famous scion of that great family was born in one of the towers. The room was called the " Chamber of the Four Lakes," for thence might be discerned Maggiore, Monati, Comabbio, and Varese. Carlo Borromeo was born in 1538—he who became the saintly and courageous Archbishop of Milan. His story is too well known to require extended notice here. He is one of the heroes of the Church at large,—the Renaissance patron of Milan. Of the Castle of Arona only ruins covered by evergreen ivy now remain,—but the memory of the great Cardinal lives in what is called " the most eloquent and remarkable work in Italy. The world of Christianity could not wish for a nobler memorial of perfect charity than the splendid statue of Saint Carlo above Arona." Erected in 1624,—along with two fine buildings,—a seminary for priests, with a notable library of rare manuscripts and books, and a church where precious relics of the Saint are treasured—a cast

PALAZZO BORROMEO ISOLA BELLA : GALLERY OF TAPESTRIES

From a Photograph

To face page 48

of his head in wax, his pocket-handkerchief, and pastoral cross in iron, not of precious metal. His primatial cross of rare goldsmith's work and precious gems he sold for the relief of the plague-stricken people of Milan.

One of the most notable works of the great Cardinal was the visitation of all the monasteries and convents of Lombardy immediately after the Council of Trent. He found faith, practice, and morals subverted, and licence, lust, and extravagance unchecked. Among the articles of the Visitation were:—" Each cell shall have a simple crucifix of wood, an " *Agnus Dei*," not of precious metal, one devotional picture, a few religious books simply bound, a table bare of cloth, a wooden bedstead and a hard mattress, a *Prie-Dieu* without adornment, no carpet on the floor, no utensils for drinking, eating, or writing. Nuns are not allowed to keep pet animals, except poultry for their eggs ; they are forbidden the use of mirrors, scents, and essences,—and each must occupy her cell alone. "

These strict but salutary regulations were not held in estimation long, for Giorgio Pallavicini, at the end of the eighteenth century, a clever satirist, records that " sumptuous beds with embroidered window-hangings, and thick expensive carpets, were commonly in use, and the cells were adorned

with silver vases filled with flowers or with hanging lamps of crystal and sensuous pictures of
' Venus,' ' Satyrs,' and other irreligious fads and
fancies."

Canonized in 1610, San Carlo Borromeo speedily
vindicated his right to saintship in miracles wrought
by his efficacy.   One, known to all the lakeside
dwellers and throughout Lombardy, had immediate attestation.   On the evening of December 17,
1630, the house of Signore Giovanni Battista
Cadolino at Pallanza was the scene of a notable
visitation.   A small picture hanging in the family
room representing the Saint with hands joined
together, kneeling before a crucifix, suddenly
exuded a copious shower of tears ! The first
member of the assembled family,—they were
gathered for their midday meal,—who observed
the phenomenon was the youngest daughter of
the house, Maria Elizabetta.   Jumping up suddenly, she cried aloud, " *Uno Miracolo !*" and,
taking down the picture from the wall, she showed
it to each in turn, the while showers of water ran
over her hands to the ground. Among the
assembled children and guests were her brother
Bernardino, her sister Marta, and her Aunt
Madonna Bernardina di Magistrio, her father's
sister. All fell upon their knees and prayed to
San Carlo for instruction what to do. A strange

voice, coming whence they knew not, but at a distance, whispered, " *Alla Cappuccini !*" whose monastery adjoined the parish church of San Leonardo. Young Bernardino, reverently wrapping a silk scarf of his mother's around the weeping picture, bore it reverently, followed by his parents and the rest of the family and their domestics, to the monastery. The Father Superior at once recognized this astounding circumstance as an interposition of San Carlo in answer to devout prayers on behalf of the plague-stricken citizens of the town. Assembling his chapter and the religious communities, a peregrination of the town and suburbs was conducted, he himself carrying the still dripping picture beneath the great processional canopy. Stations were made before every house marked with the dreaded black cross, prayers were said, and hymns were sung, and the fragrance of sweet incense was wafted over the beds of the sufferers. Immediate relief was experienced, and not only such notable people as Signore Massimiliano Viani, Signora Costanza Innocenti, and Madonna Isabella, wife of Tommaso Cadolino, were cured, but the plague was stayed in the most densely populated and most squalid quarters of the town. A *festa* was appointed, and communications were addressed to Rome. The Sacred Congregation approving the testimony of the Cadolino family and the witness of the clergy, ordered the erection of a chapel in connection with the parish church for the worthy conservation of the miraculous picture, and imposed upon the family the honourable task of maintaining the building and the altar in perpetuity. The devout citizens and country-folk flocked in thousands to render homage to their new treasure, praying humbly and gratefully to San Carlo Borromeo, and also to Saints Maximinio, Ippolito, and Bonifazio, whose bones had been buried beneath their altars centuries before.

San Carlo Borromeo was not the only Saint who came to the aid of plague-stricken towns upon Lake Maggiore. In the year 1344 a venerable priest lived as a recluse on one of the spurs of Sasso Ballaro, now called Santa Caterina del Sasso, from the simple sanctuary erected where the good hermit prayed and ruled. His name was Alberto Besozzo of Arolo, belonging to the rich and noble family of that name in Milan. He had been for years busy smuggling goods and robbing folks by excessive usury. One day he was returning from the market of Lesa, some miles down the lake, in a small open boat, when a fierce tempest tossed the water into deadly whirlpools. The frail barque was wrecked upon a sunken rock, and Besozzo, the only survivor, found refuge on a small island

far from land. He took this as an intimation that
Heaven's will required him to renounce his evil
ways, turn penitent, and remain where he had
been cast. Before settling on his island, he returned home, sold all his property, and distributed
the proceeds among the poor. Very soon the
holy man's fame for sanctity reached the farthest
limits of the lake, and penitents thronged his cell
for spiritual counsel. For ten years he remained
in his narrow hermitage, and then, owing to the
influx of visitors, he removed to an inaccessible
peak of the mountains, and there spent his time
in prayer, interceding especially for the sick and
dying of plague and famine. His prayers were so
efficacious, and withal so profitable in a worldly
sense, that with the offerings of the faithful he
built a little chapel near his mountain cell, and
dedicated it to Santa Caterina di Alessandria, the
special intercessor with Heaven for such as were
victims to pestilence. On the day of dedication,
and once every year upon the anniversary, religious processions scaled the lofty mountain to
pay honour to the holy man and to ask his inter-
cession with St. Catherine. This procession,
though curtailed in numbers and less enthusiastic
than at first, still visits the mountain sanctuary
year by year. Blessed Alberto Besozzo died in
1385, passing, as pious souls said, " *in mano degl'*

Angioli."   His epitaph may be read in the mountain chapel :—

> " Qui giace il penitento grand' Alberto,
>   Romito di tal merto
>   Che vivendo godena quà qui in terra
>   Fra gl' Angioli quel ben, che' l' ciel riserva
>   Vive, ma dormirà sino, che' l' sole
>   Cingera questa
>   E poi desto, fra quelle puro forme
>   Del ciel volgera l'Orme."

Under the wooden roof of the gateway of the God's acre are frescoed scenes from the " Dance of Death," wherein the personages are portraits of well-known people of the lake, and the backgrounds of the pictures reproduce the various towns.

The story of Angera is quickly told.   Its castle has been a bone of contention hard and sore. In the thirteenth century the Torriani were its overlords, but that bellicose Archbishop, Ottone Visconti, dispossessed them in 1276.   Giovanni Maria Visconti I. pulled the castle down in 1350, and,—with the like incontinence, that Duke Gian Galeazzo II. displayed at Arona,—rebuilt it immediately. There ought to have been a method in this madness, but nobody has yet discerned it.   One hundred years passed, and witnessed many notable events and entertainments within those frescoed walls, and then, upon the passing of the Visconti, the ambitious Borromei obtained the stronghold. Vitaliano Borromeo assumed the rank of Count ; the Rocca d' Angera is theirs to-day. With rare discernment and munificence the ancient appearance of the castle and its confines has been retained, —antique furniture and ancient curios adorn the rooms, and frescoes and textile hangings present scenes of conflict between the rival Torriani and Visconti. The windows to the west give upon the lake, and in particular upon the islet of San Giovanni, where a holy deacon in early Christian days, Arialdo, was done to death by the heathen Oliva Valvassori, " The Scourge of Angera." Among the " Lords and Ladies of the Lake " who have passed in and out of those massive gateways was Queen Isabella of Spain, one of the ill-fated beauties of the Milanese Court. By the chief portal is a stone incised :—" *Camillus Io : Baptista. —Hon : Romei,*" and here we have the derivation of the patronymic Borromeo.

Taking our way somewhat erratically before giving ourselves away to the alfresco delights of the Borromean Islands, we may pass a pleasant time by the waters of two minor lakes of Lombardy, strictly of Savoy ; and very beautiful they are— Mergozzo and Orta. The former has, alas ! lost much of its beauty and renown on account of the quarries and lime-pits which have made its banks

utilitarian feeders of the commerce of Lombardy
and Piedmont.   What repute it had was as the
backwater retreat of Maggiore smugglers, for
originally Mergozzo was a bay of its greater sister.
Orta,—sometimes called " Lago Cusio," on the
other hand, has preserved its ideal beauty and
seclusion.   It reposes in a delicious basin bordered
by verdant hills, a land of fruit and flowers, a
scene of pathos and romance.   In addition to
natural and historic interest, the banks of the lake
are busy with the works of clever craftsmen—
wood-carvers, metal-workers, and paper-makers.
Being secluded from the general run of business,
the workpeople, as well as their masters, are noted
for their scientific study of industrial questions
and problems, the outcome of their studies being
invention and adaptation, difficult to realize in
crowded cities and in busy townships.   Omegna,
Orta, and San Maurigio are the chief places on
the lake.   The first and last are almost entirely
operative and around   Orta, — Orta-Novarese,
as it is called by many,—gathers the story of the
lake.

The romance of Lake Orta starts historically
in the fourth century, upon the picturesque islet
of San Giulio, opposite the town.   The ancient
bastion of San Giulio was founded by a Greek
missionary in 379, who wandered thus far in search

MYSTIC DANCE

'

of heathen converts. He brought with him precious relics, among them a small portion of the Cross of Calvary, which, at Milan, he had caused to be inserted in the apex of his long-stemmed metal cross, from which he flew the narrow banneret of the *Agnus Dei.* The saintly man placed in the crypt of his primitive House of God the vertebræ of a deadly dragon, which he slew, —after the pattern of other saints,—in a cavern's mouth on Monte Mottarone. Centuries came and centuries went, until Giullia, the amazon wife of King Berengario, of Lombardy, took refuge, in her husband's absence in Southern Italy, where Otto, afterwards the first of her line of Emperors, sought, first to woo and then to slay her, and usurp the Lombard throne. She threw up hasty ramparts on the island, and subsequently built a stronghold, remains of which are still to be seen, and they are still called "*Muri della Regina.*"

Otto made Lagna, across the lake, his head-quarters, and laid siege to the fugitive Queen, who, after two months' stout defence, was compelled to surrender herself and her castle to the usurper. It appears Otto made a vow that if he should succeed in capturing Giullia, he would render up the island as an offering to God, and he bestowed it upon the Bishops of Novara—hence its current name. A curious story is told about the siege.

A child was born, it was said, of Giullia, whom she name Guglielmo, and dedicated him to the Church. The lad lived, became a priest and the Apostle of Burgundy, and dying in 1031, left splendid monastic foundations at Orta and at Dijon. A very beautiful villa now adorns the island of Orta, built by Signore Ottavio Pio, after the patterns of the Moorish Palaces of Ziza, and Cuba near Palermo.

III.

Baveno, Stresa and Pallanza dance merry measures with the islands Madre, Superiore, and Bella—glittering sirens in their cerulean gold-flashed bay, and reflecting in the crystal mirror of its waters the snowfields of Monte Rosa and her afterglow. Mingling with the decoying vocal echoes of the fabled "Ladies of the Caves" and Shores are human sonnets of the Religious, of the fisherfolk, and of nobles proud and fair. As the wavelets lap marble steps, or pitter-patter on rolling strand-stones, their titillations keep time with ghostly footsteps of the pageant figures of the past.

To name the Borromean Islands is to arrest the ear and start the mind off in an ethereal dream. Not even the Biblical Paradise had anything half so fair ; indeed, the eye shares with the heart the

impressiveness of illimitable delights. In the
gay cotillion danced by nymph and form, by
mermaid and merman, Baveno gives her hand
to the picturesque fishermen, Stresa to the palace
courtiers, and Pallanza to the merry monks. The
well-matched couples gyrate on shore or dive to
depths profound, and we who watch and wait have
as much as we can do to take our cue and join in
the merriment. If we are called upon to give the
award of Paris to the fairest of these islets, we have
a problem hard to solve. Each has a special
charm, equal, if not better, than the rest.

Stresa has always been an aristocratic place
ever since the lordly Visconti picnicked there in
the long ago. The Castello, now a ruin, of course,
dates from the eleventh century, and now we have
the twenty-first not very far ahead. A thousand
years are a goodish span for any locality to keep
up its reputation, but Stresa to-day is still the
resort of " Lords and Ladies of the Lake." She is
a congeries of villas and gardens as full of gay
romance as of sweet flowers. The Royal House
of Savoy,—sovereigns of " *Italia Unificata*," year
in, year out, here enjoy their *villeggiatura*. At the
Villa Ducale the Queen-Mother, beloved Margherita, recuperates after strenuous exercises
around Alpine heights ; and King Vittorio Emmanuel comes over from Racciongi, when he is

tired of sport and study, to visit the home of his grandparents for rest and relaxation.

Stresa's partner in the fantastic dance of shore and isle is Isola Bella ; they are parted only by a very narrow strip of water.   Any white-clad handsome young boatman will ferry us across and introduce us to óne of the liveried *custodi*, who can tell us what has been told to him about " the beautiful Eliza "—*Eliza bella*—whose name the island bears.   It was Giangiacomo Borromeo, the brother of Count Vitaliano, who, visiting friends at Stresa, rowed over to the nearest island of the group, then occupied by fishermen's crazy hovels and a little chapel very much out of repair.   He at once perceived that very much might be made out of the islet, so secure from alien feet ; indeed, it was just the spot he had been hunting for.   The Signore was, as all Lombardians were, and all Italians are to-day, a very amorous fellow, and he had a youthful mistress,—a child of Milan,— whom he had decoyed from home.   A jealous wife and spying friends surrounded the liaison with difficulties ; besides, the girl was not of gentle birth, although pure and lovely as the lily.   He dreamed a dream of a beauty-spot wherein to place his sweetheart, and realized his vision by the erection of a little villa upon the islet and by the dismissal of the few inhabitants.   In short, the

Signore created an Elysium where he disposed the lovely Eliza and surrounded her with nothing but things of beauty and of joy. Certainly she was a prisoner, but she had nothing to do but to minister to her lover and translate his wishes into facts. Alas for the happiness of things terrestrial, the seraphic dream vanished in cold dust and air, for the beauteous *castellana* died, from " the excess of love,"—so was it stated,—and after Signore Giangiacomo had buried her in the little chapel patch, he left his enchanted island and never saw it more.

Then, in 1632, came Vitaliano, the lordly brother of our hero, and cleared the ground once more. Giangiacomo's casino was replaced by a very much more beautiful garden of delights, and he set to work to build a palace which should have no rival in Lombardy. He cared not one whit for the Elisa dedication, but inasmuch as the name of his Countess was Isabella,—Isabella d' Adda,—the name of the island remained unchanged—*Isola Isabella — Isola Bella*. No fairer spot upon this wide earth can be found than Isola Bella di Lago Maggiore. The palace,—taken possession of in 1671 by the magnificent Count and Countess,—was never really completed, but its rooms are filled with choicest works of art and fashionable foibles. The gardens are unrivalled. The terrace grottoes echo

softly, if one listens patiently, the tales of bygone
days, and repeat bashfully the passages of love
which they have concealed.   Sitting there beneath
magnolias, camellias, and oleanders, with the
aromatic perfumes of thousands of exotics, one
requires the use of a meagre imagination only to
people those alcoves and parterres with " Lords
and Ladies of the Lake " who have clanked gilded
swords up and down the marble steps or swept the
borders and greensward with trailing skirts of silk
and velvet.   Those orange-trees have been robbed
of their delicate blossom to crown Borromean
ladies ; those laurels have given verdant leaves for
wreaths of champions in the games of love.   The
tragedies of life are substantiated in Isola Bella, for,
among the fair women who have been loved,
divorced, and evil-treated, none receive greater
commiseration than Josephine Beauharnais, the
hapless Empress Josephine.   To the Isola fled the
Cavaliere Giovanni Tempesta for sanctuary, when
incontinently he had murdered his worthy wife in
order to marry a more handsome woman—a
lady of the Borromei.

Buonaparte, too, frequented the Borromean
Palace, and many a time he sought repose and
refreshment amid the amenities of the gardens.
In the stem of a giant oleander,—whose flower was
his favourite,—he cut on one occasion his initials

and the word "*battaglia.*" It was just before the decisive victory of Marengo.

Isola Superiore,—better known, perhaps, as Isola de' Pescatori,—has quite another story. It is approached from Baveno, the fishing-town *par excellence* of the lake. Their interests are in common, and they are linked in imagery of romance, like loving partners in the glorious dance of life. Fishing-boats and fishing-nets encumber beach and harbour. No more picturesque or courteous people dwell along the lake ; they are Nature's gentlefolk, ever ready to show kindness to strangers and to support their kith and kin. Perhaps they number three hundred souls all told, and are reckoned citizens of Chignole on the mainland. At eventide, when the fishermen race home for food and amusement and rest, you will hear such vocal music as will delight your ears and cheer your hearts. The baritone and tenor of the *barcarole*, borne by the breeze and ripples, blends in delicious cadence with the women's contralto and soprano on the beach. The songs are Venetian in character, and tell in tuneful numbers of love and death, and hope and despair, with *staccato* praise of valiant deeds of yore. This island is a small Republic, and owns no obedience to the lordly Borromei, as do her sisters twain.

Baveno,—one of the sweetest spots on earth,—

gets its name from *bavero*, the embroidered cape of a
brocaded cloak—a very apt derivation, for within
her boundaries are gathered quite a dozen villages,
some on the lake, some off. No beetling cliffs or
crumbling castle walls frown down upon the sunny
plain. Baveno, like her rival Stresa is a parterre
of villas and villa gardens. The finest, and for
English-speaking visitors the most interesting, is
Villa Clara, still so called by habituées, but renamed
within the last decade Villa Bianca Scala. Built
in 1872 by Mr. Charles Henfrey, after designs of
English architects, its gables and red bricks give
it quite a British character. The grounds, too,
are triumphs of English landscape gardening, and
the beautiful English church within the gates is
Anglican outside and in. Good Queen Victoria
sojourned here in 1875, and added her august
name, with the names of British Royal Princesses
—Louise and Beatrice—to the " *Libro d'Oro* " of
the " Lords and Ladies of the Lakes " No more
gentle, charming hostess could be imagined than
Mrs. Henfrey. Her gardens were open every day
to British and American visitors, and when she,
from her boudoir window, noted the presence of
her country men and women in the grounds, she
used to sally forth, dressed in floating white muslin
and a big garden hat of straw, and welcome her
visitors cordially.

VILLA CLARA   THE LOGGIA   BAVENO

" Come in and look at my pretty things, and
have some tea." A deprecatory answer always
called forth a charming protest, " But you must ;
now come along with me !" and, suiting her action
to her words, she linked her arm in that of one
of the ladies, and bore the party off to do her
gracious will.

" You admire my flowers, I know. See, my
gardener shall cut you each a bouquet, whilst you
chat with me and tell me your news. My life is
somewhat of a solitary one, you know—my husband is much away—and there are no English
residents in Baveno. Your presence is a perfect god-
send, and I thank you greatly for your company."

She was a lovely young woman in those days,
and as good as she was comely ; but money, and
the will to spend it discreetly and helpfully for the
benefit of others, could not avert the crushing grief
that came to the lady of the Villa—called after her
own name in loving compliment by her fond husband. In 1890 Mr. Henfrey died. The blank was
more than his disconsolate widow could endure.
She left Baveno, weeping bitterly, and no one
passed those bolted gates for eight long years. In
1898 Villa Clara was in the market, and the purchaser was Signora Maria Scala Bianca, who
changed the name and the régime. Queen Victoria's trees—a cedar and a cypress—still flourish

in the grounds where Her Majesty planted them. It was at Villa Clara that she first indulged in what in after-life became a Royal custom—alfresco refreshments. The Queen loved to pitch her tea-kettle under some shady tree in the grounds or beyond upon the slopes of Monte Mottarone, and invite specially honoured guests to partake along with her suite.

Our fanciful set-to-partners shows Pallanza and Isola Madre hands-across the lake, but the comradeship is in danger of disaster through the intervention of the smallest islet of them all—San Giovanni. How Isola Madre got her name of maternal dignity two tales may show. The first is of pious origin, and links the memory of holy men and women of the past with folks at work and play to-day. The site, it is said, of the earliest Christian church in Lakeland, holy monks and nuns dwelt in security in the wild old times, and ministered to turbulent souls the sweet comforts of Mary, Mother of the Church. When "*Pallanza la Graciosa*" was in swaddling-bands, and before she began to grow, the mother-island and the mother-Church stood for her weal and healed her woe. Time ran swiftly on,—it ever does,—and men's simple faith and humble practice were no safeguards against pomp and circumstance. The beauty of the island was its undoing as a sanctuary. Never the prey of marauders, it is true, in the sense of rape and rage, Isola Madre became the apple of the eye of the discerning and enterprising Borromei. Theirs was already the Isola Bella, the cynosure of artistic girlish beauty, and of Isola Madre they made the exemplar of natural maternal comeliness. Likened to a cunningly woven basket filled with ripe delicious fruit, which Pomona offers to "Lords and Ladies of the Lake," Isola Madre, more luxuriant far than her younger rival, wins the love of all. The other story of nomenclature assigns to Elizabetta Cristina, Mother-Queen of Spain, the designation "Madre." She, like many another Aragonese bride of Dukes of Milan, was enchanted by the vision of the Borromean Islands. "Here," she said, "I could wish to spend my days, and find my grave at the end of them." Alas! the Palazzo, like a flashing crystal set in emeralds and gold, has nowadays no occupant. Scions of the noble house occasionally pay visits for alfresco delights, but their parting footsteps echo and re-echo along empty corridors, and ghosts of gay visitors glide silently through unpeopled rooms. Isola Madre, like she whose name it really bears—*Maria Immaculata*—is undefiled by steamer-smoke and the rough-and-tumble of the world. No more secluded beauty-spot for meditation can be imagined.

From the Borromean Islands to Intra's smoky chimneys is quite a short cruise by boat or foot, and yet a greater contrast is unimaginable. Intra is the Manchester of Maggiore—a land of machinery and fumes—strange metamorphosis indeed, for in the fourteenth century her name was Sant' Ambrogio di Intra—a shrine for peace and prayer. The Borromean stronghold is altered out of all recognition ; it is an iron-foundry. Still, Intra is encircled by lovely country bedight with sumptuous villas. Villa Frangosini is called the " Queen of Villas." Nowhere are magnolias and camellias so immense, and flowered with so much wealth. Count Antonio Barbo, whose town house is in Milan, is the lucky enterprising owner. There is, however, little or no historical romance at Intra. Romance there is, of course, and plenty of it, but it belongs to the ordinary day and night, and is more or less sordid in its measure and touched with commercial vulgarity.

Once round the Punta di Castagnola,—with its bright green chestnut-trees, with almost human hands, and spikes of early pink-white spring bloom, and later on hard nuts of rich autumn brown,— Lake Maggiore assumes quite another aspect, and her story thenceforward to her head is unlike the romance of her southern moiety. Minerva of the shores of literature and femininity, her brilliant

golden casque laid aside that men may be fascinated by her autumn locks and flashing eyes, now
assumes her brazen helmet and grasps her weapon
tightly, for she needs all her reserve of powers to
withstand the pirate crew. Purple flow the lake
currents—coloured by the crimson gore of men
mixed with aqueous blue. A cold wind from the
north and a broken sea of foam bid the lookout
keep his post. Nature as well as history has dif-
ferentiated Maggiore north and south. Still, there
are beauty-spots hidden away in pretty coves, and
the sternness of Vulcan at times relaxes in a
love-liaison.

Ruined castles and dismantled towers meet the
eye with martello-like frequency, but their stories
of rapine and deadly feud have vanished into dust.
As we gaze on these tokens of a sanguinary past
the terrifying cry of " *Le Mazzarditi !* " seems to
sound in our ears,—the fell pirates of the lake from
whose clutches there was no escape. They were
the irreconcilable offspring of an early race or
races of marauders. In Milan, in the year 1275,
there culminated the blood-strife of Torriani and
Visconti. The former were for the people, the
latter for the lords. All Lombardy was torn in
pieces by war, robbery, and lust, and the waves
of savagery rolled back the southern culture currents of the lakes. The Lomellini fell before Arch-

bishop Ottone Visconti ; " Torriani to the rescue !"
drove the Visconti out of the castles they had
seized, leaving them only Arona and Angera. Then
the fortune of war changed, and the Visconti re-
occupied Quassa and Castellsepiro, to be expelled
with grievous loss once more, until the militant
Archbishop was in full retreat to Cannobio. There,
rallying his forces, he was joined by the Signore
of Locarno, Simone Rusca, and Marchese Guglielmo di Monferrato, and they pushed the Torriani
back.   Battles fought on land and lake decimated
the lacustrine population and impoverished the
lake lords.   In 1358 Duke Gian Galeazzo II., for
the permanent glory of his house, dismantled the
strongholds of Arona, Invorio, Castellatto, Mia-
simo, and many others on the banks of the lake,
leaving, as he said, not " a goat foothold " for
adherents of the rival faction.   The next Duke,
—Giovanni Maria Visconti,—the most cruel of his
race,—not content to let matters settle gradually,
let loose once more the dogs of war,—to speak
metaphorically,—and alongside of the metaphor
actual savage dogs, great mastiffs, to hunt out,
drag forth, or devour all fugitives and men
marked as dangerous.

Those were days of Guelph against Ghibelline,
Ghibelline against Guelph, and no man's life and
land were safe.   Holding with the Ghibellines in

the first decade of the fifeenth century, at Cannero,
were the five brothers Mazzarditi, doughty champions in work and strife, sons of Pietro, a black-
smith of Roneo, near Locarno : Giovanolo, Beltra-
mino, Simonello, Petrolo, and Antonio were their
names. Incited by Simore Rusca, a descendant
of the hoary-headed ally of the Visconti,—they
began to harass the unfortunate Guelphs, who
happened to be in the vicinity. Their depreda-
tions grew in boldness and dimension. At length,
in 1403, they fell upon their peaceful neighbours
at Cannobio, plundered their houses, and slew all
who opposed them. The two seneschals of the
town—the brothers Mantelli—they despatched
with their daggers. Their sister Bianca, rather
than lose her life, entreated Petrolo Mazzardito to
marry her and do with her what he would, in exchange for the goods of her murdered brothers—
not a very heroic line of action, to be sure, but
perhaps excusable under the circumstances ! The
wife of the *Podestà* was carried off for ransom ; he,
good man, escaped—Giacomo Pozzo di Vezevano.

Then the miscreants set off upon their cruise of
piracy. Locarno, Ascona, and even far-distant
Angera, were laid under contribution. Pallanza,
Intra, and Arona alone repelled them ; Angera
suffered terribly ; taken unawares and in the dark
by a crowd of savage brutes, the greater number

of the men were massacred, and the young women carried off to feed ill-conditioned lust. Returning from the foray, the pirates found arrayed against them the united and armed fleets of fishing-vessels of Laveno and Belgirate, with a great flotilla from Pallanza, on its way to join her neighbours. Daringly and successfully the corsairs of Cannobio ran the gauntlet of grappling-irons and artillery, sinking instead of themselves the boats of their allied enemies. Back once more in their home waters, the ruffians set to work to fortify themselves against the vendetta at their heels. They compelled the poor disheartened men of their village to build, laboriously and almost unpaid, two castles upon two rugged rocks projecting above the lake at Cannero. One they called "*Traffiume*," the other "*Carmagnola;*" but those who wrought and those who watched in derision dubbed them "*Castelli Malpaga*"—No-pay Castles!

All trade and industry were at an end so far as the northern portion of the lake was concerned, and the robber brethren were ever ready to sally forth to destroy any useful peaceful movement in the south. Their example and encouragement made many an honest man a rogue. Bands of highwaymen haunted the valleys and the shores hand-in-hand with the pirates of the deep. At

ARRIVAL OF KING CHRISTIAN AT THE CASTLE OF MALPAGA

GIROLAMO ROMANINO

Fresco at the Castle of Malpaga. (See page 280)

To face page 72

last, in 1414, Duke Filippo Maria Visconti, hearing of the distress and anarchy, determined to subdue the Mazzarditi and their following. Capitano Giacomo Lonate, one of the Duke's most trusted commanders, was despatched with a strong force, manning many battleships at Arona. The expedition was a triumph of order over riot. The Mazzarditi were caught, like rats in a trap, in their two castles at Cannero, but, like brave men, they fought and refused surrender, until six months of starvation had lowered their courage and their vim; they paid the death penalty for their madness and their crimes.

Lake Maggiore now breathed freely after twelve years of bloodshed and misery. The two robber castles were thrown down, and happier days came to Cannobio. One hundred years after the feuds of Torriani, Visconti, and Mazzarditi had been put to silence, other Lords—not war-Lords—assumed the ownership of both communes—the all-pervading Borromei. On the ruins of *Traffiume*, in 1519, Count Lodovico Borromeo built his Castello Vitaliana, but it became a ruin, too. Where "Ladies of the Lake" flirted, fished, and feasted, nowadays the simple folk of Cannero foregather yearly in harvest-time, and make the battered walls, clothed in richest ivy, re-echo with hilarity.

Between Cannobio and Brisago is the Swiss

frontier,—for the head of the lake belongs to Switzerland's canton of Ticino,—with its custom-houses. Toll is taken, too, of water-craft sailing over the imaginary line. Brisago has belonged to Switzerland since 1520 ; she was weary of the bloodshed of Torriani, Visconti, Rusca, and Mazzarditi, and she loved her liberty. The delta of the torrent, Maggia, portentously increasing during each decade, separates Ascona from Locarno at the head of Lake Maggiore. The crown of Locarno, and, indeed, of the whole lake, is the Madonna del Sasso, which conspicuously proclaims the triumph of religion over other forces. The town has been famous from Roman times but Celts baptized it *Loc-ar-no*—the Place of the Lake—and so Locarno is the soul of Lake Maggiore. With feet at Arona and Angera, and hands at Stresa and Baveno, her graceful form reposes in the deep valley Nature has formed, and her head lies on the breast of the Madonna del Sasso. It is a notable sanctuary, built by the devotion of Locarnese noble families—the Muralti, Orelli, Magoria, Rusca, and a host of others. All feuds and passions are laid low at the feet of " *Maria Stella Maris*," now The Virgin of the Rock ; and a story must be told.

Upon the glorious Feast af the Assumption in August, 1480, a pious brother, Bartolommeo

d' Ivrea, a monk in the Franciscan monastery at
Locarno, was honoured by a supernatural visit
from Christ's Mother. It was midnight, and a
brilliant harvest-moon silver-plated lake and land,
—when the brother beheld, whilst reciting his early
" Prime," a vision of glory in his cell. The Mother
extended her hand, and pointed up the hill, and
said : " Tell the men and women of this place to
build me a sanctuary yonder !" Frate Bartolommeo sought the Prior, and told him his story,
the while heavenly voices chanted the sweetest
" *Ave*" mortal ears had ever heard. This sign was
the token of absolute truth and command. The
little church was consecrated in 1483, and then
the holy brother retired into a grotto he had
scooped out of the mountain-side, and lived there in
piety, prayer, and poverty for nigh twenty years,
and when he died, the same angelic choir chanted
over his bier the *Nunc Dimittis*. San Carlo Borromeo loved to dwell there, and to preach to the
fisherfolk and the dressers of the vines. Due to his
initiative, a greater church was built, " with room,"
as he indicated, " for all who love Mother Mary."
The church is reached by a winding path under the
shade of trees, and the devout pilgrim finds fourteen " Stations," at all of which he may rest and
meditate. These Stations are chapels with altars
and their appurtenances, but are chiefly remarkable

for the painted terra-cotta groups illustrative of the life and death of Christ. These figures have a speciality all their own ; they are not merely ideal reproductions of humanity, but are portrait studies of " Lords and Ladies " of Locarno and the neighbourhood, and are quite startling in their realism. The " Lords and Ladies " of modern Locarno are cast in another mould — men and women, of course, like their predecessors. The cult of religion yields in them place to the cult of fashion ; and where cowled monks and veiled nuns four hundred years ago crept laboriously on knee to pray, well-groomed visitors of the health-resorts make the hills ring with merry laughter.

CHAPTER II

"CERESIO"

THE LAKES OF LUGANO AND VARESE

"Ceresio," the Home of Ceres! What more delightful or appropriate name could be wished for the harvest-field of the gods which surrounds the sickle-shaped lake of Lugano! Well and cunningly did those old Romans and Greeks, who colonized barbarous Europe, give names geographical where they listed. Lugano is the Lake of Ceres, the goddess Earth's riches, mother of Persephone, the gatherer of flowers, whom she lost awhile, but again recovered with the help of Mercury, much as spring and autumn succeed each other in the yearly round.

There is a further conceit anent this divine patronage of the luxuriant Ticinese lake. Zeus and Plato, it was said, were privy to the rape of Persephone. Giant mountain gods and guardians of "Ceresio" are Salvatore and Generoso, rocky monuments of the two deities, and aptly named. The return of Persephone to Ceres produced amazing fertility, and the mother-goddess had as much as she could do with her golden sickle to gather in the harvest of the earth.

I.—LUGANO.

The social conditions of the canton of Ticino and of the inhabitants of the lake-shores of Lugano are very different from those which obtain generally in the land of the Italian lakes proper. Strictly speaking, there are *no* " Lords and Ladies " of Lake Lugano, and none have there been these four hundred years or so. Before the time of Francis I. of France the history of the canton and of the lake ran concurrently with that of the neighbouring Piedmont-Lombard lands.

Bellinzona, the ancient capital of the canton, is a thoroughly Italian town, quite Venetian in character, with three most picturesque castles— Gorbe, Picile, and Gian—but it gives place to Lugano as the most populous and best-known place in Ticino. Some maintain that Lugano is of Roman origin—the *castrum,* or headquarters, of a legion. Be this as it may, in the year 1000 the Emperor Otto II. made a grant of the whole district to Adelgiro, Bishop of Como, with the right to levy market tolls. The election to the see of one of his successors, Landulfo Carcano, a Milanese monk, was the occasion of a fierce conflict. The rival Popes, Gregory VIII. and Urban II., each nominated a Bishop. Carcano was the choice of the former, but the people of Como would not accept him, and drove him from the city. Carcano took refuge in the Castle of San Giorgio at Agno at the head of the Magliaso bay of the lake, some three miles from the town of Lugano. There he intrigued with certain Milanese clerics and nobles, and the castle became the headquarters of a strong army hostile to the orders of Carcano. The Comacine forces took the fortress by storm, and put Carcano and his Visconti allies to death ; this was the beginning of the hundred years' war between Como and Milan. The partisans of Guelphs and Ghibellines carried on the feud of blood in that fair lakeland, and the families of Vitani, Rusconi, and Torriani, and many another were opposed to, and at grips with, one another. Lugano became the prey of Como, Milan, and Venice turn and turn about.

Spanish, French, and Teuton swept the lake and its shores with warning sails and warlike hosts, but all the while the thew of the mountaineers and fisherfolk was hardening, and in the fulness of time patriots foregathered to the undoing of the invader. Under their leader, Johann von Wippingen, the men of Ticino gained their independence. After the decisive battle of Men-

6

drisio midway between Porto Ceresio and Como,
Francis I. of France, in 1516, signed a treaty which
left his patriot foemen to manage their own affairs.
Von Wippingen caused landowners and peasants
alike to swear an oath of fealty to the new Republic, safeguarding individual rights and com-
munal privileges. Each adult Ticinese was the
equal of his brother, and families, which dated their
nobility back to a distant ancestry, dropped their
titles and prerogatives, or migrated into Lombardy. Ticino joined the League of the Twelve
Cantons, and was blessed by wellnigh three hundred years of peace. Then that upheaval of all
Europe -the French Revolution of 1798—made
itself felt in the Swiss-Italian cantons. Lugano
again resisted the makers of the Cisalpine Republic, and the patriots affixed their motto—
" *Liberi e Svizzeri* "—upon their banners and their
buildings.

The town of Lugano played a conspicuous part
also in the struggle for freedom of her mighty neigh-
bour state Italy in the year 1848. She became the
headquarters for nearly twenty years of Giuseppe
Mazzini, the " prophet " of Italian unity, which
Cavour and Garibaldi carried to success.

If there are fewer tales to tell of titled famous
people of Lugano than of their kind about the
other lakes of the Southern Alps, the folklore of

CORNER OF THE "SALITA." PORTRAITS OF LADIES OF THE
MARTINENGO FAMILY

ALESSANDRO MORETTO

Martinengo Palace, Brescia. (See page 302)

To face page 80

" Ceresio " yields to none in fulness and fascination. The *Tradizioni Popolari Ticinesi* are abundant, and their hold upon townsfolk and country people is still emphatic. Go where one will—off the beaten tourist track, of course—quaint sayings and quainter customs are delightfully in evidence, and the dialects are most interesting. Let it first be said, however, that the temperament and personal characteristics of the people are dissimilar from those of their Lombard cousins. The promptings of liberty, defence, and responsibility have marked the men and women, and even the children, with a measure of seriousness which is unlike the *abandon* of the Italians. Gaiety, too, be sure they have, but one detects easily a sense of restraint in every class. The Luganese say of themselves, " In disposition we are Italian, but in action we are Swiss." Ticino is comparatively a very prosperous canton, and the peasantry are well-to-do and comfortable. No Swiss-Italian race has anything like so great a love of home and homely things as the Ticinese. They are law-abiding people, addicted to religious exercises and generous to their own, whilst they perhaps ruthlessly despoil the foreigner.

Passing in review the seven ages of mankind as exhibited around the Lake of Lugano, childish

words and ways first arrest us. In the district of
Bedano the children's morning orisons are recited
in the words which follow :

> " A letto mi vagh,
>   Quatordas àngiur che ma cumpagna,
>   Düü da pe,
>   Düü da cò,
>   Düü dra mau drizza
>   Düü dra mau sinistra,
>   Düü da indurmentàm,
>   Düü da dessedàm,
>   E düü da menàm.
>   A ra santa gloria du Paradis."

A mother nursing her baby on her knee sings or
croons ·

> " Trik, tròk, cavalott,
>   Trè stéra d 'u mè morott,
>   Pan cald, pan ciòk
>   Trik e tròk, ciapaciok."

When parents note pugnacious proclivities between their young offspring the fathers at least
look on approvingly, but the mothers check the
infantile combat with dulcet words ·

> " Tira via quel pügn
>   Parchè ?
>   Parchè l' é cent' ann ch 'u gh'è.
>   Chi ch'e mangiàd ra carua du lavigioö ?
>   Ul gatt.
>   E'l gatt induva el nacc ?
>   In d 'u tecc.
>   Alprim che palla ga tirum ı urecc."

It is easy enough to understand the meaning of these nursery rhymes ; they are like our own, and the quaintness of the diction appeals to all. To pronounce the odd-looking archaic words is quite another matter !

The children of Ticino are strenuous youngsters. The richness of the air and of the soil greatly aid the natural vigour of their parents. Their games are all of a pushful character, though often trained in a theological direction. At Arbedo they play "*Angiulin vegu via.*" The boys and girls place themselves in a row one behind the other, ready to advance, and then they separate in two divisions, one headed by "*La Madonna,*" the other by "*Il Diabolo*"—the rest are called "Angels" and "Devils" respectively. The girl called "*La Madonna*" challenges the boy, "*Il Diabolo*": "*Angiulin vegu via !*"—Let the angels pass ! To which "*Il Diabolo*" replies : "*G' o pagina che 'l diàvul ma porta via !*"—Only those may pass me who pay my price ! Then he blows a whistle, and all rush pell-mell to a point pre-agreed, the "Devils" trying to catch the "Angels," and kissing those they capture.

Another very popular game, in which adults love to join, is called "*Fare al bel galante*"—Good luck to the bravest ! The players form a ring ; one enters and takes his or her place in the centre, and then all dance round and round singing, merrily ·

> " Bel galante entrate in ballo,
> Innamorato senza fallo,
> Ghè qualcuno che vi piace ?
> Degh la man, tirell in pas."

Then the leader in the centre chooses his or her sweetheart from the ring, and they dance together round about, making what steps and grimaces they choose, whilst the other players dance round again and sing :

> " Eccola gui che l'ò trovata.
> Granda e grossa e ben levata,
> Eccola qui che la balaben
> Che la sumeja un mügg da fen
> Degh un gir, intorno, intorno
> Degan un altro, amora amora
> Mora, mora, lasselà auda
> Mora, mora, lassela scapa."

The couple in the centre kiss and then part hands, and each chooses another partner,—and so the game goes on. The couple who look, and dance, and kiss the best is accounted victorious. The game is quite the favourite in every part of the canton. There are many variations of the game under different names, but in each the daintiest figures and the prettiest faces win the day,—and so it should be, of course !

Satirical songs and greetings mark all arts and crafts, professions and conditions. An old maid is saluted thus :

> " Ra prestinera la gà trii goss,
> Vün pinin e vün l' è gross ;
> E vün la grà in dra panèra
> Trik e titrak ra prestinera."

Which may perhaps be Englished :

> " An old maid is always known,
> Whether thin or fat she's grown ;
> Be her bucket light or weighed,
> Trik and trak, poor old maid."

Masons upon buildings are chided :

" Mastru	" Master
Impiastru,	Plaster,
Stöpa bócc ;	Eat your tow ;
Mazza piöcc."	Take a blow."

As in other countries so in Ticino, the church bells have the imputed righteousness, or the reverse, of articulation. The Cathedral peal at Bellinzona sound : *" L' è or-argent-azzal-metall-tolon-l' è fer-l'è pioomt."*

The campanile of San Lorenzo in Lugano echoes the following :

> " Fra Martino campanaro
> Suona sempre le sue campane.
> E tón—li tón—ti tón—li tón,
> Li tón—li tón—e li tón—e ti toon."

At Magadino there is a very quaint saying :

> " A gh è un animal
> Che a la matin el va cun quàtar gamb
> A mezz di cun dó
> E ala sera cun trè
> Induvina cosa l' é."

It is in the form of a riddle, and the answer is : " Man, who, when a baby, goes on all fours ; in middle age on two legs ; and when old, supports himself upon a stick !" There are very many such amusing conundrums,—and most of them are uncomplimentary, — throughout the lakeland of Lugano.

The Tavernese, near Lugano, have a septet— " *La Settimana degli amanti* "—The week for lovers :

> " Lünedi l' è 'l di di spùs,
> Martedi l' è di murus,
> Mercoledi di poch da bon,
> Giovedi l' è di strion,
> Venerdi di desperàd,
> Sàbat di invemuràd,
> Dumeniza di passionàd."*

The people of Ticino hold many beliefs in signs and auguries. Thus, in order to win at the ever-

* " Monday—prepare.
  Tuesday—speak fair.
  Wednesday—take hold.
  Thursday—quite bold.
  Friday—despair.
  Saturday—repair.
  Sunday—the day for Love."

popular lottery, it is a desirable practice to get
hold of a lizard with two tails (not, one would
suppose, a too common *lusus naturæ !*), and place
it in a box with two compartments, with a full
feed of corn. Next day open the box. What
grains have not been consumed represent the
winning number. Should the lizard devour the
whole feed, then place a double feed in the box,
and examine as before.

Saliva is made the vehicle of good augury.
To spit is the correct thing if one meets a hump-
backed person, or beholds a spider running quickly
up a wall, or if one finds a clover leaf in quatrefoil.
To see a white moth flying round a lighted candle
or lamp is a presage of good news on the morrow.
If the first person we meet out of doors on January 1
is a boy, one may look for a good harvest; if a
girl, then there may be trouble at home. On the
other hand, there are signs of ill-fortunes :—If
a hen crows like a cock, then there will be an
immediate death in the family ! One must never
leave the knife in a loaf of bread, because it will
hurt the heart of the Madonna ! Never beat a
boy before a girl, or *vice versa,* or they will marry
unhappily ! When a woman combs her hair,
she must be careful to burn the hairs which fall.
Should one fix itself upon another person, it is
an indication that misfortunes are in store. We

might quote scores of such expressions on the popular belief in portents, but these will suffice to illustrate the simple character of the people of Lugano and Ticino.

There is an amusing story about a mule, which ate the grass off the church tower of Isone—a village a little north of Lugano. Villagers one summer noticed a particularly luxuriant growth of greenery upon the tiles of the Campanile, which died down in the autumn, and presented a very untidy appearance. Not knowing quite how to remove the disfiguring mass, they took counsel with a wise woman of the district. She advised them to attach a rope to the collar of a mule, draw it over a pulley, and fix it to the highest loophole of the tower. Then they were to raise the animal gently, and let him feed on the dry leaves. Almost strangled (as we may well suppose), the mule was got as far as half-way up, when, giving vent to a lusty salutation, he addressed, like Balaam's ass, his comrades on the ground :—" Be of good courage, children ; pull the rope tightly, or I shall laugh at your stupidity, and leave you to eat the grass by yourselves !"

By the villagers of Brè, and of other hamlets upon the slopes of beautiful Monte Brè,—a favourite excursion from Lugano,—May Day is

celebrated in the singing of a very delightful
" *Maggiolatà* " or spring ditty :

" Sem vegnü stasira,
    Sem vegnü da via,
    Per dar la buona notte
    A Vostra Signoria.
        Belleben del maggio,
        L' è fiorid el magg."

" In alto, in alto.
    Come l'erba al praa,
    Sem rivaa al palazz
    Dal scior cüraa.
        Belleben del maggio,
        L' è fiorid el magg."

" Quella finestrella
    Che garda vers al pian,
    Viva al scior cüraa
    Quand al và a Lügan.
      Comè 'l sa mai de bon
    Ul fiur da la violà,
    Viva al scior cüraa
    Quand al va a Castagnola.
      Come 'l sà mai de bon
    Ul fiur dal gelsümin,
    Viva al scior cüraa.
    Quand al và a Pascialin."

The quaintness of the language attests the
antiquity of the rondo, and the union of Lombardian and Swiss-German phraseology—"Beloved
be the May and the flowers of the May."

Carlo Cattaneo, the thinker, philosopher and
writer, spent many happy years at Castagnola,

which, on account of its beautiful situation, he
called, –" A bit of Paradise dropped on earth."
The sun shines on this " sweet alp of Brè " the
winter through ; its back is to the North, its face
due south. Villas, *villini*, and every sort of
tenement encroach upon flowering trees and
evergreens. Jealous of the amenities of Castagnola, the level ground above and behind the town
of Lugano has associated to itself the title " *Il
Paradiso*." Its rising background is " *Il Monte
d' Oro* "—very high-sounding sobriquets to be sure,
but admirably appropriate.

The road from Lugano to Ponte Tresa, whence
travellers pass on to Luino for Lake Maggiore,
skirts the exquisite little Lake of Muzzano, which
shares with the Dürensee, near Cortina, the renown
of being the most perfect natural looking-glass
in Europe. Photographs of either lake look quite
as well upside down, the reflections in the never
ruffled water being absolute. The natives have
from all times,—perhaps from the fabled days
of Venus,—made the mirror of Muzzano their
gazing crystal. The surface reproduces accurately
every object projected thereupon, whilst the remarkable clearness of the water reveals every
detail of the lake bed. " Go and look in
Muzzan !" is a common solution for questions of
the future or the past. Maidens see in those

THE MIRROR LIKE LAKE OF MUZZANO

From a Photograph

To face page 90

placid waters their lovers, the lads their sweethearts, whilst the craven villain's guilt is brought
home to him by those tell-tale depths. On Sundays and holidays the sedgy banks are thronged
with hopeful devotees of Fate "I saw Zuan
(Giovanni) in Muzzan." "Bella kissed me out
of Muzzan," and suchlike are the convincing
verdicts of those silent pools. Fishing, boating,
and bathing were at one time all forbidden in
Lake Muzzano, lest, unhappily, disastrous consequences should follow the breaking of the
sanctuary. The peep over and into the lake in
the full moonshine is an astonishing and bewitching experience. It has something of the same
weirdness of effect as gazing through and through
endless miles of glacier ice as one lies helpless in
the abyss of an alpine crevasse.

The Lake of Lugano is surrounded by lofty
mountains, well sheltering her shores and border-
lands from every wind intemperate. For all the
world it might be the Bay of Uri, part of the Lake
of the Four Forest Cantons — Lucerne. Their
names seem to betoken giants of a noble Valhalla,
—Generoso, Salvatore, Brè, Boglia, Camoghè,
Tamaro, Pizzoni, and Bernardo, the loftiest.
Whereever mountains run up into the sky there
caves and caverns explore their bases, and so
around the lake are many eerie openings into the

bowels of the earth. The grottoes of Osteno and Rescia, with waterfalls and ravines, are happy resorts in summer days; they have had their tragedies also. The picturesque cascade of Santa Giulia is named after a lovely maiden escaped from ravishers—Giulia da Lanzo d' Intelvi. Her lover slain before her eyes, herself thrown anyhow over mad Ramponio's saddle, stumbling, the steed threw man and girl to the ground; he being stunned, she flew and hid herself in the spray of the water- fall, and there she died, for she dared not issue forth.

Lanzo d' Intelvi is the birthplace, and has been for many a generation, of noted archi- teets, sculptors, and pavement-markers. Adamo d' Arogno, Lorenzo de' Spazzi, Ercole Ferrala, and many others, left their humble cottages, full of ability and enthusiasm, and having built cathe- drals and castles in Trent, Como, Florence, and Novara, returned as " Lords of the Lake," to enrich their native village with the fruit they had gathered everywhere, and to lay their bones in the cemetery of Santa Magherita di Belvedere. The Val d' Intelvi is one of the most exquisite valleys of Lombardy—a very worthy cradle of the fine arts.

From Lanzo d' Intelvi the summit of Monte Generoso is easily reached on foot in a couple

of hours : thence is gained the most splendid panorama of alp, and lake, and town in all Lakeland.
It is one of those rare experiences which bring the
best heart - blood bumping in one's temples, to
transport the soul and intoxicate the senses.
The whole plain of Lombardy is at one's feet, and
seated in a dry mossed stone, the grand pageants
of Milan and her sister cities pass before one's
eyes, from the warlike times of Bellovesas, the
Gaulish chieftain, six hundred years before our
present era, to the struggling days of Garibaldi,
the " Liberator " of yesterday.   Around and about
Monte Generoso have marched Celts, Romans,
Carthaginians, Goths, Lombards, Moors, Spaniards,
French, and Austrians.   Relics of those mighty
warriors are brought to light daily by the busy
plough; many are treasured in the Lugano museum.
Quite near Lugano town is Campione on the lake,
the nursery of families of masters in stone, and
wood, and iron — the celebrated Campionesi of
the thirteenth and fourteenth centuries, rivals and
compatriots of the Comacine masters on the other
side of Monte Generoso by Lario's lake.   Below
Moreoti, with its noble church and campanile,—
another Madonna del Sasso—the imaginary water
frontier-line between Switzerland and Italy is
crossed, and then the Italian Custom-house officers
on board the steamer begin to trouble travelling

"Lords and Ladies of the Lake." They are especially interested in the subject of cigars. By a comical coincidence the author, without any introduction, one day chanced upon a *doganiére* in a very accommodative tobacco shop in Lugano. Both purchased boxes of the seductive weed, and exchanged agreeable salutations in the doorway. In duty bound, the officer made his rounds of examination among the passengers on the Porto Ceresio steamer, and in turn greeted his chance acquaintance of the Tabacchierie. Embarrassment fell on both; the customary interrogations were checked whilst four eyes took in the situation. The official had erred, as had the traveller, and a mutual elevation of hats ended the episode!

Porto Ceresio, the southernmost village of Lake Lugano, points the way to Varese—a delightful walk of six or seven miles along the banks of the pleasant murmuring Brivio, between spurs of Monte Piambello and Pravello. The granite quarries of Cuasso al Monte, somewhat mar the suavity of the landscape, which here has gained the title of "*Il Deserto*." Right on the top of the workings is a solemn-looking building exactly like a monastery: it was, indeed, originally a cloister of barefooted Carmelites. The friars came to Varese in 1676, and first established themselves at Brenno Superiore, just above the town. Their emigration to Cuasso was purely tentative, for after they had developed the estate and erected their refectory and cells, they cast about for a wealthy purchaser, presciently knowing that an evil day was coming for all conventional institutions in Lombardy. *"Il Deserto di Cuasso"* was the name given in 1702 to the monkish retreat of its new proprietor, Count Vincenzio Dandolo, a lineal descendant of the great Venetian crusader Doge and Admiral Arrigo Dandolo. The culture and the chivalry of the Crusades became hereditary traits in that famous family, and Count Vincenzio exhibited all the charm of the "Perfect Courtier" in his treatment of the Religious. They were permitted by his bounty to retain the chapel and four cells, that they might say Mass daily for the benefit of his soul and the souls of his ancestors, and might also share the good things of his table. Unhappily, but perhaps naturally, the worthy friars presumed greatly upon their patron's clemency in respect of their conduct. Village matrons and maids preferred complaints against breaches of the vow of chastity. Episcopal indulgence proved inoperative, and at length the brown habits and bare heads and feet were sent about their business. *"Il Deserto"* became a forsaken shrine, and remained unoccupied for many years, until a widowed Countess of the noble House received the estate as a mortuary bequest—Elizabetta Morosoni-Dandolo, herself a Venetian of lofty and renowned descent.

From the windows of the villa,—a reformed monastery, indeed,—the eye looks right over the rising ground of Pogliana, right on to the white villas which peep out of the beautiful boskets of Bisuschio—the fashionable suburb of Varese town. It is a land of olives, magnolias, vines, and pomegranates, a land, too, of buxom mothers and graceful daughters. The menfolk, plain and simple, are noble in their bearing, and industrious and peaceful in their habits. They are well-to-do.

II.—VARESE.

" *Le Belle del Varesotto !* " is how natives of Varese and the visitors speak of the lovely scenery and delightful climate of the lake casket of Varese, with all the other enchantments of its treasures. It is perhaps a little difficult exactly to place the orthography of the place-name, but in the mythological conceit of the patronage of the celestial goddesses, which is so clearly indicative of her sister lakes, great and small, no better nor more attractive cult may be found than that of " Astræa," and the milky way of the gods. Varese is, indeed, not the only starlike expanse of

liquid moonshine in that fair plain of shimmering
waters—three other lakelets, like the Pleiades for
lustre, lend their brilliant charm to the scenery.
Biandronno, Monate, and Comabbio—they form
a flashing aqueous constellation, as though portions
of the starlit sky had been detached and fixed in
verdant landlocked frames. The Romans had
an alternative designation for the seven brilliant
stars—" *Vergiliæ* "—perhaps Varese is a corrupt
form thereof ; anyhow, it is sufficiently near in
derivation to illustrate the conjunction of the stars
and planets in the Pleiadesian corruscation which
flashlights the Varese plain of lakes.

Very quaint is the description of this chain of
charming lakes in the " Encyclopædia Brittanica " ·
" South of Varese are two small lakes,—like Erba
and Pusiano, between Como and Lecco,—of
similar character, and scarcely worthy of notice !"
But those who know the Varesian Lakeland think
and speak very differently.

Three miles south of Porto Ceresio, in the lovely
Val Brivio, is the picturesque commune of Bisuschio, with wellnigh countless villas and gardens
of the " Lords and Ladies " of Varese, and beyond,
Nature and Art have entered into partnership to
create and enrich a terrestrial paradise, which is
hardly surpassed by other beauty spots. One of
the most charming of these country resorts is

undoubtedly Villa Cicogna-Mozzoni, belonging now to the Counts of that twice ennobled family, with its superb views over Lake Lugano and the surrounding country. The villa, which is in the somewhat severe style of Tuscan architecture, and for all the world might be a Medici residence wafted over the hills and far away from Florence, is not without historical interest. In the twelfth century a monastery was founded upon the site by the Papal See for the purpose of affording seclusion to ecclesiastical dignitaries and other persons of position who had misused the world to their own undoing, and, euphemistically speaking, were cultivating holiness in retirement. When the Dukes of Milan began to stretch themselves abroad, the valley and fruit-covered hillsides of Bisuschio attracted their attention, stocked as they were with bear and deer, and many more wild things. The monastic buildings at length were seized by the Sforzas, and Duke Giovanni Galeazzo converted the cloister into a very commodious hunting-box ; and through those hallowed halls and courtyards trooped sportsmen with their dogs. Their hunting cries and the music of the hounds quite drowned the echoes of the chants of Holy Church. The mountain streams and rivulets, which danced gracefully down the flowery slopes of the Campo di Fiori into the valley, were broken

VILLA CICOGNA-MOZZONI, NEAR THE LAKE OF VARESE

From a Photograph

To face page 98

into little pools stocked as full as full could be with
trout and other toothsome fish. The monkish
rule of catching their Friday's dinner on Thursday
gave way to the constant whipping of the stream,
and the trout of Bisuschio rivalled that of
Garda in the estimation of lordly epicures. The
deliciously shady-sunlit artificial fishing lake of
Fraschirolo was formed by Antonio de' Medici,
the friend of Giovanni Galeazzo Sforza, and there
ladies fair and ladies frail joined the sportsmen
with rod and gun, with hawk and hound.

In the middle of the sixteenth century the
estate, or at least the hunting-box, passed into the
possession of the family of Mozzoni of Milan.
Francesco and Massimo Mozzoni built the villa
and employed the Campi brothers, and other
Lombard artists, to decorate the walls of the
cortili, and open loggie with frescoes in the graceful manner of Leonardo da Vinci and Bernardino
Luini. The Mozzoni intermarried with the
Cicogne, who were descended in the female line
from the Sforzas. The fairy-like gardens are due
to Ascanio Mozzoni, whose order to his garden-
architects was : " I wish to hear running water
everywhere, and to behold trees growing on
terraces." Hence is due the erection of what was
strictly called " *il castello d'acqua*," where one walks
under and over fountains of water, with water

spurting and springing on all sides. Hanging
woods and pendant arbours deceive the eye, for the
floral trees and fragrant shrubs appear to grow
right out of marble balustrades and sculptured
basins—a Renaissance Babylon of delights !

The thriving town of Varese, which is at some
distance from the lake, is of ancient origin.
Etruscan, Roman, and Lombardian relics keep
cropping up ; but its preferential history dates from
the beginning of the fourteenth century, when the
fief was held in chief by the Archbishop of Milan.
When matters went hard with the Guelphs, and
with churchmen generally, the powerful family of
the Torriani acquired it under Filippo delle
Torre. Then chance of feud and war gave it
to Filippo Visconti, whose family in turn relegated
it to the Cani, in the person of Count Facino Cane.
The Church of San Vittore was built by the Sforzas
in 1580. Varese has always been an especially
favourite *villegiatura* of wealthy Milanese, whose
villas peep out on all sides of the town from under
the well-grown chestnuts and limes. Charles V.
bestowed the " *Seigneurie* " of Varese in 1768 upon
Duke Francesco Maria d' Este of Modena, who
kept royal state in *La Corte*,—as his huge palace was
called,—for twelve busy years, with the honorary
title of Governor of Lombardy. La Corte, in the
Square of San Giovanni, in Via Luigi Sacco, was

acquired by the Duke along with its grounds from two wealthy inhabitants of the town, Tommaso Orrigone and Pietro Talamone together with a considerable extent of land in the Val de' Nicogni.

The Duke had married many years before,— for he was a septuagenarian at the time of the purchase of the estate,—Renata Teresa, widow of Prince Antonio Maria Melzi, by whose will she obtained the life interest in an immense property. Francesco Maria d' Este married her, of course, for her money, for she was of unequal birth, and a foreigner,—an Austrian of the middle-class family of von Harrach. Whether she accompanied the Duke to Varese, or whether she was dead, appears to be uncertain. At any rate, she was not at La Corte when the Emperor Joseph paid a memorable visit to the Duke at Varese in 1769. The villa,—it was, indeed, a palace,— amazed his Imperial Majesty. He had never beheld, as he admitted, anything so magnificent. " I thought," said he, " when I approached the Duke's stables I was at the palace, and I wondered what the ducal residence would be like if the housing of his stud was on so grand a scale." To do the honours during the Emperor's visit, Duke Francesco had the assistance of his daughter, Beatrice d' Este,—the child of a former marriage,—

and of the most beautiful and most brilliant woman of the Modenese Court, the Countess Teresa Trivulzio-Saluzai.

The ducal suite was as numerous and as distinguished as that of any reigning sovereign. His Master of Horse was Count Clemente Bagnesi; the Controller of the Household, Count Giulio Cesare Vezzani; the Ducal Keeper of the Purse, Count Gaspare Sanseverino; the Chamberlain of the Court, Marquis Gianpietro Amori; the Marshal of Ceremonies, Marquis Sebastiano Tibaldi; and the Governante, Princess Maria Melzi, sister-in-law of the Duke's wife. Equerries, pages, footmen, and all the ranks of princely attendants were more numerous than at the Emperor's Court. These and a full staff of domestics required commodious quarters, and consequently the original villa was quadrupled and more in size to house them all. The Varese people looked on amazed at this magnificence, but shrewdly tapped their pockets, for the presence of so many "Lords and Ladies of the Lake" meant oof and pelf for them. During the Imperial visit, and frequently enough afterwards, the Duke kept open house: every individual who ventured through the park gates was sumptuously entertained and his cattle foddered. Never were there such doings and such junkettings in all that country-side. Operatic performances, musical parties, hunting breakfasts, picnics in the woods, *fêtes galants* in the gardens, balls, banquets, and masquerades made time pass madly and merrily.

The Duke himself, though past the time when vigorous men divide their time betwixt love and sport, flirted with all the fair damsels of the company, and rode forth at the head of his hounds. Few could fly hawk or hook fish more deftly than His Highness ; but the younger sparks grumbled at " an old man still juvenile," and behind his back sneered, grimaced, and cracked untimely jokes. The appointments of the suites of rooms and of the convivial boards were rare and costly. The Duke spared no expense in cultivating gaiety and extracting joy. To say he kept a harem would not be very wide of the mark ; at all events, there were no prudes at Varese ! In person Francesco Maria was very presentable—tall, well-made, slim, active, and enthusiastic. He dressed well, usually in a white and gold Austrian uniform, but without orders, except on State occasions. One foible at least he had—indeed, he had many—the wearing of finger rings. Daily he changed them, but usually he wore rings together, all of the same description—diamonds he wore on Sundays and festivals.

The day's diary at La Corte was strenuous and

varied. The Duke rose early, and first of all received his private physician, Dottore Francesco Grossi, a practitioner of Varese. Mass found him daily as an assistant, and then to breakfast, partaken of privately in his own apartment. Official interviews, inspection of plans, papers, and personnel, followed; and then, before the midday meal in the state dining-room, the Duke was accustomed to promenade up and down the grounds, leaning on the arm of some pretty, sprightly girl or other. The afternoon was spent in excursions in his cumbersome berline, drawn by six coal-black horses. The Duke's companions were, as he called them, " *amorose dame e donzelle.*" Reading, cards and other games passed the time till supper was announced. One ever-popular form of recreation was a water-party on the lake, in a superb gilded and painted state barge—a quasi Bucentoro of Venice. The usual rendezvous were Gozzada, to the villa of his friend and crony, Giovanni Perabo; and Bisuchi, the residence of another congenial comrade, Count Francesco Mozzoni. There were always, as a *sine qua non,* a numerous band of dainty damsels waiting to welcome the gay old man, and entertain him with gossip, dances, and, doubtless, kisses not a few ! After the day's work and play were over and supper ended, coffee, and conversation, and more cards, and gambling, faro for choice, prepared the company for bed, and none were supposed to be otherwise than within their rooms when the great palace clock struck eleven. On Church festivals the Duke and all his Court made a point of hearing Mass at the Chapel of San Bartolommeo, at the Castellanza or Casterino, where he erected his own marble monument; and then all listened, devoutly of course, to the affecting sermon of the Capuccini monks. This function was made the occasion of perfervid music ; and the Duke's chief musicians,—Piccinini, Guzzangani, Parseilles, Cimarosa, and Zucchinetei, —were put upon their metal to compose and conduct novelties appropriate to time and place. In Varese the Teatro Ducale was the home of the Muses,—and between 1779 and 1790, under Duke Francesco Maria's hearty patronage, its fame eclipsed that of the famous Scala in Milan. It is interesting to record that the Opera of Barbiere di Seviglio made its first appearance at the Ducal Theatre in 1818. Many other notable *premieres* found in Varese their start for success and popularity. The spacious days of the Duke of Modena and Count of Varese closed all too briefly. In 1780 the splendid master of the revels was laid to his rest in the tomb which he prepared, and other men and manners ruled La Corte.

Midway between Varese and Milan is Saronno, with its wonderful gingerbread and still more wonderful Church of Santa Maria de' Miracoli, —the temple of honour of Bernardino Luini and Gaudenzio Ferrari,—both strictly " Lords of the Lakes " ; the former born at Luino on Lake Maggiore, the latter at Valduggia, twenty miles from Novara. Both were devout men, painstaking pupils of their common master, and in many ways examples to their fellows. The church, also known as " *Il Santuario della Beata Vergine*," is an early Renaissance structure of the years 1480 to 1490, with an imposing dome and a lofty campanile of the first decade of the sixteenth century. Its origin was very picturesque. In 1460 a little distance from Saronno, on the road from Varese, stood a simple shrine with an ancient sculptured figure of the Virgin Mary and the Child Jesus. Much neglected, ruinous, and overgrown with weeds and brambles, few gave a thought to Mary as they passed that way. But the time of restoration drew near. The story runs as follows : Pedretto, a peasant farmer in the plain of Saronno, bedridden and a martyr to gout, one night, unable to endure his sufferings, cried bitterly to Heaven for the mitigation of his misery. All at once his poor bedchamber was brilliantly illuminated, and over against the foot of the bed

FRANCESCO MARIA D' ESTÈ, SIGNORE DI VARESE, 1768-1780

From a Painting in the Municipal Palace, Varese

To face page 106

he beheld a woman of celestial beauty and dignity, who thus spoke to him : " Pedretto, poor sufferer, if thou wilt be healed, go to the old shrine on the Milan road,—thou knowest well, for I have beheld thy reverence in passing,—promise there, upon your knees, to build a church worthy of Blessed Mary, and means to do so shall be forthcoming."

At this astounding order Pedretto roused himself, shook his painful limbs, and tumbled out of bed. His gout had vanished ! He sallied forth, dark as it was, and groped his way to the ruined shrine, and spent the rest of the night in prayer. Next morning he wended his way, without any pain or difficulty, to the village, crying, as he approached the houses, " *Uno Miracolo! Uno Miracolo!*" People ran up and asked him what he meant, and how he had been cured. The cry was taken up, and " La Madonna della Via Milanesi " was acclaimed as their benefactress. Throngs of country people gathered around the shrine, sick and hale, and all who followed Pedretto's prayerful example went home sound and saved. Everyone tossed a copper or two to the poor old fellow, and there he very sapiently took up his abode in a hut he built behind the shrine, and held his hand out daily for contributions to the building fund.

The old shrine was repaired and railed in,— the iron trellis is still preserved in the portico of

the new church,—and in 1498, amidst universal
rejoicings, the foundation-stone of the sanctuary
was laid. The ancient statue of the Virgin was
carefully guarded until, on September 10, 1581,
San Carlo Borromeo personally removed it to its
present position over the tabernacle of the high
altar of Santa Maria de' Miracoli. To-day the sanctuary church attracts hosts of pilgrims who leave
behind pathetic tokens of their cure. Ex-votos have
encroached upon the frescoes of Luini and Ferrari.

The Madonna del Monte over against the town
of Varese, attracts countless pilgrims annually,
who make the "Stations of the Cross" from chapel
to chapel of the Sacred Way. The fourteen chapels
have seventeenth-century groups and frescoes
illustrating the mysteries of the Rosary. Bernabo
Visconti in 1371 endowed the *Cappellano* a
hermit priest. A century later, Galeazzo Maria
Sforza, mauled when hunting bear in the surrounding forests, was carried to the Sanctuary to hear
Mass and register a vow for recovery. Lodovico
il Moro frequently made the sacred mount his
retreat from strife and worry, and when Duchess
Beatrice died, he endowed five hundred Masses
for the repose of her soul. He and she had made
many costly offerings to the altar—rich *palli*,
altar frontals, and altar vessels. Some of these
gifts are still treasured by the clergy sacristans.

It is certainly rather a *tour de force* to descend

from these sublimities to things of modern days. Still, Italians are nothing if they are not go-ahead. One of the most sumptuous of the villas of Varese is that of Marchese Ponti,—who, by the way, has just vacated the post of syndic, or mayor. The origin of the family and the foundation of its fortunes form a romance of financial possibilities. The grandfather of the present Marquis was an obscure tradesman in Varese—a saddler and jobmaster—but quite in a small way. Reading his weekly journal, his eye caught news of the "cotton corners" in America and England. Tempted to speculate, he corresponded with an agent in Milan, through whom he acquired shares in the cargoes of blockade-running cotton ships. Beginning quite modestly, he at last achieved a record, for he became the holder of fifty thousand bales of best qualities, and was thus enabled to hold up the market. He sold his stock at a huge profit—some said as much as five hundred dollars per bale; at all events, Signore Ponti was able to set up in his native town as a wealthy landowner, and exchanged the style of commoner for that of Marquis. He built the Villa Ponti, and there entertained King Victor Emmanuele II., whose friendship he enjoyed through liberal gifts to patriotic objects. To-day the Marquis Ponti is an honoured friend of the third Italian King, and a generous benefactor of his native town.

CHAPTER III

"LARIO"

THE LAKE OF COMO

"LARIO,"—first named by travelled, warlike Romans *Lacus Larius*,—is Venus of the Lakes. The very conformation of the lake sets forth the goddess's beauteous form, and the sights and sounds and scents of her shores proclaim the artifices of her boudoir. The name, it is said, comes from Etruscan sources, and implies primacy, and in Latin times Como was the premier lake in Italy. One other derivation, maybe too fanciful, connects "*Lario*" with "*Lares*," and indicates the Latin pendant to Greek Olympus, the stately Court of gods and goddesses—the happy retreat of pleasures unalloyed. The name "Como" may, after all, be more antique than "Lario," for a considerable authority, Count Benedetto Giovio,—one of the city's most famous sons,—sees the derivation in the Greek word "*Kome*"—The Town—and Greeks may quite as well have reached "the most beauteous banks of all" as they did the "banks of marshy Rhone."

" In seno i sacri
Vasi celando, sugli ignudi scogli
Nuova Patria fondava, e dell' autica
Da Varenna scorgea l'ultimo fumo."*

In his letter to Rufus, Caius Pliny writes thus effusively of this lovely lake : " How fares Como, our common joy ? How is the charming villa, the vernal portal, the shady avenue of planes, the waterway ever green and jewelled, the pathways soft yet firm, the sun-warmed bath, the arbours both for company and for seclusion, the quiet nooks for siesta and for sleep ?" And yet Como is not for *dolce far niente* only. " It is," a writer in the eighteenth century says, " well known that every lake is the fruitful mother of industries, but there is no instance in which any other has produced so many or so famous " No lacustrine people of to-day are more busy and more enterprising than those of Como. Great sailing barges drop leisurely down the lake ; heavily laden market carts on shore creak with weighty loads, and women's heads bear up colossal burdens. Fish, flesh, fowl, fruit, foliage, and forage—such form the staples of the trade. Fisherfolk compete with country peasants in daily profitable toil, and

* " Conceiv'd in the heart—ark of sanctity
A new country forth comes right gloriously ;
Of the old world and its grand moods and manners
Is wafted the fame beyond Varenna."

every native is at any moment quite free to earn the stranger's gold and render pleasant service.

No other lake anywhere offers so many attractions and inducements for boating, but the boatman must be untrammelled by directions. Recline at ease, and look and list and smell, and worry not for train or meal or bed.   Floating upon the emerald glory, each vision is a miracle—dreamy distant peaks, near forest and precipice, inviting grottoes and ravines, with castellated crags and ensconced villages, white churches and campaniles with sweet-sounding bells, and all the delicious scents of the rarest potpourri are treasure-trove for all.   At sunset or at sunrise angels' robes and wings, ever whirling in graceful dance, float in coloured pageantry across the sky, and all the prismatic tints are shot like rainbows everywhere. There is an unseen world, it is true, and on the Lake of Como things are made clear to human vision which are dim and obscure elsewhere.

" A thing of beauty is a joy for ever."

I.

Before exploring the stories and beauties of the Lake of Como, the city claims the attention of students and lovers of romance.   Greeks, Romans, and Lombards in turn laid and destroyed its

foundations and its prosperity. The blood of
martyrs crimsoned the lovely Monte Baradillo,
but when St. Ambrose consecrated St. Felice first
Bishop of the See, the land had peace. The
"choral Father" had, too, a ready wit; for,
when Felice sent him one day a goodly basketful
of toothsome truffles, a speciality of the Larian
woodland, he replied epigrammatically:—"Beware,
my brother, lest you find truffles of sorrow,—for
the word has a double meaning,—pleasant enough
as a gift,—for which I thank you,—but disagree-
able as regards our bodily and spiritual infirmities."
In the twelfth century fratricidal war between
Como and Milan made of the former a second
Troy—albeit we lack the name of a Lombard
"Helen." Then a triangular côntest sprang up
between Papal nominees for the bishopric, and the
Monte and the city were again baptized with blood.
Fleets of warships, built by Como, Lecco, and the
Tre Pievesi,—the three northern lakeside parishes,
—strove for mastery of the deep. The great
Como ships, "*Lupo*," "*Scorrobiessa*," and "*Schifo*,"
were sunk, and the sacred floating "*Carroccio*" was
lost, with its precious guard of comely youths.

The Torriani, the Visconti, the Lecchi, and others
carried over the smiling waters of "Lario" the torch
of war. Napoleone della Torre and his three brave
sons were captured and thrust into iron cages in

the Castello di Baradillo. Bereft of hope, devoured by vermin, and insulted by the common folk, the gallant but unfortunate leader dashed out his brains against his cruel bars.

The story of the first recorded heroine of Como is told by the elder Pliny,—with his nephew Caius, —a citizen of Como. " Sailing," he writes, " lately upon our lake with an old acquaintance, he called my attention to a mansion above the shore by the city. ' From that room,' he said, pointing to a lofty chamber, ' a woman threw herself and her husband. He suffered with a terrible cancer, which caused intolerable agony. Finding no hope of recovery, she advised him to put an end to his life, but when he demurred she encouraged him by her own fortitude, for, tying herself and him together, she plunged with him into the deep water.' " Pliny was not only a romancer—he was a benefactor, too, and initiated, perhaps, the earliest Free School in Lombardy, standing surety for a third of the cost.

From Pliny's day to Garibaldi's is indeed a wide, wide span, and yet woman's grit and self-sacrifice is as conspicuous now as it was two thousand years ago. There came a day when the " Liberator " was in danger of capture at Cavellesca, a mountain village above the city of Como. When the menfolk dared not communicate with

Garibaldi and tell him of his peril, "Bianca,"—as she was called in the village on account of her fair hair,—feared not to extricate him from his dangerous position. When a truce was signed the hero rode over to thank his protectrice, and then, by one of Fortune's unexpected happenings, an accident caused his detention in her father's house. Three weeks' delightful ministry could only have one result—a proposal of marriage, which "Bianca" reluctantly accepted. A wedding was hastily arranged at Varese, but before the nuptial day closed the bride,—so much younger than her hero spouse,—eloped with her village lover, who had followed the pair from Cavellesca. "Bianca" lived to repent of her breach of troth, and became the ardent admirer of her one-day groom. It was said that she pressed Garibaldi to acknowledge her in spite of her lapse, but he refused!

The situation of the city of Como is exquisite. She is like a costly jewel set in a rich casket. Her villas, her churches, and her gardens are all enclosed in a splendid amphitheatre. Nature and Art have combined to make the Larian capital a beauty-spot, and then her outlook on the lake is a dream of loveliness impossible to put in words. The story of her people,—nobles and citizens,—is reflected in the deep green water and upon the verdure of her shores, for out of her came most of those builders who have decked her outskirts with paradises in miniature.

Of all the villas and their stories which embellish the Larian " Court of Venus," perhaps, to English-speaking travellers and students, Villa d' Este at Cernobbio presents the greatest interest.   It was erected by members of the Comacine family of Galli : Cardinal Tolomeo Gallio, in 1568, completing the work.   He died in 1607, and bequeathed the estate to his nephew Tolomeo, Duca di Vito, who in turn gave it at his death to the religious Order of Jesuits.   The Fathers held it for one hundred and sixty years, and then let the villa to Count Mario Odescalchi.   The family of Marriani took up the tenancy until General Marliano bought the property right out, greatly improved it, and restored the villa.   The next owner was the Marchese Calderara, who, dying in early manhood, left the delightful possession to his young widow, Marchesa Vittoria, who called it Villa d' Erba. Her tears and regrets were many and sincere, but youth and beauty cannot long wear widow's weeds, and the Marchesa gave her hand,—we must hope her heart as well,—to General Count Do-menico Pino,—one of Buonaparte's lieutenants,— and they added to the villa a convent for Benedic-tine nuns.   Again widowed, the Marchesa, after much pressure, in 1815 sold the villa she so greatly loved for 150,000 livres, to the representatives of the Princess of Wales, and she changed the villa's name to Villa d' Este. The story of the Princess's life at Cernobbio has been told and often, but a good story does not suffer by repetition, and there are points in the narrative which stand in need of just appreciation—biographical history is the most prejudiced form of literature.

Having nothing whatever to do with mere stodgy facts of history, nor with party views of politics, we can at once take up the story of Princess Caroline at the point when it first approaches the pageant ground of the Italian Lakes. Upon August 9, 1814, the Princess embarked at the port of Worthing in the frigate " *Saxon* " on her way home to Brunswick. She had been separated from her Consort eighteen years, and, although her character was completely vindicated and she was declared innocent of all scandalous charges, the Prince refused to have anything more to do with her. She was very unhappy at the gossipy little German ducal Court, and set off to see something of the world and find comfort amid new scenes. Her steps were first directed to Naples, where the small suite of English attendants left her, and she was obliged to fill their places with Italians, and of these Count Antonio Schiavoni became her secretary. Her itinerary took the Princess to Elba, Corsica, and Sicily. Thence she sailed to the Barbary coast, to Palestine, Greece, and Malta, and returned to Naples, and on to Terracina in the Pontine Marshes, and so to Rome. Everywhere she went she acted as the proverbial good fairy—visiting sick and poor, and distributing largesse. At Agosta in Sicily her name is still spoken with reverence—"*La buona Principessa.*" Travelling north, she sojourned at Leghorn, Genoa, and Milan. From the latter city the Princess made excursions through the plain and the lakeland of Lombardy, with a view to renting or buying a residence. The Lake of Como charmed her most : " Its delicious climate, the surrounding country, varied and lovely." Quite fortuitously she learnt that the very villa, which more than any other upon those delectable shores attracted her, was available at Cernobbio. " Its garden seems almost suspended in the air, and forms a scene of complete enchantment," so she noted in her diary.

Almost the first improvement of the property undertaken by the Princess was the planting of a double avenue of limes and horse-chestnuts along the lakeside past the villa Tavernarola, beyond the mouth of the Breggia, to within two miles of the city of Como. The idea in her mind was to

QUEEN CAROLINE AT VILLA D' ESTÈ

SIR THOMAS LAWRENCE

Victoria and Albert Museum

To face page 118

rival the famous avenue in Bushey Park. The Princess greatly enlarged the villa, laid out an English garden, made marble landing-stages for her barges and canoes, and annexed the Villa del Garrovo, built by Count Resta at the end of the eighteenth century. She established a Court, and surrounded herself with appointments suitable to her rank. Her chief lady of honour was the Contessa Oldi of Cremona—estimable alike for her amiable qualities and her heroism under misfortunes. Doctor Augustino Mochetti of Como,—formerly Professor of Botany, Agriculture, and Natural History in the University of Pavia,—she appointed her physician-in-ordinary ; Captain Robert Hannam of the British Royal Navy and Knight of the Brunswick Order of Caroline, shared Count Schiavoni's duties as English secretary to Her Royal Highness,—a man she praised as " remarkable for his high principles and undoubted devotion." A gallant young Knight of her Order, Monsieur Alfonse Guillanine, was named Equerry, and Signore Vallotti Pergami,—formerly under-Prefect of Cremona,—became Controller of her Household. The Princess further attached to herself many notable men of letters—Cavaliere Giovanni Tommassia, a well-known writer on philosophy and political economy ; Conte Girolamo Volta, Cavaliere Filippo Vassalli, with Signori

Fernando Configliadro and Enrico Cavalletti—men
of erudition and of good fame.   As legal adviser
Signore Giuseppe Marocci of Milan,—well known
in legal circles of Lombardy,—joined the princely
suite.   The Princess's first Chamberlain was Cavaliere Bartolommeo Pergami of Cremona—he it
was whose name was linked with that of his
royal mistress in the banal gossip of the English
Court.

It may be well here to take up this slander, and
vindicate both the Princess and the Cavaliere.
He was said to have been of low origin, impecunious,
but fascinating in appearance and manner.   It is
true that he had lost much money and had to sell
his family property in consequence of military
exactions, but he was well connected and had
married his three daughters well.   He had himself
been on the staff of General Count Pino in the
campaign of 1812, 1813, and 1814.   Caroline
named him Knight of her own Order, and pro-
cured for him a barony in Sicily.   Upon his
daughters she conferred many favours, and they
and their father enjoyed her fullest confidence.
She chose the Cavaliere to accompany her in her
equestrian exercises, and at all times treated him
with unusual familiarity, which, be it said, he
never attempted to abuse.   " Upon the arrival
of the Princess at Cernobbio rumours were circu-

lated " writes Madame De Mont, a devoted attendant, "unfavourable to her private life. Signs of levity and inconstancy were noted in her innocent pleasures. Her affability and generosity were stigmatized as indelicate and corrupt. Her simplicity of conduct and dislike of ostentation were said to screen caprice and secretiveness. She was accused of surrounding herself with base-born Italians, who might the more readily pander to her perverted tastes. On the other hand she is accessible to all, she has no affectation or caprice, she is gentle towards everybody irrespective of rank or circumstances, and she knows not how to be a great Princess except in doing good."

This amiable writer of " The Journal " goes on to say : " Many persons pretend to be astonished she does not receive the nobility of the neighbourhood. . . . It is true she has not sought a wide acquaintance : she prefers to devote herself to the members of her household and to the poor of the district. Still, any who wish to be presented are always received with distinction and courtesy. A society of persons of established probity, a table where gaiety and hospitality always preside, musical entertainments and private theatricals, walking, riding, and boating—such are her innocent pleasures."

The Princess delighted in nothing more than in

popping in and out of peasants' cottages on the hillsides and fishermen's huts along the lake, conversing with the simple-minded mothers and caressing the smiling babies—all swathed in their yards and yards of coarse linen. Her visits were as unconventional as possible. Dressed very plainly in a loose robe of muslin or alpaca, with a light silk Como scarf thrown across her shoulders, she loved to wear upon her head a coarse brown straw sunbonnet, untrimmed but for its bow of ribbon or its knot of poppies. Her graceful arms and hands were covered by long undressed kid gloves, and she wore low shoes to match. Upon her arm she invariably carried a biggish reticule filled with kitchen delicacies for the sick and poor, and her lady carried just such another basket. Those roomy receptacles ever returned empty to the villa. What the Princess looked like one may judge from Sir Thomas Laurence's well-known portrait of her. If her face was bonnie, her heart was just as good. Old crones told their children stories of "*La graciosissima Principessa*," and such stories linger still in every home in and around Cernobbio.

Shortly after Dr. Holland took his leave of the Princess, in 1815, an infamous plot was laid against her person and her honour. There is not a shadow of a doubt but that it originated among the evil-conditioned toadies who fanned the self-conceit of the Prince of Wales, and he, shame to his memory, took no steps to stop the slander nor to shield his wife's character. The " accomplice in the Princess's misdemeanour," so it was said, was a fascinating young Englishman—a Mr. William Burrell, travelling for health and pleasure in Lombardy. Caroline first met him during an excursion upon the lake when accidentally her barge and the young man's skiff came into collision. A favourite spaniel, which was upon the Princess's lap, was thrown into the water, and, to rescue it in response to its mistress's cries, Burrell jumped overboard and saved the pet. The episode took place quite near the shore, and Caroline insisted upon the gallant rescuer changing his clothes at the villa. He was as accomplished as good-looking, and the Princess, doubtless weary of the monotony of her life and of the want of brilliancy, perhaps, in her immediate attendants, persuaded the attractive youth to join her in excursions, attended by the very proper Countess Oldi. One brief month saw the romance ended, for young Burrell became ill, and, with his valet, made his way home to England. At Brussels tales first were rife of a royal liaison : the valet had been paid by someone to watch his master and the Princess, and at the Belgian capital he was not proof against a considerable bribe to make heavy demands upon his imagination. These confidences came, as they were doubtless intended to do, to the ears of the Duke and Duchess of Cumberland,— then on their way to England,—and the gossip filtered, with exaggerations and distortions, through the mouths and ears of the royal servants. Lord Castlereagh,—that most despicable of Cabinet Ministers,—ever seeking for materials for the manufacture of repressive measures against the Princess, seized upon the slander greedily.

The Prince of Wales at first refused to hear the chitter-chatter, but Castlereagh so inflamed his prurient mind against his outraged Consort that the Minister's brother, the Lord Charles Stuart, was sent to Milan to make inquiries on the spot. His coming was entirely unknown to the Princess, and he carefully avoided the neighbourhood of Cernobbio. At Milan he found a villain ready to hand for any dirty work, Baron d' Ompteda, formerly Minister of King Jerome Buonaparte at the Court of Vienna. For betraying State secrets and for irregularity in his administration of public funds, the Baron had been dismissed, and, mortified beyond expression, he turned his eye and ear to any ill-savoury employment against exalted personages. Lord Charles Stuart interviewed the Baron, and placed his brother's wishes before him, giving him carte blanche as to ways and means. At the time of this despicable conspiracy Princess Caroline was travelling through Lombardy with a limited suite, and, upon her return to Milan, she was amazed and indignant to find that she was an object of close police surveillance.

Baron d' Ompteda had well used the absence of the Princess from her villa. He had been there not once but several times, had conversed with the Italian servants left in charge, and by large offers of money sought to enlist them in his nefarious enterprise. Every man and woman with indignation resented the miscreant's suggestions ; they were the staunch and devoted retainers of Her Royal Highness. In the Princess's stables, however, he discovered a German groom, Moritz Crede, who had been entrusted with the convoy of two Hanoverian horses,—a present from royal sympathizers of the Princess,—and had been, by her generosity, allowed to remain and enjoy himself at Cernobbio. This fellow yielded to the tempter, and undertook to introduce the Baron into the Princess's private apartments by the aid of false keys. As chance would have it, almost the first thing the Princess heard, upon reaching the villa after her travels, was a complaint made by one of her dressers, Annetta,—a

German maid,—in which she accused Crede of attempting to seduce her. Caroline sent for the man, and, having confronted him with the girl, who relented of her confidence,—so like the sex,— dismissed him. In hopes of retaining his post in the royal service and of gaining the affections of his sweetheart, Crede made a full confession of his part in the Castlereaghian plot.

Writing from Como, November, 3, 1816, Crede gives away the case against the Baron. "I suffered myself," he says, "to be seduced and to betray the best of mistresses. It is about a year ago, and just before the departure of the Princess, that Baron d' Ompteda took steps through the intervention of a certain Ambroggio Cesati, who came to me in Como, to discover the place where my mistress slept, what apartments were contiguous, and to procure false keys. I persisted for some time in refusing to have anything to do with the matter, but, when the Baron told me that I should be a ruined man if I did not listen to him, and offered me a large sum of money, I was corrupted, although I was fully persuaded that there was no foundation whatever for his infamous suspicions. "

The Princess immediately sent for the Governor of the Province, Count Sauran, and told him about the transaction. Baron d' Ompteda was

ordered to quit the dominions of the Emperor at
once on pain of arrest and imprisonment. Every
one of Caroline's suite stood firmly and indig-
nantly for their beloved mistress; indeed, Captain
Hannam challenged the disreputable Baron to a
duel, but he evaded the issue and sneaked off.
If a motive were desired for the wish to locate
the Princess's sleeping apartments, it must, alas!
be sought not in the assignations of lovers, but
in the designs of assassins. This seems fully
proved by a strange circumstance, which occurred
at Genoa during the Princess's sojourn in that
city. Some masked men one night actually
penetrated as far as the door of her bedroom;
there they encountered her faithful valet Teodoro
Majocchio, who fired on them as they fled.
What capital the English Ministry made out of
this cruel persecution it is impossible to say, nor
can one divine the condition of the Prince-Regent's
mind in face of the failure of the foul plot. Anyhow, the Princess continued to reside at Cernobbio, but her seclusion became all the more
complete, and no strangers were admitted to her
presence. Four years later Caroline,—now Queen
of Great Britain and Ireland,—returned to London
upon the accession of her husband as George IV.
She was, however, refused admission to the royal
coronation in July. Broken-hearted, she sought

a refuge at Hammersmith—what would she not have given to have regained her beloved Villa d' Este !—and there she died quite unexpectedly at Brandenburg House on August 7, less than three weeks after her rejection at Westminster Abbey.

The villa of the Queen of England is still an attraction to British tourists. It no longer shelters a royal Court, but it has blazoned forth as the Grand Hotel Villa d' Este et Regina d' Inghilterra—one of the most comfortable caravanserais in Europe. The visitor may wander, as did good Queen Caroline, for hours through the spacious park, and traverse, as she did, its well-made roads. Shallops, like hers, are at the disposal of aquatic parties, and the blue water laps her marble steps as musically as when the royal Princess tripped up and down. The great sycamore,—said to be the finest in all Italy,—under which Caroline and her courtiers picnicked, still claims alfresco merrymakers, and, above all, the blue, blue sky of Italy casts its lofty vault,—that vault pierced by the prayers and protestations of a persecuted wife. The sun, which burnt her fair skin brown, and the cool moon still make the olive-trees glitter with gold and silver ; and the storm and rain which drenched the land a hundred years ago still work havoc around the Queen's villa. Her body lies in Brunswick, but

PRINCESS OF WALES'S QUEEN CAROLINE ENGLISH PARK

her soul hovers over Cernobbio, and, if you, my reader, are in a mind for reflection, you may lie in a hammock among the roses and magnolias and meditate upon the strange freaks of royal fortune.

II.

From Cernobbio the richly-wooded promontory of Torno seems but an arrow's flight across the glittering lake : round the point is the picturesque little bay of Molina, with the historic Villa Pliniana. The palace stands by the waterside, open to every passer-by, but secluded by the dense shadows cast by dark towering cypresses of ancient growth. The high cliff at the back projects a rainbowed cascade of intermittent splashing water, and this gives its name to the villa. We have imbibed the pathetic atmosphere of the royal residence at Cernobbio, and have learned something of the uneasiness which rocks a modern sovereign's crown. Here we are environed by enthralling memories of " Lords and Ladies " of ancient days. The actual villa was built, indeed, comparatively in recent times, for its founder was Count Giovanni Anguissola of Piacenza, in the year 1570, and his career and associates marked romantic tragedies of the late ' Renaissance.

The younger Pliny loved Molina and its shores, and dwelt there in happy guise. In a letter to his friend Caninius he describes the lovely scenery and the attractions of his retreat. " Do you," he asks, " seek to study, to fish, or to join the chase, or all these and other delectable pursuits together ? All light pleasures and joyous occupations can be enjoyed on this our Larius with the greatest ease and satisfaction." He speaks in another letter to his frequent visitor at Torno, Licinius Surra, of " the spring which rises in the mountains, runs down among mossy rocks into an artificial grotto, where one can lunch most pleasantly. Three times a day it waxes and it wanes with utmost regularity, very interesting to watch. Reclining by its brink our friends can enjoy their repast and collect cooling draughts of ice-cold water in golden goblets. . . ." Just as Caius Pliny and his company of sympathetic souls loved to feast alfresco, so to-day there is no more popular spot for merry picnic-parties along the " Lake of Lakes."

Pliny's ecstatic love of Lacus Larius was a counterfoil to his hatred of Rome—the lake and its shores were his Elysium, and he peopled it with brilliant personages at play and study. On Punto di Balbianello,—or Avedo,—he built a villa, to which he gave the name of "Comœdia,"

and in his mind connected it with the spirit of
the perfect calm from terrors which characterized
the proverbial smoothness of the Zocca dell' Olio
—the Bay of Oil. On the Punto di Bellagio,—the
countervailing promontory,—the celebrated historian placed another residence, and this he called
" *Tragœdia*," the unrestfulness of the dividing
waters of Como and Lecco suggesting deeds of
turbulence and horror. " On the shores of Lacus
Larius," he wrote to Romanus, " I have several
villas, but two of them give me most pleasure,
because I like the thoughts they give me best.
One of them, planted high on rocks after the
fashion of our Baiæ, overlooks the lake : the other,
no less like Baiæ, touches its waters. I am in
the habit of calling them ' Comedy ' and
' Tragedy '—one resting upon the comic slipper,
—so to speak,—the other tossed upon the tragic
shoe. Each has its charm for me and all my
worshipful company. . . . From the one we look
down upon fishermen below toiling with their
nets ; from the other we can catch fish ourselves,
casting our baited hooks from our slumber chambers,—aye, from our very couches, as one does
in a boat. . . ."

The Tragic Muse claims our attention more
especially at Villa Pliniana, and links the era
of the Plinys with our own. The Pope of Rome,

Paul III., with dastardly effrontery, had made
his natural son, Piero Luigi Farnese, Duke of
Parma and Piacenza. Uncomely in person and
morally depraved, the parvenu drew upon himself
the detestation of the nobles of the two duchies.
Five men of mark in Piacenza—Girolamo and
Cammillo Pallavicini, Agostino Landi, Gianluigi
Gonfaloniere, and Giovanni Anguissola—agreed
to do away with the monster. On September 10,
1547, the confederates gained access to the Duke's
cabinet, and despatched him with their rapiers.
The Emperor acknowledged this patriotic deed by
bestowing honours upon the five brave men. Count
Giovanni Anguissola was named Governor of the
Province of Como and granted a substantial
subsidy, which he spent upon his new villa at
Molina. All the same, honour did not bring him
peace of mind, and his deed of blood rankled in
his soul. Perturbed also by repeated attempts
to assassinate him, his life was robbed of all
happiness. He retired to the seclusion of the
Villa Pliniana—there at least hoping for repose
and security, but there he died, a victim of remorse
and misgiving. Alas! "conscience doth make
cowards of us all."

Among the "Ladies" who have graced the
lawns and halls of Villa Pliniana, none were more
remarkable for beauty of person, potentiality of

intellect, and exuberance of spirit than "the conspirator, wit and heroine,—whom all Europe admired and Austria feared,"—Princess Cristina Trivulzio-Belgiosioso. Born in Milan in 1808, at the splendid family palace, rich in art treasures and literary wealth, the young girl was the joy of her parents and the pride of the whole city. Urged on her majority, greatly against her will, to contract what would no doubt have turned out to be a very unhappy marriage, the Princess determined to eschew all matrimonial complications, and devoted herself to the distractions of frenzied political strife. She identified herself with the party of progress against all the conventional canons of her family and order. Marked down at last as a dangerous individual, she was warned to quit Milan or recant her apostasy. She fled to Paris, and there indulged to the full her democratic proclivities. " Citizen Cristina "— she renounced her title of Princess—returned to Lombardy in 1846, and entered most enthusiastically into the popular movement against the hated foreigner—Austria. She personally enlisted, equipped, and commanded a battalion of intrepid volunteers, which unfortunately suffered severely for the cause of Charles Albert. Sentenced to exile, and her property confiscated, she joined a force of Garibaldians in the heroic campaign against France. Then she travelled far and wide, gathering light and leading by the way, and adding classics to the literary treasures of her native land. Her speciality was the future of Italy, and, after the peace of Villafranca, she edited that notable review " *L' Italia.*" Restored once more to the land of her birth, under the Austrian amnesty of 1850, " Citizen Cristina " was allowed to recover much of her property, and thenceforward, under the inspiration of the great Cavour, she advocated convincingly the sacred cause of Italian unity. She died in 1871, leaving behind her brilliant fame in the heroic annals of patriotism.

The Villa Pliniana in quite recent times changed hands, and once belonged to Count Scipione Visconti,—a descendant, of course, of the celebrated ruling family of Milan. Another famous aspirant for the ownership of this historic villa was no less romantic a personage than Percy Bysshe Shelley, the poet-philosopher. In his " Letters from Italy," in April, 1818, he writes : " The finest scenery on the lake is that about Villa Pliniana. . . . The house, which was once a magnificent palace and is now half in ruins, we are endeavouring to procure. . . . The apartments are immensely large, but ill-furnished and antique. The terraces, which overlook the lake and conduct one under the shade of noble laurels, are most delightful." The villa to-day contains little enough to attract the curious, but the portraits of Gian Galeazzo Sforza and his proud and dashing consort Isabella d' Arragona appeal to all who know the story of Milan.

The quaint and quiet little town of Torno, hard by the Villa Pliniana, is rich with glad and dismal memories of famous " Lords and Ladies of the Lake," and of plainer folk beside. It was Lodovico Sforza " Il Moro," who called the French to Italy,—a fatal step indeed,—to aid his ambitious schemes, and they made Torno one of their headquarters. His far less able son, Francesco II., appealed to Spain to cast out the invaders. Spaniards raided Como, its city and its villages, and spent their strength at Torno, where every Frenchman was massacred, and the whole country side pillaged and defaced. Whilst the men were butchered, the women were outraged ; but one of them, Alicia,—surnames never were of any consequence in Lakeland,—leaped from her chamber window right into the lake. Death was nobler than dishonour, and her name lives in the memories of the peasantry, for her self-sacrifice has surrounded it with the halo of sanctity. You may read her story, and all about the dark deed of 1521, if you ask permission to visit the splendid

library, formed by Conte Giovanni Passalacqua,
in his stately marble villa at Moltrasio, opposite
Torno. In the church of San Giovanni Battista,—
dating from the eleventh century,—at Torno are
two precious Christian relics—a Nail of the Holy
Cross and a leg-bone of one of the Holy Innocents
of Bethlehem. A German Bishop, returning from
the Crusades, was weather-bound in his barge at
Torno, but, after depositing his treasures in this
holy shrine, the winds died down and the lake
was becalmed, and so he fared homewards, a wiser
but a poorer man.

There is one little spot of wholly free soil,—the
only one in all Lakeland,—you may almost see
it looking right up the lake between the jutting-
out points of Torriggia and Cavagnola,—which has
ever maintained its pristine freedom: it is an
island—the only one in " Lario." What the fabled
Garden of Eden was to mankind in general, the
Isola Comacina has been to Lombardy and
beyond. Called by the country-folk *Isola di
San Giovanni*, one's thoughts connect this alternative designation with the daring deeds of the
Lombards of old times, who hailed the " Baptist "
for their own. The story goes that, when King
Alboin and his army overran all Italy, the Governor
of Como, Francioni, retired to this secluded
islet, which he strongly fortified and amply pro-

visioned, holding aloft the standard of the Roman Empire. The island became the refuge of more people than it could maintain and treasures of all kinds were borne thither for safety. Peace and security were of short duration, for another war-lord, Autaris, elected King of the Lombards in 584, surrounded the island with his fleet of warships, and, although the defenders stood their ground heroically for many months, the prize was his, and rich it was in gallant men and maidens fair, with booty galore. The menfolk of the Isola were, however, not all warriors, for Francioni had welcomed and sheltered many cunning craftsmen, who became known as "*Magistri Comacini.*" Their story is a moving romance of industry.

Autaris, "the Long Haired," was not only a warrior in the Camp of Mars, he was also a suitor in the Court of Venus. Away across the Engadine Mountains,—the Eastern Alps,—upon the Teutonic throne of Bavaria, reigned a strong King,—Garibald,—who had a lovely and an only daughter. Tales of the Princess's charms had found their way across peak and glacier, and in Autaris's mind had created visions which he was determined to translate into substantial fact. The King despatched from his camp above Menaggio an embassy to his royal brother's castle, demanding the hand in marriage of the beauteous

Theodelinda. Chafing at delay in the expected response, Autaris, incognito, accompanied another embassy to the Bavarian Court. With the chief envoy he was admitted,—of course quite unrecognized,—to the royal presence, and there feasted his eyes upon the bewitching Princess. Like the Queen of Sheba's praise of King Solomon, " one half her charms had not been told," and he determined to make her his own whate'er bechanced. Advancing to Garibald with due courtesy, he explained that he had been specially attached to the embassy that he might convey to his master, who was his intimate friend, a particular description of the personal charms of Princess Theodelinda. The royal maiden was bidden to let down her hair, bare her breast, and pose gracefully before the visitors. Cupid's conquest of Autaris was complete ; he assured Garibald that the Lombard King required no further testimony, and that he was empowered to offer his daughter the Queen-Consort's crown of Italy. Then, gallantly kneeling to the Princess, he offered her a splendid goblet, which he asked her to fill with good red wine and hand round to her new subjects. When his turn came to quaff the loving-cup, he touched the Princess's hand with hot pressure, and at the same time signalled her to silence. Theodelinda, already smitten by the grand physical attributes of her father's guest and by his noble bearing, with a woman's unfailing intuition guessed his identity, and, to her father's inexpressible astonishment, knelt and kissed the sandal of Autaris. Discovered in this deed of daring-do, the Kings embraced, and the Princess's gentle hand was placed within Autaris's massive palm. The marriage ceremonies were at once set in order, and the next day King Autaris and Queen Theodelinda rode off together on their way to Como.

In the popular mind Queen Theodelinda lives still as the gracious fairy of Lake Como. On hill, in dale, on shore, afloat, stories of her and her worth are told in folklore ditties, and sung in rich *barracole*. The noble road from Menaggio to Gravedona is still called "*Strada Regina*." Queen Theodelinda made it that she might the more comfortably be borne in her litter to Bagni di Val Masino in the Valtellina country. Alas, for the joys of married life, the captivating Queen was widowed within the year ; but Autaris's people,—hers, too, by ardent love and gratitude,— besought her to seek a second partner. Whoever he might be they agreed to accept as Lombard King. Many suitors naturally wooed the Queen in weeds, but she turned her face from all but one,—a heathen prince ! Her choice was fixed upon the most valiant Prince in Italy,—spouse of the Conqueror Autaris. She could only wed a hero-warrior,—Ægilulfo, Duke of Turin. One condition only did the Queen require—the Duke's conversion and baptism, and he yielded generously, as a slave of beauty should. Together the new King and his Consort built the Cathedral of Monza, in pious memory of this victory of the Christian faith. Ægilulfo was on the point of leading an army to attack the Holy City, but Theodelinda at once stopped the expedition, for which act of grace a generous Pope, Gregory the Great, sent to the Queen at Monza a token of his approval and gratitude. This was a very unique and precious gift—no less than a finely beaten fillet of iron to fit her royal brow made from a nail of the Crucifixion of Calvary,—and now the famous Iron Crown of Lombardy. The "nail" to be sure, is nowadays seen encircling a coronet of pure gold and jewelled with four-and-twenty superb precious stones—the age at the time of its presentation of the saintly Queen. At Monza her portrait,—an ancient bas-relief,—is over the great west door : she is represented at the Baptism of Christ bearing a cross and wearing a crown !

There are two accounts of Queen Theodelinda's death and burial. There is, first of all, a well-supported tradition that, after she had buried

King Ægilulfo at San Lorenzo in Milan,—its most
ancient church,—she retired humbly to the Castle
of Vezio, which dominates Varenna on the Lake
of Como, and there ended her days happily in
pious exercises and charity. Our Tennyson has
caught the spirit of Queen Theodelinda's romance
in his nocturne on sweet and dreamy Como ·

> " The Lariano crept
> To that fair port below the castle
> Of Queen Theodelind, where we slept,
> Or hardly slept, but watched awake
> A cypress in the moonlight shake,
> The moonlight touching o'er a terrace
> On tall agave above the lake."

The poet's inspiration was that of the folklore
of the country-side of Varenna, which relates how
that, when the rising moon, topping the Monte
Grigna-Settentrionale, glints down the shadowy
Val d' Esino a silver beam, the cypresses around
and below the ruins of the Torre di Vezio, swaying
in the evening breeze, allow the brilliance to flash
upon the tasselated head of a lonely agave, which
for the moment assumes the verisimilitude of
the gracious, vigorous Queen. The daylight con-
sistency of the scene is no less eloquent of the
fragrance of saintly deeds, for the rugged stones
of Theodelinda's last resting-place are covered by
luxuriant growths of grapes and peaches, whilst
gay flowerets of the field perfume the air. In the

deep gorge below churns the frothy Fiume di
Latte, as it tears itself over rock and ruin, rushing
impetuously to the lake. Murmurs of its tragic
music rise up with its vapour and spread themselves peacefully over the velvet moss upon which
Queen Theodelinda trod.

Very different is the Monza story of the Lombard
Queen. Buried in a massive tomb of country
stone, in the north chapel of the Cathedral choir,
San Carlo Borromeo, when on his purifying visitation of the Lombard churches, marked the tomb
for ejection—because the Queen had not been
canonized ! Too unwieldy to be moved, the tomb
was uncovered, and its contents were duly identified. The corpse, or what remained of it, was
untouched, but Theodelinda's comb, her fan, her
cup of sapphire, a crystal cross,—Saint Gregory's
gift,—and the gold-embossed cover of her missal
were transferred to the Cathedral sacristy, and
there they may be seen to-day. Whichever story
may be true, one thing is certain—no shadow of
tragedy cast its baneful influence over the romance
of Queen Theodelinda's life and love.

But to return to the picturesque Island of
Comacina. After the fall of valiant Francioni the
islet became the sanctuary of many outraged
fugitives—penniless and hopeless. Its umbra-
geons trees and the eaves of its ancient church

gave shelter to the Duke of Bergamo, Goldulo, after his rebellion against King Ægilulfo. Cunipert and Ausprando, driven from their governments, at Comacina laid plans to recover what they had lost. The people of Como, ever jealous of the enterprise and the wealth of the Comacinesi, waged destructive wars against the island, and devastated it with fire and sword. The vanquished, however, appealed to Milan, and with Milan destroyed the turbulent lake city. The epic poem of the Ten Years' War thus speaks of Isola Comacina :

" Insula non dormit, nec jam tenit illa quietem,
Cogitat et vigilat, versat furiosa quid agit."

So much for the mediæval " Lords and Ladies " of Lake Como.

So placed is the Zocca dell' Olio—the Bay of Oil—and so distinctly clear upon its smooth mirrored surface are the reflections of island groves and mainland boskets, with buildings flashing white and boats of many hues, that it seems but a handshake between the quaint church of San Giovanni and the glittering Villa Arconati. Beautifully situated at Campo, upon the Punta d' Avedo,—the slowly accumulating delta of the torrents from Monte Tremezzo and Monte di Lenno,—this exquisite villa appeals to all who hurry past on the silvery waterway to slacken sail or draw in the oars. There, upon the sculptured terrace of the little port, hard by the villa, stands a statue of St. Francis d' Assisi, delicately chiselled and lifelike, and ever holding out his hands in benediction—those holy hands stigmataed by an approving Christ. Simple-hearted and devout fisherfolk accept the saintly blessing with uncovered heads and crossed breasts, and are all the better for the momentary pause from labour and for the passing holy thought. And then belated boatmen and peasant folk across the narrow strait from Cavagnola to Loppia take heart of grace when they behold the flare of St. Francis's night-cresset flickering over the shadowy waves. Though the curfew has bidden men to well-earned sleep, "*Ben San Franzese, ben not*" — Good St. Francis, good-night, — comes whispered through the gloom.

This saintly signal is due to the devotion and munificence of a worthy peasant-Cardinal, Balbiano Durini. He purchased the villa and a factory near his native hamlet, whereat to end his days in peace. He called his habitation "*Il Balbianello*—the little grot of Balbiano,—and he founded therein a Convalescent Home for sick brethren of the charitable Order The estate carried with it the title of Count, and, by an odd caprice, he addressed each inmate of the hostel

by the title which he himself refused. The villa
itself was built by another Cardinal of Holy Church,
—from designs of Pellegrino Pellegrini, the lordly
lacustrine architect sobriquetted Tibaldo,—in 1596,
Tolomeo Gallio—a notable spiritual "Lord of
Como," a famous benefactor all around his cher-
ished Lario. From Gravedona in the North to
Como in the South, churches, villas, and institutions
abound, all looking to him as restorer or founder.

Campo and its villa are associated also with
the name of another famous Larioan family, the
Giovi—or Zobii in the vernacular.

Somewhere about the time that Norman William
conquered this fair island of ours, Giacomo Zobii
obtained the unique privilege of naming both the
Prefect of the village of Stabio,—opposite the
Isola Comacina,—and the priest of its early
Church of St. Mary Magdalene. The church,
still earlier, and again later, members of the
Giovi family have endowed richly, so that, under
the auspices of the rector, all sick and needy
wayfarers may eat and drink and rest, and be
doctored too. The Ospedaletto de' Zobii is still a
benevolent institution, and the Torre di Zobii
still marks the spot where the good men and
women of the family dwelt and helped their fellow-
men—worthy "Lords and Ladies of the Lake."

Benedetto and Paolo Giovi, both born in the

city of Como, were among the most celebrated
"Lords" of their family. Historians both,
perhaps the younger,—as is usual in most families,
—rose to greater fame. The elder brother was a
devout and simple-minded scholar, who, although
his feet never carried him farther than to the utmost
shores of the lake he loved,—and he knew nothing
of the great world of Milan and of Italy,—contrived
to excavate a valuable mme of most truthful
fact and most amusing fiction. His labours he
dedicated to the city of his birth, under the happy
title " *Historia Patria* " ; to him is due the most
succinct précis pen ever wrote—piquant and epi-
grammatic too. Translated, it tells the fifteen
hundred years' story of the city and its people :
" A Greek colony of Orobii first settled here.
Gauls took it, Rhœtians, an Alpine tribe, destroyed it. C. Scipio Pompeius, and Caius Cæsar
restored and colonized it. Warlike men of Milan
burnt it. Frederic I. rebuilt it. Twice destroyed
by civil war. Discord of rival families plunged
it in calamities. With Charles V. came new hope
of prosperity " Born in 1471, Benedetto Giovio
died in 1544, and Paolo,—twelve years his junior,—
survived till 1552.·

Paolo was very much more ambitious than his
elder brother. A man of rare genius and vast
erudition, he earned the title of " *Il Varro di Lom-*

BENEDETTO GIOVIO   PAOLO GIOVIO

Fi   ι Illustrations in "Famiglie Celebr Italiana   by P G Litα

To face page 146

bardia." A famous poem of his " *Quattrodieci Fontane di Como,*" sings the beauties and the excellences of the valleys and the hills of Lario. Paolo Giovio took Minor Orders in the Church, and rose to the eminent post of Papal Secretary under no less celebrated a Pontiff than Leo X. Thirty-seven years of his life he devoted to his masterpiece in literature—a history of his own times. This remarkable composition has been made the butt of derision. Taking his cue doubtless from the weird gallery of celebrities in the *Palazzo del Banco di San Giorgio* at Genoa, whose *Sala del Consiglio* is filled with statues and busts of Genoese worthies in various sizes, the size and prominence of each worthy being accurately gauged by the amount each Signore paid the mercenary sculptor ! Paolo's contemporary narratives also differentiate the sums paid down ! He used, it was said, two pens, a golden one with which to laud his most generous patrons, and a pen of iron for bare, cold notices ! His biographer makes an amusing skit on this eminently business-like method · " He was," he says, " no greater a sinner than the rest of his profession, but he had the saving grace of not denying his perversities." Wideawake Monsignore Paolo was never at a loss for an excuse for inaccuracy or exaggeration. " Never mind,"

he laughed, " it will no doubt be quite true in
three or four hundred years !" There was,
indeed, a method in the romancer's economy, for,
when Francis I. of France ceased his patronage,
he heaped adulations upon the new Pope, Clement,
and his family, the Medici, and gained in acknow-
ledgment the fat see of Nocera and a hatful
of preferments besides.

Another characteristic work of Paolo Giovio
was his " *Descriptio Larii Lacus*," engineered
also upon " the poor or much-pay " principle.
Its publication, in 1558, six years after its author's
death, was due to an amusing circumstance.
One, Dionisio Sommentino, a notary of Novara,
was sent to Bellagio to investigate a charge of
murder among the tenants of his patron, Conte
Nicolò Sfondrate. The beauty of the situation
and the splendour of the villa, now Villa Serbelloni, enraptured the man of law. Upon his
return he recounted the delightful impressions he
had received. The Count smiled sardonically
and asked him whether he would like to dwell in
the permanent contemplation of so many attractions. With enthusiasm Sommentino responded.
" Go, then," said the Count, " and fetch me from
my library table a little pile of manuscript marked
' P.G.' There, "said he, handing his companion
the bundle, you will find every feature which has

struck you noted; take it home, and dream you are at Bellagio!" The notary took the gift and with it the determination to publish to the world the charming narrative.

Still another Zobio made his name famous as a "Lord of Como" — Gianbattista Giovio,—the very pleasant writer of "*Lettere Lariane.*" He belonged to the eighteenth century, and so did Napoleon Buonaparte,—and to the nineteenth,— the great war-Lord of Lombardy and the Lakes. In 1810 Napoleon dissolved the Italian monasteries and other semi-conventual institutions, and with them went the Hospital of Zobio, all purchased by a Como nobleman—Count Porro. His tenure, however, of the Villa at Campo was short, for he was compelled to go into exile for his political opinions, and settled in Brussels, spending the end of his days with Marquis Arconati Visconti, a fellow *refugé.* By his will he bequeathed his estate to his friend, who, being restored to his native land, gave his name "Arconati" to the villa. The Marquis died in 1880, and then his widow splendidly restored the villa and refurnished it, and occasionally visited it. Among the "Lords and Ladies" who have grimaced and smirked, or, of sterner stuff, conversed and plotted at Villa Arconati have been Silvio Pellico, Giovanni Mazzini, and Princess-Citizen Cristina Trivulzio-

Belgiosioso. They and many more made pious pilgrimages to the shrine of the famous Madonna del Soccorso, high above the lake upon the Dosso d' Avedo.

The legend of the Madonna del Soccorso is as pretty a story as any of the thousand and one which scintillate above the seven brilliant stars of St. Mary's coronal. Many, many years ago, say the goody gossips,—there was a little deaf and dumb peasant girl of Isola, who tended her father's small flock of goats and sheep in the pastures above the village. One day she wandered with her charges somewhat off the beaten track, and, lo and behold! found herself in a land of rocks and grottos. One little cave in particular attracted her, for by it grew the very biggest cyclamens the child had ever seen, and at the same time the most deeply crimson dyed. Stretching out her hand to grasp some of the fragrant blooms she was astounded to behold, within the cave's mouth, the Madonna with the Child Christ in her arms. The Holy Mother smiled upon her, and made a movement which Nania misinterpreted, and, startled, she fled from the spot, nor stayed her steps till she fell weeping in her mother's arms. To the consternation of her fond parent and her sisters, too, Nania's tongue-string was loosened, and she uttered the first articulate sounds they had ever heard: "*La Madon! La Madon! Col Bimbi! Bimbi Gesù!*"

Recovering from their surprise, the child excitedly told them what she had seen, and where. The Madonna Adeliza called her menfolk from their toil and, led by little Nania, the whole village ascended the steep slopes and reached the spot where the flock of sheep and goats still nibbled the succulent grasses. There, sure enough, within the grotto stood, not, indeed, a living *Maria Vergine*, but a sculptured figure. With the utmost reverence the pious peasants knelt upon the rocky pasture, and recited all the prayers they knew, whilst the women, shedding copious tears, folded in turn the hitherto mute child to their breasts. "*Miracolo! miracolo!*" was upon the mouths of all, and forthwith the whole company ran hastily down the declivities and made straight for the pievano's house. With cross, candle, and bell, the good priest sallied forth, attended by his village acolytes, sprinkling holy water and tossing clouds of incense smoke before the grotto and reciting many prayers. The devotions of Holy Church were rendered, and the congregation then set to work to lay the first stone of a hillside tabernacle, wherein to guard and venerate the Holy Image. A chapel and an altar were very soon upreared, and then, with great ceremony, the Bishop of Como and a goodly gathering translated the miracle-working Madonna to the church at Isola, and fixed her upon a splendid shrinelike bracket. This removal, however, was not at all to the liking of the Madonna, and one night she returned mysteriously to her grotto shrine. It was a way the Madonna of the *cinquecento* had, and characterictic of her beneficient sovereignty! Thrice was our Madonna carried, with penitential litanies back to Isola, and thrice she hurried back, at last to be allowed by her devotees to assert her will and pleasure.

In 1537 the present chapel, on its grassy, stony platform was erected, and since then " *La Madonna del Soccorso* " has rested contentedly. Very many miracles have, these four hundred years, been wrought upon that lovely mead for the relief of suffering humanity, and very many mutes have there cried out with little Nania— " *La Madon ! La Madon !*" An annual pilgrimage was ordered by ecclesiastical authority. It is still held on September 8, and attracts thousands and thousands of pious folk. Few, perhaps, of the " Lords and Ladies of the Lake " join those fervent bands—Society has another level, another cult—maybe a worse and certainly a more sordid. Would that some of the pristine simplicity of faith and practice marked our own day's work !

In times of stress the country-folk of Lario and its villages cry aloud to the Madonna of Isola, visit her hillside shrine and deposit their little offerings, leaving, in memory of their pilgrimage, little spluttering tallow candles. The approach to the chapel has become a foot-polished pavement. By the " *Via Sacra*," in small shrines and chapels, are fifteen coloured terra-cotta groups,—Biblical and historical,—teaching more vividly than book-lore the great epic of Christ and Mary. If you ask the cassocked *custode* of the church at Isola, he tells you the Madonna has been nothing but a blessing ever since Nania first proclaimed her.

III.

From the scene of sweet reveries of religious fervour over Isola, it is but a short course by land or lake to the modern elysium of Lake Como— a triangular sheet of deepest blue water pointed by Bellagio, Cadenabbia, and Menaggio—each brim full of interests, chiefly modern. A little way back from the well-worn stone landing-steps at Tremezzo stands a villa, rather inconspicuous and lacking in renown—" Villa Scorpione " it is named. A velvet, verdant sward stretches from the garden-gates to the borders of the lake, where some ancient, much-gnarled olive-trees lend weird charms to the *mise en scène*. One glorious summer's evening, in 1873,—when the Lombard sun, beating hotly upon the ice-fields of the glowing crimsoned Alps was reflected, with the refraction of its ardour, upon the green pastures and blue waters of the North Italian lakes,— a gondola shot out silently from the pier at Cadenabbia. The sky was of chameleon opal, and the trees of the wood had taken on a golden sheen of bronze. Butterflies and moths,—gay-hued or sombre,— worsting one another in daring flight ; honey-bees, —their thirst for nectar not yet quenched,—and dragon-flies,—spiking everywhere in sunbeams, and jealous of more humble glow-worms already kindling their lamps of gold,—were holding revels with the busy, noisy crickets in the superheated grass. The craft drew near the landing-stage— in it a quartet of English travellers—their object being a friendly visit to the hospitable owners of the Villa.

" *Zitto !*"—Hush !—passed from lip to lip, for the raised vocal ecstasy, the sweep of oar, or the creak of rowel would have utterly disturbed a marvellously charming idyllic serenade in view and hearing of the water-party. Slung from two hoary, widely separated arms of an ancient olive giant was a red-knotted, netted hammock, and from it trailed the white laced petticoat of a salmon silken robe. One dainty shoeless foot of the fair form reclining there,—with her gay Japanese umbrella stuck up against the golden sun, too hot to bear,—was swinging gracefully and rythmically to and fro. The face was in shadow—her form well shrunk in the meshes made recognition difficult. Below the dreaming, rocking damsel, reclined upon a couch of moss and flowers, an apple - green - velvet - costumed suitor; his head, long flaxen haired, was bare; at his throat he wore a yellow silk cravat; his knee-ribbons, gaily-bunched, matched his tie. His face, turned away from the direction of the lake, was fixed upon the object of his song,—for he was eloquently strumming a much - decorated guitar, and he was softly drooning his melody of love. Through the glittering, animated leaf-sprays of the trees stole silvered visions of a crescent moon—just rising to greet the peeping stars. Bats were all the while incontinently faring here and there, whilst nesting-birds were cooing soft good-nights to one another; all Nature was in harmony.

The lovers were Henry Brockett and Georgiana Bernal - Osborne; he the son and heir of the owner of the villa over there—she, the youth's fiancée, as good as she was fair. Now they are

man and wife together, and have been many a
year. Probably they have forgotten the idyll
they created for the delight of their fellow-country-
folk ; perhaps they did not realize it at the time.
Love is often very blind and very deaf !

Villa Carlotta claims notice further on at Cadenabbia, from the water-wayfarer, and from the
lover of the beautiful. Its name is very recent,
for, not till Duchess Charlotte of Saxe Meiningen
came as a bride to Lario in 1850, did " Carlotta "
supersede " Sommariva "—the loveliest bank of
all—the name of the first noble owner, Conte
Sommariva. The original villa, indeed, was quite
an unambitious edifice, built by the Marchese
Clerici of Como, in the middle of the eighteenth
century. Princess Albrecht of Prussia bought it
and the estate for £29,000, in 1843, and gave it to
her daughter, upon her marriage with the Hereditary Prince of Saxe-Meiningen *Regina del
Lago !"* is the unanimous verdict,—native and
foreign,—when it is sought to balance villa
rivalry on Lario. " Carlotta " yields to none ;
her throne is the highest, her crown the rarest
in the realm of Nature decked by Art. Be it
softly whispered, however, she holds no Court of
romance ; and her story is void of tragedy, but
her treasures are eloquent of human passions
and the joys of man. All the world knows some-

KING CHRISTIAN HUNTING WITH CAVALIERE BARTOLOMMEO COLLEONE

GIROLAMO ROMANINO

Fres > at the Castle o Malpaga. (See page 280)

To face page 156

thing, at least, of the loves of Cupid (Eros) and Psyche ; but reading mythology is somewhat dull work in comparison with the contemplation of the almost speaking, breathing group of sculpture in the Great Saloon of Villa Carlotta, which tells so convincingly the sweetest tale of human mesmerism.

This lovely "bit" of purest Carrara marble,— flashing white as the crystal snow,—is not the creation of a passionate Buonarroti, nor of an impetuous Cellini ; no sensuous Sansovino nor gallant Giovanni da Bologna chiselled those exquisite young forms. A serious son of Italy, a recluse indeed, born in Tyrolean Possagno,—through whose veins still coursed at fifty the fire of love,—gave to mankind, in 1800, this thrilling version of the old, old love story. Youngest of three lovely sisters, Psyche incurred the jealousy of Venus, who condemned her to love the most hideous and contemptible of mortals. Eros,—ever wide awake,—determined to make her his own, and conveyed her mysteriously, whilst she slept, to a nuptial bed, upon a lovely mountain-top. His visits were at night-time, and he vanished ere the dawn. Searching one early morning for her beloved companion she came on him pinioned by the dew. Flashing upon the prostrate, godlike youngster, her golden, flickering, lamp, she beheld no monster but the comeliest youth in Paradise. Butterfly-like she hovered over him, not daring to touch him, though thirsting for a stolen kiss. Down by his side she laid, but he, bashful, instantly arose,—brushed by her gossamer-like winglets. Appealingly she extended her ambrosial arms to retain her lover, but he winged away his flight and left poor Pysche fixed with a silver dart right through her heart. Venus chanced to pass Psyche's couch of love, and overheard her weeping bitterly, and calling Eros distractedly. Instantly she seized the love-lorn deity,—no daughter-in-law should she be, be-witching though she might be,—and clapped her in a noisome prison. Psyche was love-sick for Eros, and so was Eros for Psyche, and the gods of Olympus granted their desire, and Psyche entered the Court of Heaven, escorted by Mercury. The offspring of those amours men nowadays call " Pleasure !" Canova has most cunningly con-fected the awakening of the blessed pair,—fated to part in the first rosebud of their love—a perfect human allegory in marble. In the same saloon of the Villa Carlotta is another convincing creation of the same master-hand, a more complete contrast to the Eros and Psyche could not be imagined— " The Magdalen." Sunken, broken-hearted and penitent upon the ground, she silently proclaims

the bitterness of illicit passion. Her story is
enshrined in the life's narrative of Christ,—its
echo reaches, and will reach, to the utmost limits
of human sympathy. Centrally placed in that
villa boudoir of the "Loves" is still another
marble group,—not by Canova, but by Acquisti,—
"Mars and Venus." If the goddess had to relinquish her beauteous boy to Psyche, Mars
she held in thrall—woman, the "Superman" in
celestial cult as well as in matters of the world!
This, too, is an inspiring work, for the sculptor
has made his marble think, and plot, and counter-
plot, and all but live and move.

In truth, this very captivating salon at Cadenabbia is a precious casket, like Pandora's, wherein
are found imperishably preserved the human
passions which have inspired the lives and fortunes
of the "Lords and Ladies of the Italian Lakes"
whose romances fill these pages.

There are more things of deep interest in the
villa, and its gardens are unmatchable for beauty
and for rarity of plants and trees. Within the
beautiful little chapel of Sommariva, by the lake,
is a very chaste "*Pièta,*" in costly crystal marble,
too. Its contemplation in that hallowed fane
brings the mind of busy mankind, intent on
pleasure, to view the scriptural expression of the
mystery of Love—the dead Christ lying across his

Mother's knees. So, when the human heart has thumped out all its fierce desires, there remains nothing for the lifeless body but to lie prone along dear Mother Earth ; but, after all, " Cupid " is stronger than death, and " Psyche," the soul, never dies '

We pass out into the shadow of the giant-leaved plane-trees in the avenue by the lake, and behold the garish glories of the shimmering heat contentedly, for at Cadenabbia Longfellow is close by—the sweetest English singer of the simple life, and we read him thus :

> " I pace the leafy colonnade,
>   Where level branches of the plane
> Above me weave a roof of shade,
>   Impervious to the sun or rain.
>
> " By Sommariva's garden gate,
>   I make the marble steps my seat,
> And hear the water as I wait
>   Lapping the steps beneath my feet.
>
> " The hills sweep upward from the shore,
>   With villas scattered one by one
> Upon their wooded spurs, and lower,
>   Bellagio blazing in the sun.
>
> " And dimly seen, a tangled mass
>   Of walls and woods, in light and shade,
> Stands beckoning up the Stelvio Pass
>   Varenna, with its white cascade.
>
> " I ask myself, ' Is this a dream ?
>   Will it all vanish into air ?
> Is there a land of such supreme
>   And perfect beauty anywhere ?'

"Sweet vision! Do not fade away;
    Linger until my heart shall take
Into itself the summer day
    And all the beauty of the lake:

"Linger until upon my brain
    Is stamped an image of the scene,
Then fade into the air again
    And be as if thou hadst not been!"*

Longfellow loved Cadenabbia, and there he wrote many of his idyllic poems. He loved to gaze across the glittering water at Bellagio in its magical effulgence,—a dream land of fancy and of fact. Bellagio called to the poet; she calls to the prosaic, too, as well as to the romantic among her many visitors to-day. The call of Bellagio is to cross over and pick up acquaintance-ship with some of the "Lords and Ladies," who there have lived and died, and who haunt the villas of her crown; to cross the cloud-hued wavelets ever gyrating in brilliant ballet, and heed not siren's cry the while   But willing, very willing, though we be to rally to the signal, another cry arrests us as we step aboard our awninged gondola—a cry from the heights above the Villa Carlotta—a cry from lofty Griante to climb up to her village green and behold her beauties and listen to her story.

* From a poem in manuscript, written by Longfellow at Cadenabbia, and preserved in the office of the Hotel Belle Vue there.

It is the first Sunday in September, and the whole village, with its pretty church, withal ancient though it be, is *en fête*—" *La Festa de' Canestri* "—the Feast of Baskets—in fact, the Harvest Festival. All the countryfolk, great and small, foregather at the parish church for very early Mass, bringing with them their offerings to Christ's altar, most tastefully arranged in big new wicker baskets. An amazing variety of firstfruits is presented to the parish priest for benediction and acceptance,—living animals and birds, fresh-caught fish, fruit from the orchards, grain from the fields, and roots, newly crushed oil, and freshly trod juice of grapes; with sugar-loaves and loaves of bread, butter, cheese, and eggs, side by side with tinned meats and stuffs, and sausages and tasty jam-tarts. As heterogeneous in dress as in their offerings, the peasants and the farmers and their children, with gay banners and quaint crucifixes and lighted lanterns in honour of the Host, with exuberant grimace, gesticulation, and rush of noisy words, call forth echoes and reflections from green woods and polished stones. The men and boys, bare-headed and be-clogged, have covered their well-stitched gathered smocks with coarse linen surplices and scarlet capes; the women and girls, in highly coloured stuffs and calicoes, are discreetly veiled in black

veils and white, and all wear posies of natural
fragrant blossoms at breast or by way of coronal.
They are all members of religious communities ;
mostly of the "*Buona Morte,*" and carry their
Prayer-Books with rosaries, and badges of their
guilds. What heaven-lifting voices those lusty sons
of agriculture possess: the old men and the young
vie with one another to drown the sweeter
cadences, if nasal, of their womenfolk ! All
know, word by word, the oft-sung litanies ; all
recite the well-remembered prayers ; all march
with swinging strides decorously through lane
and pasture-land, in and out of rocky corners,
and around quaint house-ends, the *Pievano* at
their head. Halting here and there for ritual
acts of thanksgiving, until the whole district has
been well traversed, and the processionists squat
themselves down about the church once more and
await the excitement of the auction. This is a
remarkable competition, joined in by " Lords and
Ladies of the Lake," personified not only by
descendants of romantic forbears of the past,
but by sympathetic visitors from afar, Americans
for the most part. The profits of the sale are
pocketed by the *Pievano,* for the maintenance
of the fabric of the church and for its functions.
When all is over the country - people quietly
return to their farms and hovels to resume the

year's toil and to bear their burdens stoically, whilst overseas visitors carry away pleasurable impressions to store in head and heart.

Bellagio, indeed, still calls us over the fabled, fairy waters, and we fain would go, but other voices call,—voices out of fathomless deeps,— sirens of the lake. Psyche-like they yearn for lovers ; vampire-like they crave men's blood. For the nincompoop and molly-coddle care they not one whit : their lust is for the beauty of Adonis, the culture of Apollo and the energy of Mercury. They count their human prey by hundreds— submerged never to reappear. A finer oarsman than Edward Royds never stroked for his University ; a noble life was his, and full of promise ; daring beyond his fellows, and resourceful, too. A summer's morn tempted him to swim in the cool water; many such had charmed him. He took his wonted plunge, right in the middle of the lake ; his friend,—who now sets down this record,—regained the boat in safety, but Royds never scaled that stern. Somewhere in a mysterious cavern under the dissimulating flood his body rests till the crack of doom, shrouded by the floating strands of hair of cruel lake-maidens. It was a double tragedy for Caddenabbia. Cupid's gentle arrow became a poisoned dart in the stricken heart of a lovely English girl.

A TYPICAL FORMAL VILLA-GARDEN AT VILLA BOZZOLI

From a photograph

To face page 164

She drooped and died within a twelvemonth of
her lover's loss. One other domestic tragedy is
connected in the writer's mind with the mirrored
whirlpool of the lake-maidens twixt Cadenabbia
and Bellagio. Decorated for valour upon the field
of battle by the grateful King of Prussia,—
first German Emperor,—young George Lampson
was a valiant medical volunteer, although an
American, in the ranks of the allied Teuton
armies. Gifted very greatly with physical and
mental attributes, the world and its successes
were his apparently to command at will; he was a
pet Fairy Fortune. Caddenabbia was the sana-
torium for his wounds and the arena of his
pleasures. He ministered skilfully to many an
ailing sojourner by that beauteous lake, putting
by his up - to - date methods the hoary mis-
wisdoms of local medicos to shame. He treated
most successfully,—when she was suddenly taken
very ill,—the dear one, to whom in part I have
dedicated these romances of the Italian lakes.
Two years passed, and then the hero was hailed
before a Criminal Court, tried for murder, condemned, and hanged ! At Wimbledon, in Surrey,
dwelt a delicate youth, Valentine, George Lampson's cousin. In England for his health and
education, and heir to countless dollars, his was
the only life between the testator and his cousin.

A devil entered the sunny heart of the young doctor, now the husband of a charming English girl. Visits to Valentine became the order of the day, but the youth grew feebler and whiter week by week. Nothing that his cousin brought him gave more delight than boxes of rich chocolates. The post-mortem proclaimed the presence of strychnine—strychnine in the chocolate—this was George Lampson's crime! His untimely and unworthy end was not the end of tragedy. A young wife, soon to be a mother, brought forth prematurely, through the shock, a still-born child, and was, alas! buried in her offspring's grave. These were like other tragedies of the Italian lakes, which count their victims by a lengthy roll, but the great world beyond knows little of such happenings. Perhaps chance conventional paragraphs in some journal are all the record. The prime function of creation is destruction ; life is but a complexity of contradictions, and Providence, so misnamed, is a vendetta !

Many villas now constellate around San Giovanni di Bellagio, but they are modern in their vogue, yet some of them have links with a romantic past. Melzi,—the most conspicuous among them, —is of very recent date. Built by Count Francesco Melzi d' Erile, Vice-President of the abortive Cis-Alpine Republic, in 1814, it is a link with

the most shining genius of a century. Buonaparte created Count Francesco Duke of Lodi, and
on him showered numerous distinctions. Local
tradition has it that the great Corsican spent
many a strenuous hour in the delightful retreat,
working out his mighty schemes. When on
campaign he gave himself little or no time for
relaxation and pleasure. Duchess Josephine
Melzi - Barbo,—the Emperor's goddaughter,—
decorated the villa pretty much as we see it
to-day. The chapel is remarkable for an unconventional and unique figure of Christ,—a
youth in meditation,—and for two frescoes,
which are sure to strike the eye and set the mind
inquiring. They are family memorials of an
earlier Francesco Melzi d' Erile, and of his dear
friend and master the great Leonardo da Vinci.
One represents Leonardo imparting instruction to
the young Count ; the other, Francesco receiving
the master's last bequest—his studio at Milan.
Between master and pupil existed an impassioned
friendship. The family of Melzi possessed a
beautiful country house at Vaprio in the valley
of the Adda, some twenty miles from Milan.
Thither Leonardo fled for repose, or when harassed
by the attentions of the French soldiery. When
the master went, in 1576, on his way to Paris, at
the bidding of King Francis I., his boon com-

panion was his young friend, Count Francesco, more like a son or a younger brother. Three busy years only were vouchsafed to Leonardo, grown old but still ineffable, and then death took him. Broken-hearted, Francesco carried the news to their royal patron, who appointed him executor of the will and a chamberlain of his royal person. Writing to his father from the Castle of Amboise, where the comrades had resided, he concludes a sorrowful epistle thus : " He was the kindest of fathers to me. . . . Nature will find it hard to produce such another great man." In the grounds of Villa Melzi are marble busts by Canova of Buonaparte's mother — Madame Letitia — and of his first Empress—Josephine Beauharnais. The name Josephine has now been handed down for three generations in the family of Melzi d' Erile.

The Villas Trotti, Giulia, Serbelloni, and Trivulzio are all hard by Melzi. Their gardens are contiguous, each one a vision of Paradise. There is not much that may be told of some of these, but the Serbelloni,—now called Villa Crevelli-Serbelloni,—has romances not a few ; and we must put back the scene five hundred years to get at the beginning. In the fourteenth century the towering promontory of Bi-lacus was unclothed with gracious foliage ; it was a rocky headland, dominating, from its impregnable fortress, both lakes—Como and Lecco. Within its walls and bastions stood armed to the teeth men of blood and human devils,—desperadoes flying from the hand of justice.

In 1375 Gian Galeazzo Visconti subdued the outlaws, and destroyed their stronghold, and ordered henceforth no man to dwell there. The Marquis Stanga of Milan, however, loyal ever to his master, obtained from Lodovico Sforza,— regent and ruler both—the right to plant the eminence with trees and build a family residence. Vain was his handiwork, for, no sooner had he moved his family to his Larian elysium, and his guests had commenced to come and go,—amazing the fisherfolk by their frolics and their follies,— than ravagers once more pounced upon their prey, —the dreaded Cavargnoni, from Menaggio,—and the pleasaunce was laid bare. For two hundred years the Hill of Bi-lacus, or Bellagio, was a waste, and then another noble Milanese—Count Ercole Sfondrati—rebuilt the ruined mansion and afforested the promontory. His name and his date—1594 —he stuck up on a wall washed by the split waters of the lake at the point of land. His family became extinct at the end of the eighteenth century, and their property passed to the Duke Alessandro Serbelloni. At the point of the headland is a ridge of hard sharp rocks, and there, according to the story still rife in Bellagio, in a massive castle dwelt a human siren-vampire—one Adeliza, Countess of Borgomanero, who had for her iniquities been exiled from the smiling Val d' Ossola. She set up her Court, or charnel-house, in this inaccessible spot, and set as well no bounds to liaisons with every passing gallant—soldier or troubadour. Like bad Queen Giovanna II. of Naples, of later date, she had a very simple way of ridding herself of her lovers when they had given her what she craved. They were expected to commit suicide next morning, but those who shirked this quietus were dropped willy-nilly through steel-racked oubliette into the deep lake below—where there were no tale-bearers, and, of course, no return !

* * * * *

"*Alla memoria di Giulio Mylius*" is the dedication of a very beautiful bas-relief, by the sculptor Marchesi the younger, upon the wall of a marble temple in the lovely gardens of the Villa Wachs-Mylius at Loveno, a few minutes' walk from the Castello di Menaggio. The relief represents a youth recumbent upon a couch at the moment of death, with a young girl bending over him, bitterly weeping. It is a subject full of pathos, and few who look upon it can restrain a sigh or a

tear; it is the tragedy of Giulio Mylius and
Anastasie Kreutzner. Giulio lived with his
parents,—well-to-do merchants of Como, who
yearly sojourned in their Larian lake-side retreat.
One day he chanced to meet, coming out of the
cathedral, the most lovely girl he had ever seen.
She was the ward of an uncle by marriage, whose
sister had married an Austrian noble from Passau,
and both had died when their only little girl was
still an infant. An intimacy naturally sprang up
between the young people, and guardians on both
sides acquiesced in the engagement. Unhappily
Giulio was in delicate health, and his religion,—
Jewish,—was a ban to the union. He was sent
to travel and recuperate, but at Trieste he lay
sick unto death. News, lover-like, was not slow
in reaching Anastasie, and she delayed not to run
away from home and join her fond Giulio. He
pressed her to marry him, dying though he knew
himself to be, in order that his parents might take
her under their protection. The girl consented,
but no sooner was the marriage-ring placed upon
her finger than her spouse fell back dead in her
arms. Giulio's parents stood by the young widow,
and took her into their house and home. Some
two years after, Anastasie, by the wish of Signore
and Madonna Mylius, married Lucio Vigone,—a
prosperous young merchant of Milan,—and Anas-

tasie's dowry included the freehold of the Villa Mylius at Menaggio. Below the bas-relief in the garden temple is this touching inscription :

" Sul fior degli anni in stranio lido li' muore
  Fragli amplessi e le lagrime de suvi
  Al bacio vola dell' eterno amore
  E acerbo duolo è cio che resta a noi."*

The date of this pathetic romance is 1830.

From Menaggio sprang one of the greatest lights of Lario—"*Il Cavaliere Aretino*"—whose real name was Leone Leoni. A goldsmith by profession, he first became famous as a medallist, and entered the service of the Emperor Charles V. His *chef-d'œuvre* was a bronze statue of His Majesty in pure white Carrara marble, to which he added, very judiciously, flesh-tints here and there. This figure, —the size of life,—he clothed with costly steel armour, which he forged himself, to be removed at will—a great novelty in the art of the sculptor. This remarkable creation is now at Madrid, and on the pedestal are inscribed Leoni's words : " *Cæsaris virtute furor domitus* "—having reference to the chained figure of " Fury " under the Emperor's heel. Ennobled by his much gratified patron and endowed with a splendid residence in Milan,

---

* " In the flower of young life, on an alien shore,
  He died—caresses and tears for him bore
  His friends. From the kiss of love to the kiss of God
  He pass'd, but left us in grief till the last reward."

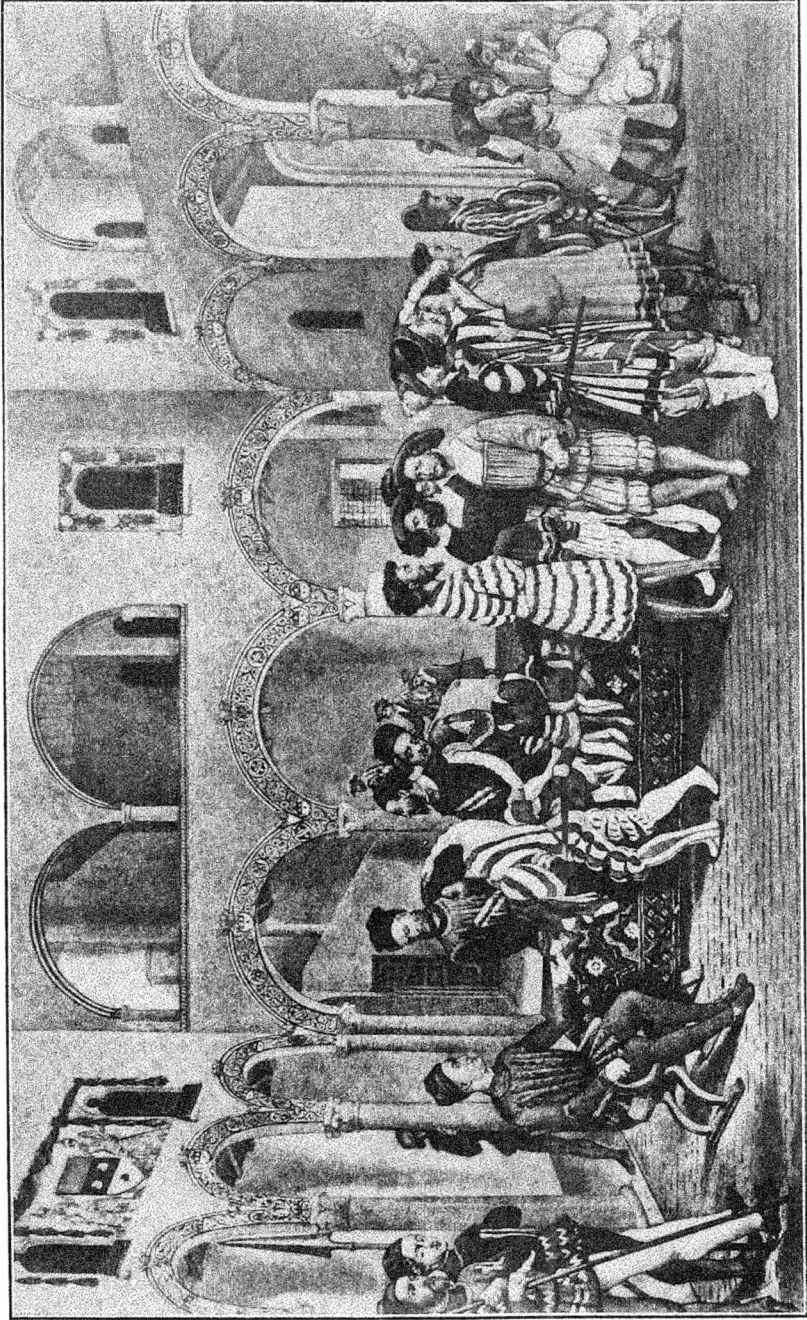

CAVALIERE BARTOLOMMEO COLLEONE GIVING OUT STATE-LIVERIES

the Cavaliere gave himself up to pleasure and
extravagance. No man loved more women, no
man fought more duels, than did the magnificent
Leoni; but his career of adventure was abruptly
ended when, having insulted Messer Giovanni
Trebbio, the Papal jeweller at Milan, by way of
denial of an intrigue with his wife, he was arrested
and sentenced to the galleys. Luckily at Genoa
he had many friends,—persons of wealth and
influence,—among them the veteran Ruler of the
city—the admirable Andrea Doria. Set at liberty,
he wrote a vindication of his conduct to Pietro
Aretino,—one of his most intimate correspondents
and admirers,—wherein he humorously attacked
the clergy for their interference with his liberty.
"I pass my time," he wrote, "in snapping my
fingers at their reverences, trusting that Providence
will one day cause such bad men to burst!"
There are many other tales about this boisterous
Cavaliere, pointing him out as a boon companion
for Torrigiano—the smasher of Buonarroti's nose!
One of these is characteristic of the rest. Thrown
into company at Venice,—whence he fared upon
his liberation from durance at Genoa—with
Titian, he invited the great master's son to
accompany him to his native place Menaggio, that
he might admit its greater charm over the Dolo-
mite village of Cadore. His guest had about

him a considerable sum of money, which the
Cavaliere claimed, and when young Vecellio
acknowledged the superiority of the Larian domi-
cile, not content with a mild request, he followed
up pretensions by a challenge to fight it out. The
young man only yielded when he had felt more than
once the sharp pin-pricks of his adversary's steel!

Quite aptly here a quotation from James
Addington Symonds comes into mind : " So extraordinary were the social circumstances of Renaissance Italy, that almost at every turn, on her sea-
board, in her cities, from her hilltops, and by her
lakes, we are compelled to blend our admiration
for the loveliest and purest works of art amid the
choicest scenes of nature, with memories of
execrable crimes and lawless characters."

Looking from Menaggio, or Loveno, to Bellano,
the lake is at its widest, and as we row across
in a stout market-boat, the snowy giants of the
Alps stand out of the azure sky in gaunt relief—a
notable panorama. Bellano is a very busy little
place,—she always was,—and ambitious too. Here,
in days long passed, the feuds between the Torriani
and the Visconti,—which devastated almost every
part of Lombardy,—raged savagely. The former
at first had the upper hand, for Napoleone della
Torre conquered the Valtellina, and led the village
maidens,—after the manner of the Latin Lombard

conquerors,—tied behind his war-chariot. He died in 1278, and then the Visconti drew conclusions with his adherents at the bidding of the outraged villagers. The Visconti retained Bellano for their own ; Azzone of that ilk made the port a pendant good work to the church erected by his uncle Giovanni, Archbishop and Lord of Milan.

Upon the stone pier, jutting out well into the lake, is a monument, not of a Visconto or of a Torriano, but of a gentler "Lord of the Lake"— the poet Tommaso Grossi, born at Bellano in 1791. He graduated in law at Pavia, and then in Cupid's University at Milan, where it is said " he made the women cry." They cried their eyes out for grief at the wrongs he told in his tragic poem, " *Ildegonda*," put forth in 1820. The sex went mad indeed over this touching story—Ildegonda veils, Ildegonda kerchiefs, Ildegonda bonnets, Ildegonda shoes, and Ildegonda stays were all the mode. And who, pray, was fair " Ildegonda "? The visionary daughter of the Valtellina chieftain, whom a Visconto had wronged in the long-buried past. She was a mediæval maiden, whose father dwelt at the lofty Castle of Teglio, this side of Tirano, where he kept in awe his vassals. Consigned to the charge of the nuns at Sondrio, whilst the war-dogs were let loose, gallant young Rizzardo of the hamlet of San Giacomo discovered his loved one's retreat. They fled together, heedless of danger and of consequences, but Cupid had not taken Fortune into his confidence, and, alas! the fugitives were captured. Ildegonda, parted from her lover, was carried back to Sondrio, and Rizzardo relegated to a dungeon at Teglio. There, after a manufactured charge of heresy, the love-lorn lad was burnt for a heretic, and poor little Ildegonda fretted out her sweet young life, and joined her swain in Paradise. Tommaso Grossi died in 1853, leaving, besides his lovely epic, other poems and stories of the good old times. The last year of his life he spent with the patriot poet-writer, Alassandro Manzoni, the graceful author of "*I Promessi Sposi.*"

And now our tales of "Lords and Ladies" of the Lake of Como are wellnigh told, but before we bid adieu to the "Glass of Venus," we must speed over the dancing wavelets, and find out what Gravedona and her neighbours have to tell us. The head of Lake Como bristles with fort-resses, now mighty ruins, significant of warring times—Rezzonico, Musso, and Corenno, and the restored Palazzo del Peco, with four great towers, at Gravedona, wherein :—

> " In the long while of times of yore,
>   When slain men lay in crimson gore,
>   And maidens fair, the prey of rape,
>   Were had to view within the gate."

The name of a Mediceo clings to the stones of
Musso—Giangiacomo de' Medici, " *Il Medeghino* "
—the Trimmer, we may call him. His father
was a cousin of Giovanni delle Bandenera, his
mother a Serbelloni of Milan. Giangiacomo came
into possession of the Rocca di Musso surrepti-
tiously. In some way or other Franesco Sforza,—
the last of that ruling House,—was beholden to
" *Il Medeghino*," and to square his account he gave
over the fief of Musso which had fallen to him to
Giangiacomo, with an emphatic proviso—that he
should undertake to kill Martino Visconti, who
was a thorn in the Duke's side. This deed was
promptly executed, and in 1525 Giangiacomo de'
Medici became Lord of Musso and Captain-
General of the Lake. He maintained a fleet of
armed vessels, and a fighting force of several
thousand men. In turn he served himself of
Frank, Spaniard, Milanese, and Swiss, and when
he had set them fighting one another, he became
the arbiter with the laurels all his own. Plunder,
intrigue, and murder reigned unchecked, and it is
marvellous how the astute *Capitano* kept his
head, his castle, and his purse. At last prudence
gave way to impetuosity, and he arrayed himself
against his quondam patron, the Duke of Milan,
who was only too pleased to place his heel upon
the Condottiere's neck. In 1529 favourable terms

of peace were made, whereby Giangiacomo was despoiled of his Castle of Musso, and his titles of Marquis of Musso and Captain-General of Lario and Lecco were merged in the less romantic Marquisate of Marignano, in the plain of Lodi. The rest of his days he spent in the service of intriguing Dukes and Marquises, his weapon ever ready to stab an undesirable to the heart, and few soldiers of fortune have as many victims upon their list as had he. A splendid monument covers his remains in Milan Cathedral, erected by his brother, Pope Pius IV., who was a cordial patron of his villainies. It was said that all Milan mourned for the Marquis of Marignano. It was a work, indeed, of supererogation, but perhaps, like most base men, he had his good points, and they appealed to the populace. People do not probe too deeply the private life of their heroes; if a man is masterful and successful it is sufficient—details are matters of indifference. Thus the world judges its idols.

The Palazzo del Peco attracts the eye of all who pass by Gravedona. It is, perhaps, the biggest building on the lake, and certainly the most imposing. Built for that Larian benefactor and potentate, Cardinal Tolomeo Gallio, in 1586, by his protégé Tibaldo of Val Solda, his Eminence, marking the zenith of his career, "placed his head at Gravedona, whilst his feet were at Cernobbio." His was the freehold of the Tre Pievi, or three parishes, Gravedona, Serico, and Dongo, and, besides his properties near Campo and Como, he owned estates at Scaldasole near Pavia, at the Bagni di Lucca, and elsewhere. It was said of him that, "travelling seven days direct between the Palazzo del Peco and his titular church in Rome, he never slept out of his own house." Away back in the twelfth century the unruly forbears of the Pievensi gained an unenviable notoriety. "Pardon all but the perfidious men of Gravedona!" was the sentence of an outraged Emperor, Frederic Barbarosa, when at Constance he granted peace and privileges to the defiant Lombardian rallies. Two years later these turbulent families gained the freedom of their lands, but another tyranny, far more deadly than the Teuton scourge, settled down on Gravedona and her sister Republics. In less than a single century the Holy Office of the Inquisition was set up in the Tre Pievi under Peter of Verona— St. Peter, Martyr. His zeal for persecution first broke out at Florence, where, smarting under a scandal of his cloister at Como, he resolved upon revenge. He first pounced upon, as Inquisitor-General of Pope Honorius III., the harmless benevolent institutions of the capital city—" The Brethren," " The Band of Love," " The Disciples of Chastity "—and other such dogmatic societies, who, beside being lukewarm in their love of Rome, were accused of being favourable to the Ghibelline cause. For nineteen years this " Scourge of God " relentlessly ploughed lake and land, tracking to their doom luckless and inoffensive countryfolk and folk of higher grade. Burnings for heresy were seen in every hamlet on the lake, and at Gravedona the fires of persecution devoured whole families. At length the deep rancour of the survivors found vengeance for their wrongs, and on April 21, 1252, Peter the Inquisitor,—with another brother of his Order,—were decoyed into a wood at Barlassina, midway between Como and Milan, where terrible sword-thrusts clove their skulls in twain. Canonized by Innocent IV. the following year, St. Peter Martyr's shrine in the ancient Church of Sant' Eustorgio in Milan, — a very splendid monument, — became a holy place for pilgrims from afar. The Saint's head, with its great gashed wound, and the blood-covered blade, used to be exhibited to the curious and devout on payment of a fee.

Gravedona contains many interesting monuments of the earliest Christian days, and miracu-

THE MARTYRDOM OF T. PETER THE INQUISITOR

lous Madonnas not a few. Among quaint epitaphs upon forgotten worthies one runs as follows :

" Grande patentia hio portava perffa che l' arma sia Salvada.
Per l'avarixia che a abinda l'anima mia a son perduda."*

The saintly figure to which this is inscribed is that of a man who wears across his breast a scroll bearing the single word " Gravedona."

The women of the Tre Pievi still wear their distinctive dress, a brown Benedictine smock, without sleeves, reaching to below the knees, and girt about the waist by a leathern strap. The bodice is of white linen, and a woollen petticoat is worn below the scapular. This costume is the record of a vow made by the whole community, when in 1450 pestilence, flood, and famine, in quick succession, devastated the northern shores of Lake Como.

The ruined Castle of Fuentes,—once the key to the valleys debouching upon the head of the lake,— a few miles beyond Colico, was built by the Spanish invaders in 1603, and its destruction dates from the triumph of the French in 1796. It gains its name from Count Ignacio del Fuentes, the Spanish Governor of Lombardy, and its reputation as a terror-spot from the atrocities practised upon its unhappy prisoners. One of these was the

* " Patience great I exercised my soul to save.
Lost my soul !—to avarice myself I gave."

celebrated Antonio Maria Stampa of Gravedona. The only ostensible reason for his seizure was that he was " an outlandish sort of man, given to much musing and the study of evil things, and a suspect." He wrote during his captivity an imaginary history of his time and town, full of extravagances. His unfortunate family also felt the sting of persecution ; their goods were confiscated, and they were compelled to undertake menial offices for the garrison. Over the rude blocks of tumbled masonry of the old fortress kindly Nature has spread her carpet of greenery. Walnut-trees grow in courtyards where mailed warriors strode, and grape-bearing vines cover secret chambers where sorrowful maidens wept, and each poured out " a woman's soul, most soft, most strong." Perhaps Venus after all had such a second self when she had conquered Mars !

The fascination of Lake Como is indescribable !

CHAPTER IV

LECCO

LAKE OF LECCO—BRIANZA—CASTLE OF MILAN

LECCO is the will-o'-the-wisp among the North Italian lakes; not, indeed, that she aqueously is here and there and everywhere, but her name betokens her character—the coin of echo, the acme of daintiness, the blush of temptation—in short, Diana of the Gods! Artemis of mythology was sister of Apollo, goddess of the chase, and protectress of the young and the suffering. Her love, Endymion, she kissed in sleep, and the loves of this well-matched pair illustrate the association of Lecco and the Brianza. By inversion of the metaphor—the pleasure-grounds of the " Verdant Land " enshrine the sportive deity, whilst she looks out languishingly upon the mirror-face of the beautiful sleep-dowered lake.

Diana is the fascinating inspiratrix of the Brianza. The Lake of Lecco is her bath; a bevy of bewitching Bacchantes encircle her with

crystal-emerald lakelets,—each a water-nymph of
rare enchantment — Annona, Pusiano, Segrino,
Alserio, and Montorfano. The resplendent pendant Diana wears on her pulsating bosom is
metaphorically the diamond jewel of Lake Garlate,
with its pearl-drop of Olgiate. The chaste feet
of the fascinating goddess,—perfect in shape,
elegant in step,—rest, or pitter-patter as she
wills, within the Sforza Castle of Milan !

> " Che qui tra gioghi Briantei primiero,
> Il colle Gernezian erge le cime,
> Come ite belle fanno, arte e natura.
> Ricco per l'acqua del Pusiano, il Lambro
> Contortuoso giro in due lo parte,
> Ora tente sorrendo—ora tra sassi
> Con un ingrato mormorio spumando."*
> (From " *Il Gernetto*," poem by ABBATE LODOVICO
> POLIDORI).

This stanza was composed within the lovely
gardens of the villa of Conte Giangiacomo della
Somaglia—called " *Il Gernetto*," which belonged
originally, in the middle of the fourteenth
century, to the Milanese family of Rozzini. The
prospect from the terrace embraces the whole

---

* " Would'st gain Brianza's sweet enchantment ?
Speed thee to Gernezian's escarpment,
Source whence, embellish'd by Nature and Art,
And enrich'd on sweet Pusiano's part,
The Lambro wanders—now tortuously,
Now softly murmuring,—now noisily
Rolls ungrateful rocks, smooth and froth-fretted."

gorgeous " *Pian d'Erba* "—the Plain of the
Verdant Land — a delicious title for the whole
Brianza."

I.

The Lake of Lecco has something of Scandinavian grandeur ; five majestic mountains, like
giant fingers of a colossal hand, enclose its deep
green waters—sleep-rocked and echoing. The
" *Resegone di Lecco,*"—brother to the Rohzahne of
Bozen,—resembles a great saw on edge, its teeth
piercing the azure sky. Nature has been somewhat harsh to Lecco's lake ; but its firs and
brambles are attractive by their strength and
boldness, and hide as many gay romances as do
the sentimental acacias and nuptial myrtles of
idyllic Brianza. Rugged natural buttresses and
dark mysterious chasms re-echo the sounds of
mountain storms. Avoided by superstitious
rustics, they shelter mountaineering " Lords and
Ladies " and chamois-hunters up to the line of
everlasting snow on great Monte Grigna. Upon
the eastern side of the lake scarce can man or beast
find foothold ; great precipices hang over the
water. On the west are sun-kissed shores and
shady coves, with luxuriant vegetation—Limonta,
Vassena, Onno, and Malgiate.

Lecco itself is an unimportant town, but is one

of the great gates of Lombardy. A solid stone bridge, strong to stand for centuries—the *Ponte Grande a' Visconti*—spans the narrowing waters of the lake. Built in 1335, by that mighty warrior, Azzone Visconti, it was one of the wonders of the world, with its bastions, towers, and draw-bridges. The Sforzas destroyed and then rebuilt this link with the cities of the plain. Restored when all but a relic of a desultory past, in 1609 by Conte de Fuentes,—he who built the Spanish castle by Riva at Colico,—it was blown up by retreating Russians in 1798, but, since repaired, is still rugged in its stanchness.

Anyone who would know the story of Lecco, as intimately told of the seventeenth century at least, should read Alessandro Manzone's romance " *I Promessi Sposi* " and his other Lecco tales. He is the Lecco Hare, and those who read and mark his masterpiece find him the best companion in their walks abroad. Born March 7, 1785, at Milan, by mere chance, he belonged to a noble family and an old, of the Val Sassina, beyond the Lake of Lecco. His ancestral home was the castle, or mansion, of Caleotto, overlooking the historic road to Bellano on Lake Como. Pietro Manzone, Alessandro's father, married Donna Giulia, elder daughter of Signore Cesare Beccarii, a member of that famous Lecco family. His

PILGRIMAGE CHURCH OF LASNIGO

From a Photograph   (See page 200)

PONTE GRANDE (OR VISCONTI), LAKE OF LECCO

From a Photograph

To face page 186

early years were spent on his father's farm, but, sad to say, a black cloud appeared on the domestic horizon—his parents were at variance. At last Madonna Giulia's patience was exhausted, and, in 1804, she left her home and children, With a friend of her youth, Carlo Imbonati, she went to Paris, where he died the following year. The Madonna brought his body back to Italy, and buried it at Brusuglio, near Milan, and then she returned to Paris. It has been asserted that Signore and Madonna Manzone were legally separated in 1792. Anyhow, her seven children knew little of a mother's care, and yet their love for her was not cold, for Alessandro and his sister Enrichetta followed her to Paris.

Beginning as a poetaster in 1801, the call of the " *Incantevole del Cielo di Brianza* "—the heavenly enchantment of the Brianza—was too strong to be resisted, and back the loving son of Lombardy returned to the country of his fathers. He fixed his temporary home at the hamlet of Costa, near the little town of Galbiate, high above the lakes of Annona and Garlate. Hence he journeyed to Milan, to and fro, and in 1818 joined the staff of the newly established " *Concialiatore*," having for his associates, Lodovico di Bienne, Samuele Biava, Giovillo Scalvini, Tommaso Grossi, and other kindred spirits. The " *I Promessi Sposi* " was given to the world in 1821, in succession to many other tales and verses. There m Lecco is the scene of his narrative and the Leccoese his heroes and heroines. He speaks of buildings fair and foul, reveals their secrets, and re-incarnates their woes and joys. He gives distressing details of family feuds and of the marches of foreign armies. He tells again the tales of Sigisimondo Boldoni of Bellano—how the people of the country fled to mountain fastnesses, and how the Teuton hordes swept bare the fair land like locusts—diseased and verminous. Many victims, beside Boldoni, died from infection, imported from the North. He whispers gently of lovers and their vows, of parted sweethearts, and of the avenging dagger. Families he names as becoming rich by brigandage, and records the insecurity of life, with the inevitable findings of justice. Across the Ponte Grande moved the life and fame of Lecco. Floods of wild waters and of wilder soldiery crashed against arch and buttress, and, across it have fought, point to point, *bravi* and their prey, and maidens have been deported for the pastime of " Lords of the Lakes " in Lombardy. Pageants, too, of fair " Ladies " have passed serenely where men fought, for Lecco was a principal portal of the great cities of the plain. Alessandro Manzone died in 1873.

The " *Archivio Storico Lombardo* " has many thrilling stories of Lecco and the Leccoese ; many of them in connection with the *bravi* and other brigands of the border. The municipal authorities time out of mind held deliberations and passed sentences upon the daring deeds of highwaymen and their kind. Six very deep-dyed villains,— Claudio, Salvadore, Carlo, and Orazio Zanetti, four brothers, with their cousins, Lodovico and Zambiano Bolognini, having been banished from Venetian territory—the two first also from the Duchy of Milan—for deeds of darkness done, had transferred their scene of operations to the neighbourhood of Lecco, and were at last captured red-handed, and on June 29, 1649 were arraigned for justice, heavily fined, and cautioned. The public prosecutor,—not a very desirable post in those wild days,—Dr. Ambrogio Arrigone, incurred the resentment of the nefarious brotherhood, and his death was decreed. One evening, when no moon illuminated the deep underwood, the six defendants in the recent trial crawled stealthily towards the threatened official's dwelling, on the outskirts of the town. They learned that the doctor was detained in Lecco on legal business, so back they struck to meet their victim unaccompanied, in the narrow high-walled street. Quite unsuspectingly the poor man fell among the thieves, who stripped him of his clothing, and then brutally clubbed him to death with their guns. The reprobates fled and hid themselves in secret places known only to the peasantry, who, however, dared not expose them. The Sindic and other magistrates of Lecco summoned them to surrender on pain of proscription in every commune, and warned all the neighbouring States not to harbour them, but to hand them over if they fled across the border. In the end two of the brothers and one cousin,—Carlo, Orazio, and Lodovico,—were captured, and, without a trial, run up to the gallows, which stood ever ready, as Alessandro Manzone has gruesomely recorded in his " *I Promessi Sposi*," for malefactors. Only one of the six actually escaped— Salvadore—his immunity being, in fact, due to his name, so judged the populace, who had more faith than we have in the protection of patron Saints. Claudio and Zambiano were drowned by the upsetting of a boat on the lake. Even so the end of brigandage was not reached. If *bravi* are no more a class apart, the brigand pure and simple still shows his masked face in unwonted places ; and the smuggler-poacher thrives in every hilly district.

Almost every cottage by the lake, or on the hill, has relics of the good old days—loot from lordly wayfarers or sober citizens. Ancestors of peasants and of townsmen of to-day danced measures on the greensward or hard highroad with courtly "Ladies of the Lakes." Curio-hunters have here a rich field unexplored, for Visconti relics are not at a premium in the commune of Lecco. To be sure some of these tokens of butchery and pillage are in the treasuries of churches,—votive offerings by sinful souls rebuked, seeking accommodation with Heaven.—and here they will remain, for clergy in Italy are on their guard now that connoisseur millionaires are on the prowl!

Everybody who is interested in Lecco, town and lake, and in the lakelet of Annona fails not to toil up the mountain path from Civate, through the Val dell' Orco, to the hermitage chapel of San Pietro. It was a favourite retreat from the frenzied world for contemplative Benedictines, and it has a romantic history. Whilst following in the chase one day, in 757, through sportive Brianza, Adelicco,—son of Desiderio, the last King of the Lombards,—was struck in the eye by an arrow which glanced from a tree. Knowing that blindness was to be his fate, he, upon the spot, vowed to build a Mass-chapel for the service of the holy brotherhood, where daily prayer should be offered for the recovery of his sight. That dilapidated building is still one of the most unique churches of Christendom. Twenty-seven red marble steps,—the age of the afflicted prince,—lead to the entrance. The devotion of " Creeping to the Cross " has never ceased from that day to this, and pious peasants, sightless and seeing, make the pilgrimage with confident faith and ardour. Within the little fane ancient frescoes, alas! much faded, still decorate the walls and vault. Three awesome creatures dominate the shrine, a griffin, a chimœra, and a dragon cut in quaint stone bas-relief: the latter, ready to devour a little child, gave rise to a superstition, which haunts the chasm over which the chapel hangs. It is of a horned serpent, which devours unguarded and truant children, and "*Il Dragone di San Pietro!*" is still named to overawe the disobedient; although the valiant Saint withstanding the reptile is the conventional St. Michael! The arrangement of this primitive Christian temple is that of a basilica. In the "*Scurolo*" or "Confessional," used to be preserved links of St. Peter's Mamertine chain; these had their healing properties, for bites of mad dogs, touched thereby, were instantly healed.

Throughout all the " Verdant Land " of Brianza, and from beyond the Lake of Lecco, year by year, thousands of pilgrims wend their way to

San Pietro, singing ancient litanies. Perhaps the first of these, and greatly distinguished for her virtues, was the Empress Ermingarda, consort of Charlemagne and sister of Prince Adelicco; her effigy is to be seen in a bas-relief behind the altar. In the eleventh century another famous personage climbed the Sacred Way,—Arnolfo de' Capitani, Archbishop of Milan. Tired of a world of faction and a hierarchy of greed the holy man sought the green solitude of Civate for fast and prayer. He it was who stilled the fierce strifes of Guelphs and Ghibellines and gave peace to embittered partisans. He died upon his wooden bedstead before the altar of the chapel. Two other saintly men among many more found solace in the little cloister, Liprando da Compito and Leone da Parego; the former a confessor, for the Christian faith bereft of ears and nose and hands—mutilations of the heretical Nicolaitans; the latter, the warlike Archbishop of Milan, who strove to stem the usurpation of the Torriani, but in vain, for he died a fugitive.

San Carlo Borromeo, in his plenary visitation of Lombard holy houses, climbed up to San Pietro in 1571, to see for himself what the lonesome Benedictines were about. Their abstinences, their poverty, and their sincerity he gladly acknowledged; but, when they sought ritual

indulgences, he quietly remarked to the Prior :
" Better leave well alone, and mind your business !" Other visitors, too, besides ecclesiastics
and pilgrims, have been wont to rendezvous in
the wild valley of the Orco—huntsmen and
viragoes of the chase. The King of France,
Henri III.,—yielding to the attractions of the
Brianza and its lakes,—took up his residence at
the Castle of Civate, on the shore of Annona, and
thence, one day, he espied a lovely girl. She was
wending her way home with a pitcher of water
poised upon her head, and the King—his identity
quite unknown to the maiden—craved a cooling
draught. Like another Rebecca the maiden's
grace and coyness quite enslaved the amorous
Sovereign, and, willy-nilly, back she went to Paris
in the royal train—Agnese da Civate. What
became of her at the French Court we know not
exactly, but, when, by the tragic death of Marie
de Cleves, in 1574, the King's heart was broken,
none so daintily ministered to him as the village
maid of Annona.

II.

The Brianza is the picturesque, undulating,
and fertile country which rolls away from the
gates of Milan right to the apex of the highland
triangle, which separates the Lakes of Como and

Lecco. The axis of the configuration is at Erba, like the pivot of a fan,—whence an alternative name is derived—"*Piano d' Erba*"—the "Verdant Land." It is watered by the prattling Lambro, flowing refreshingly through the Val Assina, which drains that exquisite chain of lakelets—Annona, Pusiano, Segrino, Alserio, and Montorfano—and then runs on to join the Adda below Milan. It is an ideal Eden, for nowhere in all fruitful Lombardy does the generous sun ripen sweeter grapes and mulberries, or paint magnolia, oleander, and pomegranate blooms with more fragrant hues. The scintillating leaflets of the olives are brilliant gold, the berries of the verdant laurels shining coral, and the dewdrops within expanding roses, lilies, and carnations are opal-tinted pearls. The thin-as-air meshes of great spider webs are silver-gilt strands, shot-silking the morning dew-dress of verdure, and the almost imperceptible brushing of variegated butterfly wings cast coloured shadows upon the shimmering noon vapours. So much may perhaps be said of many another terrestrial paradise, but the Brianza rejoices in an atmosphere of unrivalled brilliancy, perfumed with more than the fabled scents of Barbary ; and, when the sun-god has paled before his lunar mistress, then the glint of flying insects' wings excites the diamond fires of hidden glow-worms. These are special charms of the "Verdant Land."

Where Nature has been so bountiful, Art has not feared to tread, and out of luxuriant coppices of flowering trees and shrubs,—some exotic in their origin,—there peep forth the white or painted walls of elegant and commodious villas, each holding a Court like a Queen in the midst of exquisite gardens The white *campanili* of village churches vie in loftiness with solemn cypresses, and the melody of their bells mingles at all hours of the day with the musical cadence of zephyr-moved foliage. One of the most celebrated and perhaps most ancient of these *castelli* is the Villa di Tassera, overlooking the villages of Erba, Carcano, and Alserio. There Federigo Barbarossa spent many a happy day in the far-away year of 1160. In 1500 it became the property of the Ospidale Maggiore, in Milan, through the munificence of Duke Lodovico "Il Moro." One hundred and fifty years later, the hospital funds being low, the estate was sold to the rising Milanese family of Turbonato, who held it for two hundred years. Many times has it changed hands since then, and has sheltered distinguished inmates. Ismail Pasha, ex-Khedive of Egypt, died there in 1878.

Not very far from Villa di Tassera,—now

called Villa Adelheida, after the wife of its present owner,—nine miles from Como, on the highroad to Lecco, is Castello di Carimate. Dating from the troubled times of Bernabo Visconti,—who, in 1380, gave it to his bride, Donna Regina della Scala of Verona,—it became the dower-house of the consorts of the valiant Visconti. In 1386 Giovanni Galeazzo, of that ruling family, gave it to his wife Caterina della Torre—a significant matrimonial contract between the two great factions of Milan. Filippo Maria Visconti, in 1415 made the property over to his wife in due order—the imperious and frail Elizabetta Borromeo, whose intrigue with Domenico Ajcardi, Master of the Horse to her consort, led to her imprisonment and supposed death at her husband's hands. By a strange fatuity of circumstances Ajcardi earned Filippo Maria's eternal gratitude, for, by his revelations of the conspiracy of Malatesta, Arcelle, and Beccario,—the very year of the unhappy Elizabetta's tragic end,—he saved the Visconti house and fame. For reward he received the dower-house of Carimate, and was created Viscount of Scaramuzza. Three Dukes, in turn, of the supplanting Sforza dynasty, confirmed the gift to the Ajcardi, who in gratitude affixed the name of Visconti to their own, and at the same time added the arms of Sforza to

their escutcheon. A very splendid ceremonial
was witnessed in the castle hall in November,
1493, for the Ambassador of Massimiliano, King
of the Romans, married by procuration in his
Sovereign's name, Signora Bianca Maria, daughter
of the Duke of Milan.

The day following the nuptials Duke Galeazzo,
Maria, and Duchess Isabella, with the Regent
Lodovico and his consort Beatrice, accompanied
the royal bride to Como, escorted by a very
gorgeous cavalcade of " Lords and Ladies of the
Lakes." After entering the city a halt was
called at the Cathedral, where a solemn *Te Deum*
was sung, and then the royal party were conducted to the Archbishop's palace for a splendid
banquet and to pass the night. Next day the
Queen and her suite embarked upon four great
barges, gaily adorned and lined with men-at-
arms, bearing flaunting banners. The vessels
were offered for their worthy duty by loyal folk
of the town of Torno on the lake. The old adage
came true, " winds and waves wait for none,"
for the flotilla had much ado to make Bellagio,
the crew and passengers all suffering grievously.
There Marchese Stampa entertained his distinguished guests, who after an inauspicious start
next day were compelled to run back for shelter to
the hospitable harbour. On the fourth day Queen

GALEAZZO MARIA SFORZA

PIERO POLLAIUOLO

Uffizi, Florence

To face page 198

Bianca Maria bade a last adieu to Italy: for at Colico she entered her consort's litter and was borne over the Alps towards Vienna.

Upon the death of the Duke, in 1494, Lodovico " Il Moro " seized the castle and there established his sweetheart—Cecilia Gallerina. Later on the Ajcardi - Visconti regained possession, restored the buildings, and remained its lords till 1795, when Cavaliere Lodovico Visconti,—they had dropped the " Ajcardi "—the last of his race, died. Carimate now belongs to the Conte di Pirocco of Como. To go back to the Ajcardi, Marquis Domenico's son Giorgio, by another criss-cross arrangement,—common enough in those times of feud and counter-feud,—married Caterina, the daughter of the plotter Giacomo Beccario, and Filippo Maria Visconti gave him the estate of Zelada, on the Ticino, not very far from Abbiate-grasso. He rebuilt the old Visconti castle and strictly preserved the forest, where he and his friends were accustomed to hunt bear and deer, —the Marchioness Caterina and her ladies being usually of the party. Zelada passed ultimately to the family of Sangiuliano, whose descendant, Count Antonio, still resides in the again half-ruined castle.

The highroad from Erba to Bellagio,—a grand stretch of twenty miles,—crosses the Lambro, and, skirting the narrow green strip of merlin-haunted Segrino, makes up the lovely Val Assina. Nowhere are views more varied as each corner of the zigzag road reveals the scenery. From a broad ledge, looking down, near Asso, through the umbrageous foliage of chestnuts, the whole Lake of Lecco is in view, lying two thousand feet below. A little farther on, at Magreglio, both arms of Lake Como are revealed, and then, near Lasnigo, the Tremezzina, with its sparkling bays and shining villas, attracts the eye. From Cevenna we gaze down over Bellagio and take in the splendours of the northern portion of "Lario" to Domaso, with the grand range of Alpine sentinels all white with snow arrayed against the blue, hazy sky. At Lasnigo we linger to contemplate the eloquent solitude of its pilgrimage church. The whole busy world is out of sight and sound, and there is nothing to divert our thoughts or steps. A typical *Via Crucis* lies before us, and, involuntarily, perhaps, we pass upwards between two rows of fourteen shrines. The story of Calvary is told in stonewrought numbers in a thousand places else, but here the weather-battered "Stations" and the grass-grown steps, —leading up to the lofty, lonely towers,— by the very severity and harshness of it all, become illuminative to the dullest apprehension of the tragedy of Calvary. Reverie peoples the scene with kneeling, praying devotees, and their folklore hymns and the Latin chants strike imaginatively upon the ear. In the ancient church the reek of incense and wax has cleared away all mouldy smells, and the fire of ecstatic monkish exhortation has left not only echoes, but something of the enthusiastic flame of perfervid devotion. You may sit in the sweet meadow grass, or upon a ruined, chiselled stone, and sit and sit, whilst you realize that the world and its votaries are vanities of vanity—Lasigno is truly a Gate to Heaven, though a rough one visually.

Thus are you minded, but, if you like to ascend Monte Cippei,—seen in the illustration behind the pilgrimage church,—you can look right down the Pian di Tivano to Nesso, on the Lake of Como and on past a shoulder of Monte San Primo, to the wood - sheltered lake-hamlet of Lezzeno with its mysterious "*Grotta del Bulgaro.*" This is the land of witchcraft and cryptic deeds,—tradition has it that in the fifteenth century, this,—the one gloomy spot in a land of everlasting sunshine,—was the hot-bed of necromancy, and the nursery of valley charlatans. The entire province of Como was affected by a wild desire, fomented by the agents of the Holy Office, to harry, hunt, and exterminate the witchwives and their werewolf associates. It was believed that their incantations brought distress, disease, and death upon man and beast alike. The visitations of plague, the prevalence of family feuds, and the blighting of marriage offspring and of cattle, and every human ill was assigned to their fell agency. Proofs were ready to hand with which to flout every wretched and suspected individual. Confessions of nameless crimes were extorted under the cruellest of tortures, and devilish punishment far outweighed the miserable victims' turpitude. Depositions of such wretches attested by clerical witnesses, are preserved in the archives of every town and village in Lombardy. A frenzy of blood-thirstiness wrapped the whole country in a monstrous crusade ; the cry everywhere was, " We shall be better off when the witches are all burnt !" Between 1416 and 1516, it has been computed that more than ten thousand poor creatures were done to death. The memory of those awful scenes has not yet faded in the valleys of the Brianza, whilst endless superstitions still terrify the harmless inhabitants. Almost everybody, wears an amulet or charm to ward off uncanny influences, and general resort is had to herbs and decoctions as specifics against witchery. Witchhouses and well-marked witch-rings still remain in and about dark Lezzeno, and up and about the Pian di Tivano—to approach which no man or woman ever dares. Still, for all this haunting mistrust, no merrier people are there than the shepherds of the Pian di Tivano and the silk-working girls of the Val Assina. Surely here, if anywhere, simple human happiness has reached its zenith : Leonardo da Vinci might at any time have found endless exuberant subjects for his rollicking peasants ; and Fra Angelico graceful maiden models for his dancer in Paradise. Certainly there are old crones minding goats or gossiping on doorsteps, shrivelled and ominous. With distaff and spindle they are incarnations of Buonarrotti's " weird wicked Sisters three."

There are yet other stories to tell about " Lords and Ladies of the Brianza," and, first of all, the pleasant voice of Giuseppe Parini calls us to his natal village of Bosisio, smiling serenely upon the eastern shore of sweet Lake Pusiano—which, by the way, he called "*Il vago Eupili mio.*" Who would have thought, however, that the exceedingly dull, loutish lad,—as Giuseppe one while was,— would grow into the most brilliant mimic and most caustic critic of the gay world of Milan ?

His "*Giorno*" is a marvellously lifelike travesty of the men and manners of his day. He imagines himself introducing a young noble

of Lombardy to all the gallantries and foibles of
the Milanese. Two modes, divergent and irreconcilable, divided or united the votaries of
fashion—the most scrupulous and ridiculous conventions of town life, and the burlesque of simple
shepherd occupations in the country. Parini's
" Lords and Ladies " are excruciatingly funny
folks : his dialogue is full of subtle irony. No
handsomer man than he nor of more distinguished
carriage paced street or lane, but smart society
was afraid of him, or rather of his skits, whilst
everyone roared at caricatures of other men's and
women's conceits ! Fortune came to Parini not
through the brilliancy of his lampoons and dia-
tribes, but seriously, through the princely Borromeo and Serbelloni families in the drudgery of
tutoring their sons. He was fond of referring to
the days of struggle when he was wont to cry
out in anguish both of mind and body :

> " Ch' io possa morire
> Io ora trovo m' avere al uno comando
> Un par di soldi, non che due lire
> Per domano !"*

Hence, perhaps, his sobriquet " *Il   Povere
Parini !*" When he died in 1799 all Lombardy

> * " May I drop if I know
>   Where to look for a sou,
>   Much more for two lire
>   Which to-morrow are due."

was much the poorer for a personal loss and for the loss of a real reformer of cant and humbug.

On the highroad and off between Monza and Lecco are very many villas, with stories of " Lords and Ladies " galore. Twelve miles from Lecco is Castello di Merate, of very ancient origin, the appurtenance of the monastery of San Pietro di Civate. Away in the tenth century Archbishops of Milan,—from Auberto da Intinicardi,—entertained Emperors—from Corrado to Barbarossa. The Religious lost it in the fourteenth century, and then the all-pervading Visconti set to work to build the battlements with men-at-arms and to fill the dungeons with prisoners, bold and fair. Quite near at hand is the Villa Belgiosioso, built, too, upon antiquated ruins,—the property of Marquis Francesco Ferrante Villani-Novalta. Perhaps this was the Villa di Merate where Paul Musset first beheld Princess Cristina Trivulzio-Belgiosioso, and, struck with her saucy contour, her pallid skin, her " Mona Lisa smile," and the subtlety of an indefinable charm, drew her in caricature, with a prominent nose and chin à la Dr. Syntax, and an eye looking round the corner ! Be it said, however, for the fair charmer's fame, she inspired fear as well as admiration in her visitor, and whilst he mocked her behind her back his conduct was perfectly restrained in her

presence ! Men in face of clever women are
arrant cowards '

The name Belgiosioso meets one again at the
Castello di San Colombano, near Curate on the
Lambro. It is a time-worn relic of the tenth
century, and, later, it became the cradle of the
celebrated Landriani family—peers of the Visconti
and Torriani. In 1164 Federigo Barbarossa regarded it as one of the keys to Lombardy, and
fortified it accordingly ; but, when his time was
passed, the Milanese pillaged it, and the Visconti
and Lodigiani struggled with the earlier owners
for possession. A wily priest stepped in whilst
the rivals were squabbling, and Holy Church as
usual gained the guerdon. Petrarca, the friend
of Archbishop Giovanni Visconti, spent much time
at the Castello, and spoke of it as—

" Largamenti noto e fortissimo di amore."

In 1372 a very beautiful *castellana* came to San
Colombano—Bianca di Savoia, the consort of
Galeazzo II. Visconti : she obtained the fief, and
set to work to build the tower—still called "*La
Cucina di Bianca di Savoia.*" Once more the
Church obtained the mastery, and for fifty years
the monks of the Certosa of Pavia farmed its
revenues, until Francesco Sforza took a fancy to
it, and, in the name of the city of Milan, seized

HUNTING IN THE BRIANZA

From an Illustrated MS. by Gaston de Foix, 1391   Bibliotheque National, Paris

To face page 206

it and kept it for himself. The property now belongs to Prince Emilio Barbiano di Belgiosioso d' Este—whose very name speaks volumes of romance! In 1864 the whole property passed to the Trivulzio family by the marriage of Princess Giulia Barbiano.

At Olgiate, near the delicious little lake,—hid by deep bending foliage but glittering through the greenery,—is the Villa Sala-Trotti—ten miles from Lecco. Originally the nursery of the Vimercati family, the Sale of Treviglio acquired it, and laid out the exquisite gardens:—"*Essi diedero mano ad abbellore con grande spesa il giardino, ad eressero l'oratorio ai SS. Ambrogio e Galdino.*" * This dedication, so to speak, is characteristic of what one sees almost everywhere in Brianza villa-land. The adjuncture of flowers and prayers is absolutely poetic, and the ascription of saintliness to members of the family points the quaintest of morals. Wales may present a wholly unearned increment of family hagiography, but Lombardy equals the Principality in hidden stores of saintly people! Very generally the addition of the Saint of the family is made plausible by linking in such

* " Took in hand to embellish with great taste the garden and to erect the Oratory of Saints Ambrogio and Galdino." (Galdino was a scion of the house of Sala, who had gained canonization for the edification of his family and the illustration of their pedigree.)

14

popular patrons as Sant' Ambrogio or San Carlo Borromeo. Would that the family record never knew anything but the high-water mark of the most respectable member thereof ! A family which had not furbished up a Saint thereof was not considered worthy of Society.

The dedicatory sentence above recorded was put up quite lately, in 1887, when Signore Geronimo Sala was joined matrimonially to Signora Minia Trotti. Royalty has not thought scorn of the charming villa and its attractive owners. Good Queen Margherita,—King Umberto's gracious widow,—delights to stay there ; and with her, too, are usually Princes and Princesses of the Royal Savoy House. These are, of course, all of them " Lords and Ladies of the Italian Lakes ! "

At Cernusco,—almost one township with Merate,—is another historical villa—that of the Visconti di Salicito, but built pretty much in its present proportions by the Alari family of Lecco, in the sixteenth century. They were wealthy landowners and eminent vine-growers and wine-merchants,—indeed their name is still preserved on labels of a full rich red wine, " Alaro," beloved of connoisseurs. Much esteemed by Duke Lodovico " Il Moro," it became a fashionable beverage, until he and his courtiers began to feel the effect of too liberal libations in the form of gout and

eczema ! Happily there was an antidote,—by
some esteemed more tasty still, if less potent,—
quite as accessible—the thin dry vintage of Tivano,
which accommodating chief medicos prescribed
for willing victims ! The wine of Lezzeno " the
Haunted " was somewhat less medicinal in quality,
and therefore, *bon-vivants*, like the brothers
Giovio of Como, adopted it as their usual beverage.
It possessed a delicate bush and an exhilarating
colour, and appealed to jaded palates. By many
" Lezzeno " was mixed with " Griante " and
" Varenna " on the principle that ham and eggs
are more to be commended than ham alone !
Those to-day who know their Italy know also
what the " Lord and Ladies of the Lakes " knew
well, and drank with gusto ; but one must take
heed in moments of seraphic assimilation, for
Lombardian wines are stronger far than human
heads, though of the strongest !

Well, to return whence we have much digressed.
The Alari were Counts of Tribiano,—famous, too,
for generous wines,—and not without Imperial
patronage, for that brought still more grist to the
family mill. Count Giacinto, in July, 1598, was
a splendid figure as he rode a magnificent white
charger, clothed like his master in cloth of gold,
at the head of the noble cavalcade which conducted the Archduchess Margherita of Austria to

Milan to wed Duke Filippo III., the Spanish Viceroy of Lombardy. Something like a century later another Count Giacinto Alari-Tribiano built anew the villa, and added thereto glorious gardens and orchards. He and his family were sportsmen and sportswomen all. They revived the glorious hunting-fishing parties of Duchess Beatrice d' Este-Sforza. The eyes of another illustrious " Lady " were fixed upon the amenities of Villa Cernusco in the eighteenth century.

In August, 1771, there came an Imperial courier with a missive from Count Karl von Firmian, the Emperor's Commissary, addressed to the Count of Tribiano, in which it was stated that the Empress Maria Teresa wished to have the villa. The Imperial command was on behalf of her son the Archduke Ferdinand and his bride, Princess Maria Beatrice d' Este. The Count met it in the best way he could, for he knew the transaction meant the absolute abstraction of many, many lire from his banking account !

Chivalrously, even loyally, enough he responded to his Sovereign's request, and placed himself, his household, and the whole estate unreservedly at the Empress's disposition. Alterations and additions were imperative, and all these " the Perfect Courtier " undertook, and then, with the advent of the Imperial couple, the Count and his family were absolute strangers to their ancestral home for five years of impoverishment. Happily the unwelcome visitors were called away to Monza, where they made their home in the new palace, built expressly for them by Giustiniano Piermarini. Count Giacinto's son's wife, Countess Anastasia,—widowed with no issue,—to whom the estate was willed absolutely, married a Visconti of Saliceto, and hence the name.

III.

Il Castello Sforzesco di Milano—the Sforza Castle of Milan—is one of those world-famous palace-fortresses wherein are enshrined the forges of rulers' fortunes and the looms of peoples' liberties. The original building,—a rectangular edifice, with four great flanking towers and a huge curtain-wall,—was built in the middle of the fourteenth century by Galeazzo Visconti II., who called it *Castello di San Giovio*, from the adjoining gate of the rising city.

Within this lordly building Visconti's daughter, Yolanda, was married, in 1368, to Lionel, Duke of Clarence, son of Edward III. of England. The family was eager to attain equality with European reigning Houses, and, knowing the financial straits of the English crown, Galeazzo made over-tures to the King—offering an opulent dowry with his fair young daughter. Edward appointed Humphrey Bohun, Earl of Hereford, as his envoy to Milan, to judge of the noble maiden's charms and to handle her marriage portion. So very pleasant were the Visconti to their distinguished guest that he did not hasten to fulfil his mission, and two years were spent in dilly-dallying negotiations. At last a settlement was reached, and Donna Yolanda welcomed her royal bridegroom at the Castle of Milan on June 1. The English Duke's progress from the French coast had been magnificent. At the Louvre his stirrup was held by the Dukes of Berri and Burgundy, and the King himself assisted him to dismount ; at Chambéry the Count of Savoy, as Yolanda's uncle,— brother of her mother, Countess Bianca,—entertained Duke Lionel sumptuously, and accompanied him across the Alps to Milan. The marriage was celebrated in front of the old basilica of Sant' Ambrogio on June 5, and the festivities which celebrated the happy event baffled the descriptive powers of the chroniclers. Duke Lionel took home to England his fair bride, with her two millions of gold florins,—a portentous sum in those days,—together with the revenues of many Lombard towns. In his saddle-bags were the title-deeds of the ancestral castle

of Alba, on the River Tanaro, in Piedmont,
famed for its rich " Barbaresco " and " Barolo "
wine. The royal train included two thousand
persons, and many noble Milanese accompanied
the bride. There is a story that Lionel, going
with his bride first to view his castle of Alba,
died there suddenly of poison on October 7, four
months after the marriage at Milan. The wedding
ceremonies were graced by the presence of two
poets,—since then of sublime renown,—Francesco
Petrarca and Geoffrey Chaucer—indeed, the latter
was one of the official advisers of the English
Crown, and knew his Milan well.

Whether or no the bride was the heroine of the
delightful " Story of Griseldis," Chaucer, anyhow,
was struck with her beauty, her docility, and her
refinement, and he thus gave utterance to his
delight :

> " Her name is Bountie set in a woman heade,
> Sadnese and Youthe, and Beautie pridelese,
> She's Pleasaunce and Governance and Drede."

Petrarca, first a guest of Milan in 1348, with his
bibliophile friend Guglielmo da Pastrengo, visited
all Lakeland from Garda to Maggiore ; he was truly
one of the most distinguished " Lords " thereof.
Honoured by the Visconti, and the bosom friend
of Galeazzo II., the poet coquetted with his
Lombard friends, brave and fair, for quite a dozen

years. Pusiano had equal charms with Vaucluse, and perhaps, had he not met Laura, he might have had a Berta of the Brianza—a "Lady of the Lakes " !

Galeazzo II. was not only a judicious match-maker, but a sapient legislator and an intelligent builder. He wrested the Government from his ambitious uncle, Bernabo, who had established himself as overlord of Eastern Lombardy, and had extended the Visconti sway to Pisa, Bologna, Perugia, and far-off Spoleto. Galeazzo, the founder of the grand Cathedral of Milan and of the unique Certosa of Pavia, greaty enlarged the castle, and dwelt there in such sumptuous state that the Emperor Wenceslaus,—who sold him the Duchy,—once exclaimed :—" The Duke of Milan is a wealthy Sovereign, whilst I am but a needy Count !" When Giovanni Galeazzo died, in 1402, chaos and anarchy reigned in Lombardy, as in the troublous times of Archbishop Ottone Visconti and when the Visconti-Torriani feuds were at their height. The three sons of Giovanni Galeazzo succeeded their father : Giovanni Maria, Filippo Maria, and Gabriele Maria. The first was assassinated by his cousin Bernabo's sons, " in revenge for insults to their father." Duke Filippo Maria,—to divert men's minds from internecine vengeance,—led campaigns against Florence,

Venice, and Naples with varying success. When
he died, in 1447, the direct male line of the
Visconti came to an end—Gabriele Maria had died
childless in 1408. The populace, wearied by
exactions and tyranny, denounced the dynasty,
and, directly the dead Duke had been interred,
they razed the walls of the Castle of Milan to the
ground. A public vow was solemnly recorded
that "no man shall ever set one stone upon
another : it shall be a desolation and a warning."
Milan and all Lombardy became the Republic
of Sant' Ambrogio, with a purely democratic
Government, and all the "Lords and Ladies of
the Lakes" retired to their country seats, or hid
themselves in their city mansions.

A master-hand grasped the fortune and the
fame of Lombardy,—much as he could the reins
of two high-mettled steeds,—when, in 1450,
Francesco di Muzio Attendolo—" della Sforza "—
caused himself to be proclaimed Duke of Milan.
Son of the great Condottiere Muzio Attendolo, he
first saw light in his father's birthplace, Cotignola,
in the Romagna. He married in 1418 Polessena
Ruffo, but she died in 1420, leaving him no child.
To assuage his grief he gave his whole soul to
the profession of arms, emulating the heroic deeds
of his famous father. The Serene Republic of
Venice appointed him Captain-General of North

Italy—the Venetian dominions reaching almost to the walls of Milan. To strengthen his hold upon Venetia and Lombardy, very adroitly the Condottiere contracted in 1441 a second marriage with Bianca Maria, the only child and heiress of Filippo Maria Visconti. The citizens, completely overawed by their new master, besought him to rebuild the castle, "for," they pleaded, "the defence and adornment of our good town." With this petition they proposed to assign a year's revenues from the taxes on wine and meat (averaged at 36,000 ducats per annum) to cover the expenses of restoration. The *Rocchetta* was erected upon the ruins of the original Visconti castle, and an entirely new palace was built on the other side of the courtyard,—the *Corte Ducale*, a very splendid edifice,—a fit residence for the powerful Sovereign, and suitable for the functions of the new Court. With the assistance of masters like Bramante and Leonardo da Vinci, the Duke's ideas were amply realized.

The Castle of Milan under the new auspices speedily became the rival of the palaces of Florence, Ferrara, and Mantua. *Litterati* and artists foregathered thither, and beauty and fashion flocked there too. Ruling Princes and famous Captains made it their rendezvous, and notable goldsmiths and armourers offered their services. Among men

FRANCESCO SFORZA AND BIANCA VISCONTI

of mark who were drawn to the Court of Francesco
and Bianca Sforza, was the knight-errant troubadour King René of Anjou — the most highly
cultured and the most fascinating Prince in Europe.
He came to greet the Milanese rulers, but as well
to gain Duke Francesco's alliance in his attempt
to assert his ancestral rights to the kingdom of
Naples, usurped by Alfonso of Aragon. With
reference to the new Castle of Milan, Giacomo da
Cortona,—one of the Duke's School of Architects,
—wrote an account of the royal visit. "The
King," he says, "was here this morning, and went
all over the castle on foot with the Duchess, who
was perfectly indifferent about her rich velvet
gown trailing in the dust and dirt. He saw the
masons and wood-carvers preparing the medallions
with the ducal arms which are to be placed over
the gateway, and he climbed up to the very top
of the tower. He was much pleased with all he
saw, and when he heard that all this had risen
from the ground in three years, he could not
contain his amazement, and would hardly believe
such a thing possible."

Duke Francesco died in 1466, and was succeeded
by his dissolute son Galeazzo Maria, who, two
years later, married Princess Bona of Savoy.
Under their rule the castle was completed and
superbly decorated. The late Duke and Duchess

had been content with moderation in personal expenditure, but Galeazzo Maria and Bona launched forth into wild extravagance and household ostentation. For their wedding the Duke borrowed all the rich tapestries he could find from the houses of Milanese nobles and citizens, with which to hide the bare walls of the various rooms. There had been hitherto no permanent Chairs of State for the Ruler and his consort. Now two splendid thrones of elaborately carved walnut, overlaid with gold, and covered with carpets of richest cloth of gold and fine embroidery, were placed upon a dais in the principal hall of audience (these State seats are still preserved in the Cathedral Treasury). The Duke inherited the cultured tastes of his father and mother, and in his Duchess he found an artistic ally. Remains of the rich adornments of the castle are still to be seen in the different apartments—now filled with Art treasures. The ceilings in particular are notable,— in one room, Duchess Bona's boudoir, her motto— "*A bon droit*"—is many times repeated, under her cognizance (a white dove encircled by flames of fire),—all upon a brilliant crimson ground. The *Sala Verde* had upon its walls the Sforza emblems, —the golden bucket, with the Duke's initials,— and portraits of the Duke and Duchess. It was said that this apartment was decorated in a single night, in readiness for the nuptials of their daughter Bianca with the Duke of Savoy. So impatient was the Duke, that the work was hurried on without sufficient precautions as to the security of floor and walls being taken. This haste had for its result a tragedy. Upon the morning of the marriage, after the guests had assembled to greet the bridal pair, the floor collapsed, precipitating the lordly company into the basement of the palace! Although many Lords and Ladies were grievously injured, only one succumbed; but, alas! it was the young bridegroom himself who came to such an untimely end. No doubt the "Evil Eye," or some fell influence, was at work to wreck the prospects of the fair young bride, for no sooner had she put off her mourning for Duke Charles, than she was affianced to Prince Stefano,—the eldest son of the King of Hungary,—but he was accidentally drowned the day before the wedding!

When Duke Galeazzo Maria was scarcely seventeen years of age he loved a beautiful Milanese girl of noble family — Lucrezia Landriani—and had by her, in 1463, a daughter, who was christened Caterina. The infant was taken charge of at once by her father's mother, Duchess Bianca, and brought up as a daughter of the Ducal House. She was a remarkable child in many ways—excessively precocious in acquiring knowledge, and fearless, like a man. A letter to her mother is extant, dated 1468, inquiring about her health, which was very indifferent ; indeed, she died in the year following. Duchess Bianca Maria also died during the same year, and then Duchess Bona adopted the motherless girl, and educated her along with her own children. When she was ten years old Caterina was betrothed to Count Girolamo Riario, a natural son of Pope Sixtus IV. It was said that, casting about for territorial dignities with which to endow his offspring, His Holiness pitched upon the Lordship of Imola as a desirable possession. It had been surrendered to the Duke of Milan by Taddeo Manfredi when in financial dfficulties. Sixtus gave Duke Galeazzo Maria the goodly sum of fifty thousand gold ducats for the fief of Imola and the hand of his illegitimate daughter was thrown into the Riario bargain. The young couple were married on the bride's fifteenth birthday, and took up their residence in Rome. The same year Count Girolamo acted as proxy for his putative father, the Pope, in the Pazzi Conspiracy, within the Duomo of Florence, where Giuliano de' Medici was assassinated, and Lorenzo, his brother, grievously wounded. The Count returned to Rome, and gave himself up to unbridled lust and profligacy, and died by the hand of a Florentine *bravo* in 1490.

CATERINA SFORZA-RIARIO-MEDICI (WHEN EIGHTEEN YEARS OLD)

MARCO PALMEZZIANO

Forlì Museum

To face page 220

Countess Caterina, left a widow, spent very little time in bewailing her dissolute spouse ; they had lived apart ever since the tragic events in Florence. She was a virago indeed, for when people pointed at her and called her a heartless coward, she used to bridle up and reply, with undisguised scorn : " I sprang from a race of men who have never known fear, and who have never done a base action !" Caterina Sforza-Riario married again, and this union was pregnant of great consequences for Florence. She became the wife of Giovanni de' Medici, "*Il Popolano,*" and by him the mother of Condottiere Giovanni de' Medici,—"*Delle Bande Nera,*"—whose son became first Grand Duke of Florence, Cosimo I., "Tyrant of Tyrants." Perhaps the hot blood of the Sforzas coursing through Caterina's veins gave pushful character to her son and consummate cruelty to her grandson ! There is another romantic story anent strong-minded Caterina. She had a very comely valet, one Giacomo Feo ; he was but nineteen years of age and she eighteen at the time. Her loveless wedlock required consolation elsewhere, and the physical attributes of the young fellow appealed irresistibly to the love-lorn girl. It was said, indeed, that she secretly married her lover, and so legitimatized her child by him. What happened to Feo no one has stated—it is better so perhaps : he served his purpose, and that was sufficient for the virago. Virago she was in every Italian sense of the word ; a woman of vast mental ability and high culture,—five hundred letters of hers are extant,—Caterina Riario-Medici is the Renaissance female type of martial ardour and heroism. As Princess of Forli and mother of " *Il Giovannino*,"—born in 1498 at Forli,—she gave many and ample proofs of the indomitable pluck which were in her. As a " Lady of the Italian Lakes," or as the Commandant of a garrison, Caterina Sforza stands out as one of the heroines of the fifteenth century.

The Castle of Milan and its Art treasures attracted from afar visitors of all ranks and interests. Among them came Lorenzo "*Il Magnifico*" from Florence, and King Christian from Denmark—both upon diplomatic errands bent, and incidentally on the lookout for matrimonial contracts. There were several Sforza " Ladies of the Lakes " and many other well-dowered damsels in Milan—very eligible partners for royal and princely knight-errants. Such welcome guests were always notably entertained, and Milanese hosts vied with their likes in Florence, Venice, and Genoa in the magnificence of their banquets and the lavishness of their field-sports. Time out of mind the Brianza and its network of lakes and rivers were the rendezvous for sporting expeditions. Roebuck, boar, woodcock and heron, pike and trout, were preserved most carefully, and ladies and their cavaliers made records of their game-bags, and held picnics in the woods, and water-parties on the lakes.

The Duke and Duchess of Milan were the first notable visitors who fared to Florence to congratulate Lorenzo de' Medici upon his succession to the Headship of the Republic. The retinue which accompanied them was so gorgeous that it filled the people of the Tuscan capital with amazement. They were, however, dumbfounded by the magnificence of the reception accorded by the Medici. Macchiavelli instances the visit as mainly responsible for the vast increase in the luxurious habits of the citizens.

The Feast of the Nativity in 1476 saw the Castle of Milan prepared for a series of grand entertainments. Christmas Day passed serenely, but on the morrow the Duke,—although he had a premonition of misfortune, and turned back twice upon trifling pretexts,—assisted at Mass at the Church of San Stefano as usual, accompanied by a notable suite. Leaving the sacred edifice, he received the good wishes of courtiers and citizens, and he was radiant with happiness. He had, however, hardly stepped from beneath the great portal than the truth of that well-worn motto, "*Sic transit gloria mundi,*" was once more terribly affirmed. Stabbed from behind by five of his most intimate associates, he fell and expired immediately ! The awful news was borne swiftly to the Duchess, who, although stunned, had sufficient presence of mind to order the castle drawbridge to be raised and the garrison to man the walls. She folded her little son Giangaleazzo, barely seven years old, to her bosom, and bore him for safety to the highest tower of the Torre di Bona di Savoia. The city received the intelligence of the Duke's assassination calmly ; it was a good riddance, men said, for his pride and extravagance had become unbearable. No attempt was made to overawe the castle inmates ; indeed, at a convention of the nobles and citizens, held at noon on the day of the murder, Duke Giangaleazzo was proclaimed, and Duchess Bona was named sole Regent of the State. Three years sufficed to bring the new condition of affairs to a crisis. Both during her consort's life and after his death Duchess Bona's intimacy with Francesco (" Cicco ") Simonetta, the Duke's principal minister, was a subject of suspicion and a source of scandal. His position as sole adviser to a woman still lovely, a woman cultured and ambitious, was one of extreme delicacy and danger. He was one of Duke Francesco's most trusty

BONA DI SAVOIA, DUCHESS OF MILAN

ANTONIO DE PREDIS (OR BERNARDO MARTINI ?)

National Gallery, London

To face page 224

ministers, and upon the Duke's death he became paramount adviser of Galeazzo Maria, and the virtual controller of the Duchy. Among his many benefactions was a notable one to the chapter of the Cathedral of Como, in memory of his governorship of the city. In recognition of his generosity the authorities placed his statue upon the façade of the sacred building in the second row from the Broletto, and there it is to-day—evidently a portrait-bust. Once it is said a rival spoke derogatingly of his minister to Francesco, who at once took him to task. " So necessary is Cicco to the State and to me," he said, " that if he died I should be compelled to have him in wax !" His career ended tragically, for on the evening of October 17, 1479, whilst engaged in a *tête-à-téte* in the Duchess's boudoir, the door was forced by *bravi*, in the pay of Lodovico Sforza, Duke of Bari, and the paramour, torn from his *innamorata's* arms, was carried off to the Castle of Pavia. Short shrift had Cicco Simonetta, for without even the pretence of a trial he was beheaded in the forecourt on the morrow of his arrival.

The morning after Simonetta's arrest Duchess Bona was missing ; perhaps she feared a like fate might be in store for her. She fled to Abbiategrosso in company with a young fellow, for whom she entertained an infatuation—Antonio di Tusso, a carver at her table. He was a youth of singular beauty of person, and possessed of a soft appealing voice, but of low origin. Her little son, the young Duke, just ten years old, she forsook, and, under Tusso's influence, renounced her motherhood, and then she journeyed on to Paris. Lodovico Sforza seized the regency in the name of his young nephew, and became virtually ruler of Milan and Lombardy. In the early prime of life, just thirty years of age, he had, strange to say, evaded successfully the darts of Cupid; but fate was against him, for the year that witnessed his accession to supreme power, saw also his betrothal to a child of six—Isabella d' Este, the younger daughter of Ercole, Duke of Ferrara. This was certainly a very unpractical road to matrimony, and one very difficult to diagnose in the case of so astute a man as " Il Moro." It was, however, Ercole d' Este's *tour de force* in the " Lists " of Hymen, for such an eligible son-in-law as Lodovico could not be allowed escape. With Laban-like wisdom of the serpent— or the dove—the Duke of Ferrara managed, after a few months' diplomacy, to substitute Beatrice, his eldest daughter, for the younger, his projects for a Medici son-in-law having failed. Lodovico and Beatrice were married in 1490, and Isabella was reserved for the Marquis of Mantua.

The young Duke Giangaleazzo, too, had been
enslaved by the bands of Hymen, and had, in
January, 1489, married the Spanish Princess
Isabella d'Arragona, to whom he had been betrothed by his mother, Duchess Bona, acting
within her indisputable rights as a Princess of the
House of Savoy. Duchess Isabella found upon
her arrival at Milan that the domestic arrangements within the Castle were not a little compli-
cated. The Duke and his uncle,—who still held
to his self-imposed title of Regent,—had each
imposing households within the precincts,—the
Duke at *Corte Ducale*, Lodovico at the *Rochetta*.
So long as Lodovico was unmarried, perhaps,
this condition of affairs was endurable, but when
he brought home to Milan his Ferrara bride, and
established her as mistress of a portion of the
castle, the situation, so far as the Duchess was
concerned, was excessively embarrassing. Isabella
was no match for Beatrice, and she was faced by a
double degradation, as she deemed it. She, the
daughter of an ancient Royal House, her father
the Duke of Calabria, and heir to the Kingdom of
Naples, browbeaten by such second-class high-
nesses as Duke Ercole of Ferrara's daughters! All
the trouble, however, came from herself, and she
made herself miserable. She cared neither for
their frolics nor for their culture, and as for their

fashions, they were indelicate and ridiculous. Her misfit self-environment became at last intolerable, and the unamiable Duchess appealed to her father for redress. " If you will not help me," she wrote, " I would rather die by my own hand than bear this tyrannous yoke, and suffer outrages continual under the eyes of my servants."

The appeal entered into sympathetic ears, for King Alfonso,—as he had become in 1494,—hated Lodovico Sforza with a whole-hearted detestation—" the arrogant and ill-bred," as he dubbed him. He could, however, do nothing but urge his daughter to assert her undoubted priority in rank, and to keep, so far as she could, Lodovico and Beatrice at a distance. Perhaps what irritated Isabella as much as anything was,—as she judged it,—the ill-breeding of the Milanese ladies with whom she had to associate. The nobility of Milan certainly was democratic, not to say plebeian. First enrolled as the "*Società de' Gagliardi*"—Union of the Fittest—each rich family in the twelfth and thirteenth centuries was empowered to build its *Torre*, or embattlemented mansion, within the city boundaries. Such families were the Torriani, Landriani, Visconti, Gallerati, Mozzoni, Rho, Dognani, and Scotti.

A very favourite hunting-box of "Il Moro" and

Beatrice was at Cuzzago, on the slopes of the
Brianza Hills, some ten miles from Milan.   Many
letters of the Duchess are extant descanting upon
its attractions.   It was here and at other country
residences that Duchess Isabella began to unbend
and enter into the fascinating occupations of the
two Ferrara Princesses.   Perhaps the best description of their sporting expeditions is the story told of
the happy doings by Galeazzo di Sanseverino.
Referring to the presence of the two Duchesses, he
says, writing to the Marchioness of Mantua: " We
had a grand fishing expedition on the river, and
caught an immense quantity of large pike, trout,
lampreys, crabs, and other sorts of smaller fish, and
we proceeded at once to dine off them, and eat until
we could positively gorge no more.   Then directly
we had dined, to assist our digestion, we played
bowls with great energy ; and after we had played
for some time we went over the villa, which is
really very beautiful, and, among other things,
contains a portal of carved marble as fine as any at
the new works at the Certosa.   Next we examined
the result of our sport, which had been laid out in
front of the villa, and I picked out the finest
lampreys to take to His Highness the Duke.   When
we had done this we all rode off to another hunting
and fishing box, and caught more than one
thousand large trout, and after choosing the best

for presents and for our own most sacred throats, we tossed the rest back into the water. Then we once more mounted our horses, and began to let fly some of those fine falcons of mine, which you saw at Pavia, all along the river-side and they killed a number of birds. By this time it was nearly four o'clock, and we rode on to hunt stags and fawns, and after giving chase to twenty or more, we succeeded in killing two of each kind. Then we returned home, and reached Milan after dark. My illustrious Lord took the keenest delight in hearing all about what we had done, far more, I verily believe, than if he had been there in person, and I believe that the Duchess will in the end reap a substantial benefit, and that Lord Lodovico will give her Cuzzago, which is a place of rare beauty and considerable value. . . . I have cut my shoes to pieces and torn my clothes, and, moreover, played the fool into the bargain, and these are among the rich rewards one gains in the service of the fair sex. However, I will have patience, since it is all for the sake of my beloved Duchess, whom I will never fail in life or death. . . ."

Galeazzo di Sanseverino again wrote on February 11, 1491, to the Marchioness of Mantua: 'This day being a festival, I started at break of day with the Duchess (Beatrice) and her ladies, all

LODOVICO SFORZA, "IL MORO"

G A. BELTRAFFIO

Trivulzio Gallery, Milan

To face page 230

on horseback, for Cuzzago. I had to ride in a chariot with the Duchess, who was a little lame, and Dioda. We joked and sang twenty and more jolly trios—Dioda was tenor, the Duchess soprano, and I bass. We played endless tricks with one another. I do not really know which of us was the most foolish." Di Sanseverino later on asserts that Lodovico did actually bestow the villa and estate of Cuzzago upon his illustrious spouse, and that she partially rebuilt and refurnished the mansion, which had been a favourite residence of the Visconti, and still contained many objects which had belonged to that extinct ruling family.

The very year dated by di Sanseverino was remarkable for the marriage of Donna Cecilia Gallerina to Count Lodovico Bergamino of Cremona. The match was due to Duchess Beatrice, who, when she discovered Lodovico's secret, insisted that the girl, then a quasi-prisoner, but mistress of "Il Moro," should be released from the Castle of Saronno and settled in life, and should take her child by Lodovico with her. Lodovico resisted for a time, but at length yielded to his wife's insistence. Cecilia Gallerina had captivated "Il Moro" in 1481, when she was a young girl of seventeen. He had sufficient good sense not to introduce her at the Milanese Court, but made over to her the rights of the castle where she resided, and where he made constant visits. She was a beautiful woman and highly accomplished, and, furthermore, blessed with rare tact. She at once fell in with Duchess Beatrice's proposition, and, acting most discreetly, never appeared at Court even after her marriage. That Beatrice was jealous of her husband's attractive mistress need not to be said ; indeed, her jealousy took a very natural course. One day, it was said, Lodovico sent to his wife's boudoir—it was her birthday—a costly gift, a splendid robe of cloth of gold, so stiff that it stood by itself. One of her ladies, however, told her that Cecilia Gallerina had just such another. Without making much ado Beatrice promptly returned the costume to Lodovico, and sent a message that she declined to accept any gift which was a duplicate of a present to his mistress ! That Beatrice bore no ill-will to the fair favourite personally was abundantly testified by her remarkably kind conduct later on, when she admitted that " no one could do anything else but love such a fascinating woman." Her sister Isabella also greatly liked Cecilia, and actually wanted her to pay her a visit at Mantua.

Further light is thrown upon the manner of life of the Milanese Court by a letter from Lodovico,

April 12, 1491, to Isabella at Mantua. "There is," he wrote, "actually no end to the pleasures and amusements which we have here. I could not tell you a thousandth part of the tricks and games in which the Duchess of Milan and my wife indulge. In the country they spend their time riding races, and galloping up and down with their ladies at full speed, trying to throw the latter off their horses. Now we are back in Milan they are still inventing new forms of distraction. They started yesterday in all the rain—in fact, with five or six ladies wearing cloths or towels on their heads—and walked through the principal streets to buy provisions. But because it is not the custom here for women to wear cloths on their heads some of the market-women began to laugh, and made rude remarks, upon which, I hear, Beatrice fired up and answered saucily, so much so that they all but came to blows. In the end they came home safe and sound, but muddy and bedraggled, and were a fine sight! I believe when your Highness is here they will go out with all the more courage, since they will have in you so bold and spirited a companion, and I am sure that if anybody dares to be rude to you they will get back as much if not more than they gave. . . ."

One of Beatrice's favourite protégés was

Gaspare Visconti, whom she dubbed " Court poet."
He speaks thus of her

> " Donna Beata e Spirito pudico,
>   Deh ! fa benigna a questa mia richiesta
> La Voglia del tuo sposo Lodovico.
>   Io so ben quel che dico
> Tanta è la tua virtu che cio che vuoi
> Dello invitti corde disponer puoi."*

There was no regular theatre in Milan until the
spacious days of Duchess Beatrice, but, due to her
patronage of Niccolo da Correggio and his company, the first Scala Theatre was erected in 1493,
and opened with a mask, " *Mosposa e Daphne*,"
delightfully suggestive of the influence of the
sportive consort of Lodovico.   There, too, Beatrice
was wont to listen with rapture to a comely youth,
Angelo Testagrossa, whose sweet mezzo-soprano
voice thrilled her inner soul.   She called him
" *Voce d' un Angelo*," and no musical picnic was
complete without him.   His notes seemed to
tremble upon the sensitive leaves of the acacias,
and to drop from the fragrant petals of the
oleanders.   Indeed, Beatrice pictured herself in a
fantasy of Apollo and Daphne—beauty and song

* " Resplendent lady and most chaste spirit,
    Alas ! for me that thy richest merit
  Is the will of thy spouse Lodovico.
  Still I, too, will go where'er thou listest,
  For thy charms command in me the chiefest
  Joys of my heart, and life's sweetest echo."

transformed and eternal. Perhaps the lad's perfect figure enforced upon her the truth of the proverb : " *Perche ne la forma sta il tuto*,"—Beauty of form is first after all.

Duke Giangaleazzo died in 1494, and his widow, at Duke Lodovico's invitation, retained her own apartments in the *Corte Ducale*. Duchess Beatrice treated her with the utmost kindness and consideration, and, sharing her mourning, restrained her ardour for sport and gaiety. By a singular mutual arrangement Duchess Isabella was endowed by Lodovico with his Duchy of Bari, and when she had at her leisure packed up her belongings and selected a sufficient suite, she started off to her distant home on the Adriatic. She took with her her only daughter Bona. Little Bona, another wee " Lady of the Lakes," was sought after by suitors before she had left her mother's leading-strings. The Duchess, however, had a scheme in her head which she at first strove to carry into execution. Lodovico Sforza's son Massimiliano appeared to be an ideal husband. Whilst complacent to a very full extent in all that concerned their grand-niece's welfare, both Duke and Duchess placed a veto on this union—another bride was destined for their eldest son.

In 1494 Duke Lodovico invited,—unhappily for his own security as it turned out,—Charles VIII. of

France to undertake a campaign against Naples. The expedition was eminently successful, but on the return of the King to North Italy he very inconsiderately absorbed Lombardy, and the Duke fled to Germany. For twelve years France retained her hold upon the Duchy of Milan. The conduct of Charles was the more treacherous because on his entry into Italy he had been royally entertained by the Duke and Duchess, and treated them quite reciprocally.

The first meeting of the King and Duke had been at Asti in Monferrato, where Lodovico was accompanied by Duke Ercole d' Este of Ferrara, his father-in-law, Asti being the advanced post of the French progress in Italy. Duchess Beatrice left Milan a few days after the departure of the Duke, but she wended her way to the North, and took up her residence at the Castle of Annona, upon the very beautiful lakelet of that name in the Brianza. There was, of course, a method in this diversion, for the Duke had not a little misgiving as to the possibilities of a French invasion in spite of his invitation to King Charles. The royal visitor was in due courtesy bound to pay his respects to the fascinating and accomplished reigning Duchess, so an excursion to the North would have the advantage of diverting the French from the City of Milan. Accordingly, on September 11,

BEATRICE D' ESTÈ, DUCHESS OF MILAN

PIERO DELLA FRANCESCA

Pitti Palace, Florence

To face page 236

Duchess Beatrice received the King with the greatest *empressement* and with unparalleled splendour. Surrounded by her Court of eighty ladies of good birth from Milan, Asti, Alessandria, and other places of importance, Charles, vizor in hand and sword in sheath, advanced to the centre of the great audience-hall, when the Duchess, about to curtsy lowly, was raised by the gallant Sovereign, and kissed not only upon the hand but on the cheek—a very welcome recognition of her rights as a sovereign Princess. Then, illustrious courtier that he was, he passed to Signora Bianca, wife of Galeazzo di Sanseverino, and greeted her ; in short, he kissed the whole bevy of fair dames and damsels ! The King and Duchess conversed for quite a long time, and then she proposed certain amusements for her royal guest, to which he quite delightedly acceded. Beatrice has, in a letter to her sister, Marchioness Isabella of Mantua, recorded the day's delights. " About half-past five," she wrote, " the King came, in a very homely fashion, with his suite of noble lords and knights—a goodly following—and remained about three hours with me and my ladies, on such a familiar and amiable footing that nothing more charming could be desired by anyone. He wanted to see the ladies dance, and then he asked me to do the same, and he found it all quite bewitching."

This tactful Princess had called all her wits into play to dazzle as well as amuse the dreaded monarch, who had a man's weak points all the same—admiration and love of pretty and sprightly women !   He had, moreover, a fondness for pomps and vanities of fashion.   Charles was just twenty-four years of age ; he was the spouse of a lovely woman, as wise and rich as she was beautiful— Anne, daughter and heiress of Francis II., Duke of Brittany, who was at the time of Charles's invasion of Italy only eighteen years old.   He and his courtiers were amazed at the magnificence of their reception, and particularly at the gorgeous-ness of the Duchess's apparel.   Her jewels greatly outnumbered Charles's ; she was weighed down with chains and collars of solid gold and flashing gems, and her fingers were completely covered with fine rings.   She wore upon her head a Ducal crown of gold, studded with huge diamonds and rubies.   The Duchess's robes were cloth of gold and silver tissue worn over the richest petticoats of costly green silk velvet ; her train was a mass of curious embroidery in calabalistic figures and designs of witchcraft—so at least they seemed to be to the French visitors.

King Charles remained at the Castle of Annona for quite a considerable time, fascinated by the brilliant *castellana*.   Thither, too, flocked

" Lords and Ladies of the Lakes," all arrayed most richly as for a tournament. The Duchess amused her royal guest with riding expeditions and stag-hunts. Each day she went forth to meet the King in splendid raiment. One day,—mounted on a pure white steed caparisoned in cloth of gold and crimson velvet,—she wore a habit of green cloth and a lace chemisette open at the breast. Her well-curled hair was tired with gold cord and pearls, and tied with silk ribbons floating down her back. She wore a crimson, wide-brimmed felt hat turned up at the side, with six red feathers and a jewelled brooch. She sat astride, as did her suite of twenty beautiful girls,—each attired like herself. Six chariots followed, lined with cloth of gold and green velvet, filled with ladies of her Court magnificently dressed.

On the third day of the royal visit Charles was indisposed, and could not accept his beauteous hostess's challenge to the chase, but remained quietly in his quarters. The Duchess despatched her ladies and the French courtiers to the forest, but she very adroitly spent the morning in the villa gardens, when, quite unexpectedly, Charles came upon her. What passed there it would be quite unkind to divulge—it was one of Cupid's stolen opportunities, and the wicked little Prince enslaved the amorous King, so that he had no

16

escape ! At dinner in the evening the Duchess again welcomed the King, clothed in lustrous green satin—green was her favourite colour, as we may well suppose ;—the body, back and front, was stitched thickly with flashing jewels, and had the appearance of a cuirass. The sleeves were tight, but puffed on the shoulder, and entwined with bands of rubies. Her bosom was bare,—the chemisette merely covering her corsets,—and round her throat she wore the biggest pearls Charles had ever seen. Upon her head Beatrice had a jaunty little red velvet cap, after the French fashion, with an aigrette of green feathers, and a great pear-shaped pearl surrounded with diamonds and rubies.

The King had completely recovered from his indisposition, and was the merriest of the merry at the feast. After a judicious rest Charles challenged Beatrice to a minuet, and desired his courtiers to find partners too. Beatrice,—a past mistress of dancing,—had not the slightest difficulty in stepping and posturing in the French way, very greatly to the King's delight. He paid her numerous compliments, of course, and, among the rest, he said : " Madame, I have never seen a dancer half so accomplished nor anything like so graceful as your Highness is, and your ladies are quite wonderful, and have won the hearts of all my lords, as you yourself have mine !"

Charles passed upon his way, and Beatrice never saw him again until he appeared in 1500 before the walls of Milan, and demanded the keys and the person of her husband! Was man ever more base? was lover ever more fickle? but perhaps the fascinating Duchess did not share the exile of her lord! Was Beatrice fickle, too?

In close attendance upon King Charles was one of the most famous soldiers of the century, Le Chevalier Pierre de Terrail, commonly called Bayart, son of Aymon, the Lord of Bayart,—" *Sans peur et sans reproche.*" The rendezvous at Annona was quite to his liking, and no man in all that splendid cavalcade bore himself more chivalrously. Duchess Beatrice was smitten by his fame and person, and reluctantly resigned him to the fascinations of Signora Anna Sforza, whilst she diplomatically inveigled the young King. Thus Mars and Vulcan were both disarmed by Venus!

Signora Anna Sforza was one of the great " Ladies of the Lakes," not only by her relationship to Lodovico and Beatrice, but on account of her association with the lakes of the Brianza; for she had been brought up with her sister Bianca Maria,—who married the Emperor Maximilian,— chiefly at the villa of the Sforzas on the Lake of Annona. Her marriage was arranged in connection with that of Beatrice. She had been be-

trothed to the eldest son of Duke Ercole d' Este—
Prince Alfonso—when they were both infants,
and Alfonso accompanied his sister to Milan for the
wedding festivities, with the view of escorting his
bride back to Ferrara. The parting of Anna Sforza
with her loved ones in Milan was, as historians
have recorded, " sad, for everyone was oppressed
by the thought that they would never see her
more." This presage of sorrow was fulfilled within
a twelvemonth, for she died in giving birth to her
first-born. " She was very beautiful and very
charming, with a sweet temper and gentle disposition, but there is little to tell about her, because
she lived so short a time "—so a quaint chronicler
sums up her story. One of Alessandro Moretto's
most striking pictures is entitled " Santa Giustina." In a beautiful landscape is the standing
figure of a magnificent woman, young and of noble
bearing. At her feet kneels a richly clad Prince,
and beside her is a unicorn. This may very well
be a portrait-study of Anna Sforza-d'Este ; anyhow, the kneeling Prince is Alfonso d'Este, and
the unicorn is the emblem of chastity.

Duchess Beatrice surrounded herself with *litterati*
and artists, the most distinguished in Europe ;
and whither her fancy led her they followed—wor-
shippers at the shrine of the " Sforza Sappho."
In the Brianza, upon the Lakes, in Lodovico's

LUCREZIA CREVELLI

BERNARDO MARTINI (ZENALE)

Newall Collection

To face page 242

many villas, along the valleys of the Adda and the
Lambro, and north and south of Milan, poets recited their stanzas,—Gaspare Visconti and Niccolo
da Correggio,—musicians strummed on organs of
gold, and ebony, and inlaid pearl, and on resonant
lancewood and silver violins,—Lorenzo da Pavia
and Jacopo di San Secondo. Jehan Cordier, a
Flemish poetaster, was the Duchess's constant
companion. At Annona, Cuzzago, and elsewhere,
his mellow tenor voice,—alfresco or *in camera,*—
blended delightfully with her clear soprano. He
was a priest also by profession, and sang the Mass
so deliciously that often enough he moved the
Duchess to tears and emotional utterances.

The gardens of her villas,—scenes not only of
pastoral delights and musical distractions,—were
sometimes vocal with acrimonious altercations
following gay supper-parties. The ladies quarrelled over the merits of their favourite *condottieri*
and their most favoured *cavalieri,* and sometimes
the disputes waxed hot, so that it needed all the
smartness and effrontery of jesters, dwarfs, and
other comical people to prevent dangerous rup-
tures. Leonardo da Vinci's advent to Milan was
hailed delightedly by the Sforza Princesses. He
undertook to stage-manage the Court festivities,
and splendid was their rendition. A ballet of
peasants of the Brianza had, in particular, great

success : the *maestro* dressed the men in red, the girls in blue,—the Sforza colours,—and posed them to form the names " Lodovico " and " Beatrice." With his own hands, too, he modelled the tournament champion's wreath of gold and silver laurel-leaves, which Duchess Beatrice placed upon the brow of Galeazzo di Sanseverino, the husband of Duke Lodovico's daughter Bianca. Leonardo, too, reset all Beatrice's jewels and designed her dresses—a frivolous occupation for such a serious genius ! He also relaid out the gardens of the castle, and erected gorgeous triumphal arches.

All roads led to Milan and its castle whilst Lodovico and Beatrice held their state therein. The Duchess has left a name for great personal activity. Daily she heard Mass privately ; then, breakfast over, she rode off with her ladies and scoured the countryside. Dinner in due course was followed by cosy card-parties,—*Scartino, Réveil des Morts,* or *L'Imperiale,*—and supper by dance and song. Her dresses were often remarkable for singularity : one, of stiff yellow satin brocade, bore in embroidery a representation of the Port of Genoa ; she wore with this a black Spanish lace mantilla, and had red carnations stuck in her hair and in the corsage. Anna Sforza rivalled her sister-in-law in the gorgeousness of her attire. At the entertainment of King Charles VIII. and Le

Chevalier Bayart, at Anonna, she wore stiff cloth of gold covered with the letters of the alphabet in raised silver-work on blue velvet. Another of her confections was of corded white silk, with lions embroidered in natural colours. Both these great ladies affected Marchioness Isabella's taste for coloured velvet mantles lined with black satin, and stitched all over with *passementerie*.

Duchess Beatrice died January 2, 1497. She had in the afternoon driven through the city to pray at Duchess Bianca's tomb, and afterwards had, with intense pleasure, watched her ladies dance some new measures. Three hours later she gave birth prematurely to a dead son, and died as soon as her labour was ended. "That night," the chronicler Corio noted, "the whole sky right over the castle was on fire, and the walls of the Duchess's gardens fell down with an appalling crash, although no earthquake or any other uncanny omen chanced." The Duke was stunned; he was a changed man. He put himself, his household, and the castle in deepest mourning, and day followed day witnessing to his devotion to religious exercises. Duchess Beatrice's name was, by his order, placed upon every public building in Milan, and in all the streets, encircled by a wreath of cypress. He lavished money on the churches for Masses and Requiems, and took no further interest in the affairs of his Duchy. At length he shut himself up in the castle, and there remained until the ever-active foes of Lombardy came banging at its portals. Even then he made no effort, but pleaded with Beatrice,—her love, her help. " As long as the *Rocca* stands I know that I shall be safe !" Still, in the midst of his desolation he gave a thought to his mistress Lucrezia Crevelli, for he executed a legal document in July of the same year, making very ample provision for her son Cesare by a grant of the lands and revenues at Cuzzago and Saronno.

On September 2, 1499, Lodovico secretly left Milan, and, *incognito*, made his way to Innsbruck. Four days later the French, under Giangiacomo Trivulzio, Marquis of Vigera, entered the city, and received from the Governor the surrender of the castle. It and the whole city were given over to unrestrained pillage. The looters revenged themselves especially upon the apartments of the late Duchess. Her furniture, her pictures, her treasures, and her wardrobe were all scattered and destroyed, and her name was torn down wherever emblazoned. Why this savagery, addressed to the memory of the accomplished and beautiful Beatrice, was perpetrated no one has declared; she was, and always had been, the friend of the people, and popular with all parties. Rumour certainly had it that the general frenzy was directed by no less a personage than Trivulzio, who thus took revenge for the rejection of an unworthy suit ! It was mean and sordid, to be sure —the foam of a troubled sea of jealousy : Trivulzio *versus* Sforza, with the concentrated hate of a disappointed lover !

Sad, indeed, became the state of the Castle of Milan in the possession of an ill-conditioned French garrison. " It was now a place of dirty booths and dirty tales. The French are a dirty people— Captains spit on the floor, and soldiers openly outrage women in the streets !"

Cecilia Gallerina had not been the only rival to Duchess Beatrice in the affections of her husband ; his liaison with Lucrezia Crevelli was a still more serious menace to her peace of mind. Beatrice, however, philosophically entered into the sentiments of the time ; she was Lodovico's lawful wife, and no mistress should oust her from her position. She would do as all other women did—grant her lord the freedom she took herself. Marriage was a ceremonial contract, and by no means limited the passions of the heart, the eye, the ear ' Perhaps Beatrice secretly felt keenly the intrusions of Lucrezia, for she had come to her at Ferrara as a child to play with, and had accompanied her to Milan as a confidential attendant. Cecilia, Duke Lodovico had discreetly kept away from the Court and castle, but Lucrezia he kissed before his wife's face at Milan. The only way Beatrice had to save her own reputation and Lucrezia's was to attach her as closely as possible to her own person. The Duchess never left the palace without Lucrezia at her side, and she never excused her presence when in residence at the castle. This was doubtless a mistaken sort of espionage, for Lodovico and Lucrezia had their meetings all the same.

With the passing of Lodovico " Il Moro " and Beatrice, the glory of the Sforza dynasty ended. The happy days, however, of " *La Sforza Saffo* " were revived in 1513, when her eldest son, Massimiliano, was called to the vacant Duchy. The first guest of honour was his aunt, Marchioness Isabella of Mantua; but, alas! the reign of beautiful and cultured Duchesses of Milan was nearing its end. The " Ladies of the Lakes " fled before the new invasion of the " dirty French " under King Francis I.; but they were once more driven out, and Charles V. proclaimed Beatrice's second son, Francesco Maria, Duke of Milan. He brought to the dilapidated castle his bride, Princess Cristina of Denmark, no more than thirteen years old. They reigned subject to the will and fancy of the Emperor; and when the Duke died, in 1535, Charles's son Philip received the Duchy, which he and his successors held for two hundred years.

CRISTINA DI DANEMARCA, DUCHESS OF MILAN

HANS HOLBEIN

National Gallery, London

To face page 248

Duchess Cristina, widowed at twenty-six, seems to have been chosen as an eligible successor to Jane Seymour, third consort of Henry VIII. of England. With this in view, Holbein was sent off to Brussels to paint her portrait—the Duchess of Milan of the National Gallery. Negotiations fell through, and the royal widow married, in 1540, Francis, Duke of Lorraine, and was again widowed three years after. She died in 1590. Then followed the Austrian domination, to be swept away by the forces of Napoleon Buonaparte. The Austrians made of the grand old castle a barracks and the French a brothel; and then, for one hundred years, ruin and desolation reigned supreme, and the stones of the venerable buildings cried aloud for deliverance. In 1893 a new palace arose like a phœnix—not, indeed, to be the theatre of brilliant Courts, but a gallery of art treasures. The memory of the Sforzas is retained by the *Ponticella di Lodovico " il Moro "*—the bridge over the disused moat, with its beautiful *loggia*, passing over which those who love the old, old stories may, perhaps, hear eerie voices, and see, at dark, weird phantoms. " Lords and Ladies " of the past still haunt the ancient precincts, and chide the modern modes of " Lords and Ladies " of to-day.

CHAPTER V

"SEBINO"

LAKE OF ISEO AND THE VALLEYS OF BERGAMO AND BRESCIA.

ISEO,—*Lacus Sebinus* of the Latins,—in shape resembles nothing more nearly than the flickering flame of a candle ; and this is quite as it should be, for one of the derivatives of the name is " Psyche," —the Spirit or Soul of Humanity. Iseo is the Psyche of the Paradise of the Italian Lakes. Ensconced in the greenest of landscapes, and gazing up into the bluest of skies, the reflections upon her gently rippling waters are delicious opal hues of emerald and sapphire. The lips of delicate wavelets are kissed by the sweet-scented zephyrs from the gracious plain of Lombardy, but are ever and anon ravished by the strenuous breezes of the Val Camonica. Her verdant locks of myrtle and laurel are the tokens of the poetic romance of her story. Drama and tragedy she tramples under her well-shaped feet—the cities of Bergamo and Brescia, so to speak,—whilst " she dances," as Castiglione says, " all day long in the lustful sun."

Like the sensuous form of the idyllic Goddess of
Love, wrapped in diaphanous veils of mist and
mystery, Iseo is ever spanned by scintillating
rainbows. All the livelong, golden day, and into
the silvered moonshine, the human entities around
the lake laugh and sing right merrily. The air is
like the effervescence of rare champagne : it
exhilarates mind and body. Maybe harvest and
vintage are prolonged through winter's solstice,
for spring seems to grasp the hand of autumn.
" *Doux et frais, comme une éclogue de Virgile,*"
voiced Georges Sand's encomium of the delights of
the Lake of Iseo. The very name,—like that of
Cupid's sweetheart,—has in it the echo of ecstasy,—
life's heart's passions foaming over. That volatile
French " Lady of the Lake " roved over land and
sea to find an Elysium, and when she discovered
Iseo, she brought her second self, Lucrezia Floriana,
—such a suggestive appellation,—to realize the
ideal life under the red-purple vine pergolas and
the silver-gilt olive-groves of Sebino.

The very lovely marble group, " Psyche and
Cupid," at the Villa Carlotta, on the Lake of Como,
is a dream creation almost incarnating the loves
of the mystic pair. Canova has caught absolutely
the spirit of idealism, and his *chef-d'œuvre* is the
realization of the spirit and the life of Lake Iseo.
The charms of Psyche are displayed everywhere

upon its bosom and its shores. " Fauna " and
" Flora " may be goddesses of a sublime Paradise,
but they reign, too, here seraphically in every
created form. Insects and plants are all Psyche's
own. Dragon-flies flit gorgeously among the snap-
dragons ; butterflies poise elegantly upon butter-
cups ; fire-flies are instinct beneath fritillaries ;
honey-bees quaff the nectar of honeysuckles ;
cheerful crickets sing amid shimmering grass and
fragrant herbs ; and the gossamer spider weaves
his tinted silken web, wet with crystal dewdrops,
here and there and everywhere. What would you
more ? It is—

> " Psyche ! Psyche ! all the way !
> Awake, my love, awake."

The voice which cries on Iseo's shores must be
the voice of Psyche ! Everything and everybody
is full of delightful unrestraint—full of tranquillity
and peace ; nowhere is human life so simple,
nowhere love more free.

I.

Sarnico is the first station on the Lake of Iseo.
There, and at every town and village along the
shores, are painted houses which overhang the
water. To drop into the most delicious of all
natural baths is a matter of the greatest ease ; but

this characteristic has in it an element of danger,
and Psyche of the sirens' haunt may become the
vampire of the unwary, even in gracious, smiling
Iseo, so deep are the intrigues of Love! "Take
care," says a time-honoured caution on the spot,
"or the Maddalena will thrust out her hand and
draw thee down!" The name itself, "Sarnico,"
has in it a suggestiveness—its meaning is "catching cold."

At Predole was, in years gone by, an ancient
castle, but in 1404 the Ghibellines of Lovere, at the
head of the lake, came down from the Val Camonica, eight hundred strong, led by their valiant
Captain, Giustiniano Camillo, not alone to strike
a blow at the Papacy, but to revenge the destruction of rich olive-woods. Iseo,—the busiest town-
let upon the lake, and its sponsor,—has a ruined
castle also; but the town's associations are rather
with a living present than a decadent past, for
dyers, silk-weavers, and coppersmiths are thriving
craftsmen. In the middle of the lake is the very
picturesque islet of Santa Maria d' Iseo, with its
sanctuary of the Madonna della Purificazione,
built by the warlike family of Oldofredi, as "an
accommodation with Heaven," in the fifteenth
century. There, side by side, each second day of
February,—the feast of Candlemas,—are lighted
by devout Bergàmese their decorated *candelore*,

and by no less pious Bresciaese their equally well-adorned *seriole*—good pilgrims all. The peasants dance Lupercalian measures, and illuminate their cottages with gilded candles; and these things they did even before Pope Gelasius in 499 Christianized the heathen festival. Many beautiful villas nowadays adorn the meads and glades of Iseo : upon the rocky islet of Loreto, with its monastic church of San Paolo, dating from 1470, Duchess Felicita Bivilacqua—La Masa, of Verona, built the fine Gothic castle, funds for which were furnished by the drawing of the first prize in a lottery of the Banco Nazionale. The castle was purchased in 1900 by Commendatore Vincenzio Ricchieri, and it is now called after his name.

Vello is most appropriately named—the place of wool or hair. Sheep's fleeces as rich as those of Spain in Renaissance times are washed, and fine carded wool is spooled. Tenderest fluffs thereof hold capricious revels in the air : to catch them is the difficulty ; hence the common saying, " Vello ! vello !"—Here it is !—a will-o'-the-wisp of Psyche ! Vello looks across to Riva—the fairest shore of beauteous Iseo—where every fragrant, shady, flowering bush rejoices in full growth, and crystal sand lines all the beach.

With respect to Pisogne, near Lovere, and one of Iseo's many beauty - spots—a haunt of the

CASTLE OF DUCHESS FELICITA BIVILACQUA-LA MUSA   LAKE OF ISEO.   A LOTTERY PRIZE

From a Photograph

To face page 254

elves and nymphs—there is a very piquant story.
The fine church of the Madonna della Néve (Our
Lady of the Snows) stands boldly upon a spur of
Monte Guglielmo; and natives of the village
desired Girolamo Romanino, the Brescian master,
to paint the walls with frescoes. One of his subjects was " St. Christopher bearing the Infant
Christ," but the amount (one hundred and fifty
livres) offered by way of remuneration was so
beggarly that, to put his patrons to shame, he
depicted the Christian giant with a very scanty
dress. When protests were raised, Romanino,
with a wink in his eye, replied : " Short skirts,
short pay !"—and the painter passed on to adorn
other sanctuaries in the Val Camonica.

Lovere is the chief place on Isco's banks ; one
looks thence right down the lake, and right up the
Val Camonica—a perfect situation for a *villeggiatura*. The town has a twofold reputation : it is
in miniature Tunbridge Wells joined to Newcastle
—an odd adjointure. Mineral springs attract the
ailing, and iron and cannon foundries the militant. Many world-famous families of artist-
artisans have had their origin in Lovere : the Belli,
the Zambellini, and the Capodiferri, perhaps the
most renowned. They were sculptors in stone, in
metal, and in wood, and they and their likes were
noted for skilful *intarsia* work. Sons of these

17

artificers travelled all over Italy embellishing churches and palaces with their beautiful handiwork. The mother church of Santa Maria in Valvendra has frescoes by Romanino, and the replica of the monument by Canova to Count Achilleo Tadini's only daughter Teresa, who, unhappily, was crushed to death by the fall of an arch at Volpino in the Val Camonica. She and a merry party of young people had gone off for a picnic in the woods, and the maiden, the happiest of the lot and the most venturesome, had dared to cross the ancient structure to gain a wager. The Tadini Palace was in 1828 converted, by the munificence of Count Luigi, into a public picture-gallery, with four hundred paintings by celebrated Italian masters, and many other art treasures.

The great charm of Iseo, and of Lovere in particular, was " discovered " by a very remarkable Englishwoman—a true " Lady of the Lake "—Lady Mary Wortley Montagu. Writing to her daughter, the Countess of Bute, July 21, 1747, she says : " I am now in a place the most beautifully romantic I ever saw in my life." She had, it seems, been recommended by her doctor at Brescia to visit Lovere for the sake of the waters. She goes on to say in her letter : " It is the Tunbridge Wells of this part of the world to which I have been sent by a doctor for the ague. I have found a good lodging, and a great deal of company, and a village in many respects like the Wells, not only in the quality of the water, which is the same, but in the manner of the buildings, most of the houses being separate at little distances, and built on the sides of hills, which, indeed, are far different from those of Tunbridge Wells, being six times as high. They are really vast rocks of different figures, covered with green moss and short grass, diversified by tufts of trees, little woods, and here and there vineyards, but no other cultivation, except gardens like Richmond Hill. The fountain where we drink the waters rises between two over-hanging hills, and is overshadowed with large trees that give a freshness in the hottest time of the day."

In another letter to her daughter, written six weeks later, Lady Mary describes her residence, and gives other interesting information. " I have been," she wrote, " here six weeks, and still am at my dairy-house, which joins my garden. I believe I have already told you it is a long mile from the castle, which is situate in the midst of a very large village, once a considerable town, part of the walls still remaining, and has just vacant ground enough about it to make a garden, which is my greatest amusement. It is on a bank, forming a kind of peninsula raised from the River

Oglio fifty feet, to which you descend by easy steps cut in the turf, and either take the air on the river, which is as wide as the Thames at Richmond ; or, by walking up an avenue two hundred yards on the side of it, you find a wood of one hundred acres, which was already cut into walks and ridings when I took it. I have only added fifteen bowers for different views, with seats of turf. I am now writing to you in one of these arbours, which is so thick-shaded the sun is not troublesome, even at noon. Another is on the side of the river, where I have made a camp-kitchen, that I may take the fish, dress and eat it immediately, and at the same time see the barges which ascend and descend every day to and from Mantua, Guastella, or Ponte de Vie (Pontevico ?). This wood is carpeted in their succeeding seasons with violets and strawberries, inhabited by a nation of nightingales, and filled with game of all kinds, excepting deer and wild boar, the first being unknown here, and not being large enough for the other."

Upon a subsequent visit to Iseo in the year 1752, Lady Mary speaks of the lake as follows : " The lake itself is different from any other I ever saw or read of, being of the colour of the sea rather deeply tinged with green, which convinces me that the surrounding country must be full of

minerals, and it may be rich in mines yet undis-
covered, as well as quarries of marble, from which
the houses are constructed, and even the streets
are paved, which are polished and laid with art,
and look like mosaic by the variety of colour.
These 'streets' are very narrow, and only afford
space for wheelbarrows, and are nearly two miles
long, lined by a mixture of shops, palaces, and
gardens. Some of the buildings are already
tumbling down." Lady Mary's own habitation
was a ramshackle *locanda* sort of building, but
the garden was the most spacious in Lovere.
She describes the habits of Loverese society, and
speaks of opera being sung, and other entertainments, but commends the early hour of closing
—10 p.m. In the season there was,—and perhaps
may be still,—a round of assemblies, whist-parties,
and routs, whereat the gentlemen were accustomed to appear in light-coloured nightcaps and
gay nightgowns, whilst the ladies were in their
stays and smock sleeves, with petticoats. These
costumes had a special name—" *I Vestimenti di
Confidenza !*" Perhaps such vesture is *à la mode*
elsewhere to-day ; so " *honi soit qui mal y pense !*"

To the north-east of Lovere runs the Val
Camonica, right away to Edolo, at the foot of the
giant Adamello,—with its mantle of eternal snow,—
and then on till it joins the Tonale Valley, beyond

the boundary of Tirol. The scenery is wild and beautiful; peasants are happily at work in their daily plot, and shepherds pipe and feed their flocks serenely. The cry that goes up to Heaven from the ground is not the bitter lament of the dour husbandry of Barbizon : it is the hum of a pleasant land. Yet upon every eminence is the ruin of a castle of wild days long past, and under the crumbling stones lie buried deep down, unshrouded and uncoffined, the dust of gallant warriors old and young. Their spirits haunt the gnarled trunks of forest-trees, and their fierce battle-cries re-echo uncannily in many a gloomy cavern. "God rest them !" cry we all, and then we pass again into the sunshine and the life of men. Cheek by jowl with these dilapidated strongholds are ancient churches of the Catholic religion ; their sweet bells sound from white, lofty *campanili,* as they did when men sounded thence the dreaded tocsin.

At Breno is the mother church of the Val Camonica ; it and all the churches of the valley are frescoed—many by Romanino, who chose to depict Scriptural scenes with the portraits of living people of the parishes ; hence the pictorial history of the Val Camonica is of quite unique interest. In the "Life of the Virgin," at the Church of the Madonna at Breno, in particular, the artist has painted "Lords and Ladies of the Lakes" attired and occupied in their accustomed manners. Everywhere, too, are scenic exhibitions of the "Dance of Death," and in every parish is a branch of the "*Buona Morte*," which numbers its members, rich and poor, noble and simple, indiscriminately. The confraternity is of Lombard origin, and was first established at the Palazzo Lazzaro, in Milan, in 1483.

The country about Lake Iseo,—and in particular the Val Camonica,—abounds in quaint customs and folklore. Peasants still regard the day as ended at sundown, and the hours of slumber belong to the morrow. When they lie down to sleep they wrap their great cloaks around them, much as they shroud a corpse at burial, with the commendatory prayer of the "*Buona Morte*," and twine their rosaries around their fingers. When they wish to prognosticate the weather, the children seek for snails, and sing over them :

> " *Lumaga bota coregn*
> *Ch' ei te ciama quei de Boregn*
> *Ch' ei te ciama quei de Sù*
> *Bota fo i to cornaciu.*"*

---

* " Oh, sweet little snail so shy,
Shall the wind be cold and dry,
Or moist and warm shall it be ?
Sweet snail, show thy horns to me."

St. George is looked upon as the patron of the nuptial day, and as many weddings as possible are celebrated upon his April festival. He shares, in these valleys of the Alps, with St. Christopher the greatest popularity among the Christian Saints. Most of the country churches have frescoes of the two patrons. At Zave, above the Lake, on the south wall of the ancient parish church, is a much-faded painting, dated 1486, representing the legendary story of the Christian Perseus liberating Andromeda, on the banks of the Red Sea, from a fierce and hungry dragon. The reptile is in the agonies of death, and the Christian maiden appeals to St. George to take her away : " I pray thee, noble youth, take me up beside thee on thy steed, and let me flee from this place " This appeal is still made by country brides on the bridal morn, when the happy groom gallops up to claim the maiden of his choice.

Throughout Lombardy an ancient patriarchal custom lingered long, and is still observed in the remote villages of the Bergamesque and Brescian Alps. After the actual marriage ceremony the newly wedded pair part once more, and each spends the first night in their respective parents' home. In the Valley of San Martino, indeed, the bride remains with her mother for fifteen days, but the groom has access to her at his will. At the end of this probationary period he wraps his wife in a great cloak of skin, and bears her bodily away. The Bergamesque and Brescian valley-dwellers celebrate their marriages with extra-ordinary hospitalities. Every relative, even the most distant, within reach is bidden to the feast, and absence is only condoned by the forfeiture of a considerable gift in kind. The same gustatory celebrations mark the funerals of the heads of families, so that it is a common saying :

" *Ai spusalese e ai mortore
Sa conos ol parentore.*"*

To be sure, a considerable difference was ob-served in the conduct of the company. At funerals bands of hired mourners—women for the most part—assembled at the house of death, and ceased not their lamentations till the priest had com-mitted the corpse to Mother Earth. There is a record at the hamlet of Gandino, off the Val Seriana, dated July, 1460, which imposes heavy fines, payable to the Commune, if the burial is delayed beyond the third day. Gandino is notable for its treasures of the goldsmith's craft : the people are past masters in the artistic manipulation of the precious metal.

One reason why St. Christopher's legend is

* " No marriages or funerals
Without the gathering of relations."

cunningly painted on the west fronts of the churches is that he is credited with the virtue and power of bearing away the evil of an unprepared or sudden death. The church at Bienno has a fresco, painted before 1500, of the "Christ-bearer," with the words: "*Christofori (imago) visaforis mane erit jnimica doloris.*" The Saint's reputed destruction of a deadly serpent points the same story.

On the festival of St. John Baptist the herdsmen of the Val Camonica offer to the proprietors of the pasturages the first cheeses of the year. They have been in the making ever since St. George's day, and are, in consequence, called "*Giorgine.*" A similar cheese is presented to the legal official of the Commune when a tenant takes up a fief. Because farm-girls are much occupied in the cheese manufacture, *Giorgia* has become a common female name at Vello, one of the loveliest stations on Lake Iseo, with its woods of limes and chestnuts, and its wealth of wild-flowers. There is a curious custom, purely Greek in origin, of treating the bark, leaves, and flowers of limes for the alleviation of fistulæ and boils. They soak them and knead them with their feet into a pulp, and then, mixing it with olive-oil, they spread the plaster over the painful spot. If the application is made on St. Sebastian's Day, the cure is absolute. The Vel-

THE LADY MARY WORTLEY MONTAGU

J RICHARDSON

Collection of the Duke of Newcastle

To face page 264

loese, indeed, speak of Iseo as "*Lago Sebastio*" (Sebastian's Lake), perhaps a corruption of "Sebino," after all. In recent days of simple faith the Christian Apollo, the arrow-pierced beau tiful youth, was regarded, at any rate by his women and girl devotees, as the gentle succourer of the plague-stricken and the wounded.

Naturally we should expect to find charms and divinations against storms on the Lake of Iseo and in the hills, and this is one of them. The peasants keep very carefully the straw which has been used in the "*Presipio*," or "Bethlehem," of the village churches until the first day of Lent, when it is burnt, and with the ashes the priests mark the foreheads of the devout. The residue of the burnt straw is then mixed with withered olive-leaves, and cast by children into the air to avert danger to their fisher-fathers and brothers in the boats.

To the north-west of Lovere a good road leads over hill and dale, carpeted with sweet herbs and wild-flowers, to Clusone, in the Val Seriana,—a delightful name, indeed, from the same root as "*Serico*" (silken)—the Valley of the Serio—the "Silken Ribbon River." The valley is famous as the home of artistic workers in metal. The rich families of Lorenzoni and Vertova and many others came thence. All the synonyms of Psyche are delightful, are they not ? The nomenclature of her country of Iseo is full of charming suggestiveness. Bondione is the highest village of the valley ; thence, in a couple of hours, may be reached Psyche's waterfall—*Cascato del Serio*—leaping down for one thousand feet in three flashing falls into a romantic caldron, enclosed by snow-capped mountains. It is the most fairy-like waterfall in Europe, and the play of light upon the spray reveals the butterfly wings of the goddess, ever swaying to and fro as she searches diligently for her Cupid ! From Clusone,—where there is a very remarkable " Dance of Death " frescoed on the wall of the village church,—it is but a short stage down the valley to Bergamo.

II.

One of the most remarkable " Lords of the Italian Lakes " was the celebrated Condottiere Bartolommeo Colleone. His fearsome name was wont to be called over refractory youngsters by worried parents anywhere upon the marches of Venetia, what time the Serene Republic dominated Northern Italy. No more redoubtable soldier of fortune ever laid his sword at the feet of ambitious or needy Sovereigns and States, and no warrior served more successfully the warlike Queen of the

Adriatic. Much of his romantic story has for its setting the city of Bergamo and its adjoinng country, and, in particular, the Castle of Malpaga on the way to Treviglio.

One other castle within striking distance of Malpaga claims, with respect to Bartolommeo Colleone, prior notice, inasmuch as the little hamlet at its foot was the cradle of his race. Built up bit by bit by many successive war-lords, the Castle of Trezzo occupies the very centre of historic battle-grounds; it was the chief prize of every victor in the fight. The outlook over the wide, fertile plain of Lombardy is superb, for, perched upon a rocky eminence above the swirling Adda, it has no rival. Here Frederic Barbarossa placed his armoury and war-chest in 1158. Hither, too, Ezzelino "the Terrible" of Bassano, Papal Imperial Vicar, dragged his miserable victims to mutilate and torture with unspeakable barbarity. At the end of the thirteenth century the great nobles of Milan fought out to a finish beneath the castle walls their relentless feuds, until the unconquerable Visconti gained the mastery. Within a dungeon of the keep Giovanni Galeazzo imprisoned his uncle, the redoubtable Bernabo, and strangled him treacherously in 1385. Now peaceful owners,—the Conti della Masterani,—patronize irrigation and industry, and the turgid waters of the river no more run red with blood of men, but are redolent of busy crafts.

One of the towers, now a heap of ruins—*Torre di Colleone*—overlooks the smiling village Solza, where, in the year 1400, Bartolommeo first saw light. His father, a plain, honest yeoman,—Paolo Colleone,—who married a village girl,—Riccardina Valvasori de' Saiguini,—looked back for ancestry to a Guelph warrior, one Gisilbertus Co-Leone,—as the cognomen was originally spelt. He enrolled his name in 1101 as a citizen of Bergamo, upon his qualification of ownership at Trezzo, Solza, and Chignolo. Bernabo Visconti, before his fall, had been a resident at the castle, and had employed Guglielmo Colleone, Bartolommeo's grandfather, as under - bailiff and confidential agent. He invited him to reside within the castle precincts, treated him almost as an equal, and then changed his mind and drove him out, offering him the choice of immediate death or seclusion in the monastery of Pontidro in far-distant Val Sabbia. What the poor man's offence was is not recorded—perhaps a denouncer of treachery—anyhow, *bravi* in the pay of Visconto stabbed him to death within the cloister.

Paolo Colleone naturally resented this atrocity, but, being a prudent man, he held his peace, and bided his time to revenge his father's murder ; and, as one of those employed by Giovanni

Galeazzo Visconti, he paid Bernabo out in kind. Giovanni Galeazzo died at Marignano in 1402, and then his executors quarrelled amongst themselves concerning the disposition of the property, and divided it without regard to will or reason. Paolo Colleone put in a plea for services rendered the defunct Visconti, and, this being disallowed, he, assisted by his friends, seized the *Torre di Colleone*, and held it against all comers. When his comrades asked for their share of the booty, he declined surrender, and then, with all the ease in the world, so characteristic of the time, they hung up their leader to a rafter in the guardhouse. Madonna Riccardina found her husband's dead body, and loudly bewailed him, hurling invectives at his assassins; so, with commendable despatch, they gagged the struggling woman, and locked her up in a dark hole underground. A child's cry struck on the ears of one of the conspirators, and, more merciful than the rest,—they would have cut the babe in two,—he carried little Bartolommeo into the woods, and then sent him on to Bergamo to the care of his mother. The hands which held the castle keys were not entirely unkind to the Madonna, for within a twelvemonth not only was she released from durance vile, but her little boy was restored to her, and she was allowed to live in peace at Solza.

At twelve years old young Bartolommeo was a
well-grown boy, handsome, strong, and venturesome. Very much against his mother's wishes, a
career was indicated for him beyond the boundaries of his forebear's misfortunes ; she, perhaps
naturally, wished him to remain at home—her
only child, her only solace. He had no fancy for
the grovelling life of a countryman, nor for the
studious occupations of the cloister ; art did not
affect him. His fine physique pointed to the
strenuous profession of arms ; but for a lad to
enter thereupon money was required, and powerful
influence. It was obviously impossible for interest to be made with the Visconti in Milan.
Bergamo, a city of craftsmen, had no attractions
for the budding warrior. At Piacenza,—that
most pleasant city of the Emilia,—was a school of
servitor boys, about which the village-folk of Solza
prattled, and young Bartolommeo listened to
what was said. Filippo Arcelli, Lord of Piacenza,
had just established a college there, somewhat in
imitation of the famous School of Vittorino da
Feltre at Mantua, for healthy, well-developed
youths, irrespective of rank and wealth. The lads
he accepted were supposed to be content not to
rise much in the social scale, but to qualify as
horsemen, huntsmen, keepers, and so forth, in
noble families. After much ado, Madonna Riccar-

dina consented to send her boy to Piacenza, but he never settled there. He scorned the society of grooms and gardeners, and, fired with the martial ardour of his sires, Bartolommeo grasped his nettle and ran away.

At eighteen the ambitious youth, after many wanderings, found himself at Naples, the capital of the notorious Queen, Giovanna II. He was certainly just the sort of lad that ill-conditioned Sovereign liked to behold ; and, discovered by one of her agents, she would have made him a royal groom. Tidings of the Queen's turpitude were rife throughout Italy, and Bartolommeo declined the royal service ; but, oddly enough, he entered that of the Queen's right-hand man, Condottiere Forte Braccio, who placed him in his stables. This, of course, was not at all what he wanted, and he speedily forsook Braccio for his rival Caldora, and was by him placed in command of twenty horsemen. Then, with admirable shrewdness, Colleone transferred himself to the following of Carmagnola, then commander-in-chief of the Venetian military forces. He had at last achieved his aim in life—he had become a soldier of fortune. In the steps of his leader he was appointed a Condottiere in the service of the Serene Republic in 1433, and for ten years did doughty deeds on behalf of his appreciative masters. Bartolommeo

18

Colleone's name was now laurel-wreathed; his fame spread far and wide, and Sovereigns in need of pushful captains plied him with offers and with bribes. Among these was the Duke of Milan, Filippo Maria Visconti, and the young Condottiere closed at once with his proposal. By the stiffness of his terms and conditions, he wiped away for ever the stain of his ancestors' murders, and struck an even balance with their murderer's successor. The Duke gave him castles and estates, and a splendid pension with which to keep up his state; but, in 1450, Bartolommeo Colleone retired from the active profession of arms.

The Castle of Malpaga was the property of the Serene Republic, and upon it and its lordship the Condottiere fixed his gaze, until, for the good round sum of one thousand gold ducats, he became its owner, the actual sale being effected April 29, 1456. "The castle,"—so Martino Sanudo, the reliable Venetian historian, has recorded,—" was occupied in the name of Venice by the Captain-General of Bergamo with a force of one hundred horsemen, who made a brave show against the Duke of Milan."

Colleone set to work at once to occupy his property; the castle he practically rebuilt, redecorated and furnished it, and gave his attention to the picturesque arrangements of the gardens.

TOURNAMENT AT THE CASTLE OF MALPAGA

GIROLAMO ROMANINO

Fresco at he Castle of Malpaga. (See page 280)

To face page 272

When the improvements were completed, he brought home, festal-like, his dear wife, Madonna Thisbè, and his beloved daughters, Ursina, Caterina, and Medea. The whole countryside rejoiced in the Condottiere's happiness ; his father's comrades and his mother's friends now became his own, and humble little Solza was proud and demonstrative.

Well might his neighbours be proud of their distinguished fellow-countrymen, for he raised them all by example, precept, and patronage, till every family felt the impress of his strong personality. Schools were opened for the instruction of young people, very much after the manner of that at Piacenza, and Colleone took good heed to the morals of his pupils. The military training of young men had the Condottiere's solicitude. From the borders of the Lake of Iseo and the valleys north of Bergamo came stalwart sons of the soil to learn the profession of arms. The curriculum was strenuous, for, not only were his soldiers busy in their drill, but athletic contests were made compulsory. The strongest men in Lombardy wore the Colleone colours. No other property was so fully developed as Malpaga. Works of irrigation brought the waters of the Serio to the castle walls. No cattle-rearing or game-preserving had such excellent results as were achieved under the

Condottiere's direction. In short, Malpaga and its surroundings became a model for all the other landowners of Lombardy.

Princely state was kept up at the castle, which became famous as the most perfect example of a feudal castle of the century. Colleone's household and garrison were picked representatives of physical fitness and graceful deportment; six hundred men sat daily at his lordly table, and strangers of every rank and station were entertained with unstinted hospitality. Colleone surrounded himself with men of letters and women of brilliant wit. Yet, in the midst of great activities, which caused Madonna Thisbè endless anxieties, the master of the castle lived a comparatively quiet life. He cared less for talk than for books, but he was ever ready with smart repartee. When asked with surprise by one of his prince-guests, why he troubled himself so much for others' weal, and patronized festive revels, and especially favoured attractive women, he replied : " I am much more surprised that so young a man as your Excellency should ask such a question, and that you should apparently be overcome with hatred of the fair sex; as for me, I love them all !" Probably woman was the Condottiere's special weakness ; he craved a male heir, and Madonna Thisbè only gave him daughters.

The most interesting guest entertained by Condottiere Bartolommeo Colleone at Malpaga was King Christian I. He had been to Rome upon a pilgrimage "for the good of his soul, and in propitiation for the sins of his ancestors," as the chronicler has it. King of all Scandinavia, and bearing a host of sovereign titles, he was accompanied by an imposing suite—the Dukes of Lauenberg and Olten, the Counts of Milligen, Barby, and Hüffenstein, and many more nobles. At Treviso, upon his Romeward journey, a mission from Duke Galeazzo Maria Sforza had saluted the King, and offered him Milanese hospitality; but Christian was bent on visiting the most famous soldier of the day, and the Duke was mightily displeased at His Majesty's preference of Colleone.

The Condottiere, courtier-like, assigned Malpaga to his royal guest, and went under canvas with his household. He laid out a camp as in time of war with stockade, ditches, stores, and munitions, and received King Christian on May 12, 1474, in full battle array, with one thousand mounted men cuirassed, and one thousand highlanders on foot— a moving and splendid spectacle. Banquets, tournaments, sports, and dances formed each day's programme, and Scandinavians and Lombards became the best of comrades—true and free.

In the royal suite travelled a gigantic Dacian,—

" the strongest man on earth,"—the King's champion. Bout after bout, wherever the royal cavalcade had halted, had proved him invincible ; and the Condottiere's athletes fared no better than the rest. One day, however, the Dacian found his match at Malpaga, when a young man came to parley with the guard. Zorzio da Spinone,—a mountain village in the Val Cavallina beyond Bergamo,—twenty-five years of age, and a perfect young Hercules, who followed the calling of a charcoal-burner, challenged the champion to a wrestling match. Colleone was informed of the young fellow's intention, interviewed him, and, struck with his splendid physique, ordered him to be fed, and washed, and shaved, and clothed suitably. "Go forth," he said to Zorzio, "with courage ; fear not, and if thou bearest thyself well, thou shalt receive a finer prize than thou canst name, for I will not that we should be brow-beaten by this bold Dacian !'" The champion duly entered the sports ground of the castle, and the whole garrison with their visitors foregathered to cheer their men. The young charcoal-burner successfully parried the giant's feints, and, when he was a little winded, deftly seized him under the haunches, and had him in a trice upon his head, his feet in the air, and then he laid him flat upon the sward ! Thunderous applause greeted this achievement,

and King Christian, shaking the victor by the
hand,—with true sportsman spirit,—gave him a
ring from off his finger, and a heavy purse of gold.
Colleone was as good as his word, and Zorzio remained at Malpaga as standard-bearer and chief
of the bodyguard. As might have been expected,
the victory of the Lombard lad was not without
its romance. Some few days after the victory in
the sports ground another stranger advanced to
parley with the castle guard, but this time it was
a maiden shy, but by no means forlorn. Berta da
Trescore, the next village to La Spinone, had
followed her man to Malpaga -for he had told her
what he had heard about King Christian's Dacian
strong man. She was just the sort of comely
damsel—wholesome, smart, and vigorous—that
appealed to the maiden-loving Condottiere, and
Colleone entered at once into the romance. He
dallied with her, as was his wont, but the girl's
spirit and devotion to her village lover arrested
further liberties ; and, with Medea, his daughter,
as bridesmaid, and himself *in loco parentis*, Zorzio
and Berta were joined in matrimony upon the
spot !

King Christian remained at Malpaga ten days ;
and, on parting with his host, he gave him a
splendid painting he had purchased in Rome, and
graciously accepted as Colleone's offering the

finest suit of Milanese armour in the castle. Accompanied by the Condottiere, the King and his escort reached the city of Como on May 23, and there he found a fleet of roomy vessels, chartered by the Duke of Milan, ready to carry him to Colico. The King's barge had a lofty tent or awning of cloth of gold; its crew was liveried in scarlet cloth, and rowed with gilded oars. Four troubadours and a band of musicians, with the royal cooks and butlers, were in the next vessel, ready to feed and cheer the royal sailor and his suite. Such a splendid flotilla had never passed up the lake. The citizens of Como and the fisher-folks and peasants on the shores lavished festive decorations and illuminations in honour of the royal " Lord of the Lake," and so the Scandinavian " pilgrims " hasted on to their far-off home, intoxicated with the delights of Lombardy.

Bartolommeo Colleone paid his adieux to King Christian at the quay of Como, and then returned to his Castle of Malpaga for rest, and to carry on his works of benevolence. Madonna Thisbè, too, was weary after all the gaiety and ceremonial · she missed the help of her two married daughters, Ursina and Caterina. The former was wife of Count Gherardo Martinengo; the latter of his brother, Count Gaspare—both of Brescia. The two Countesses were, it seems, prevented from journeying to Malpaga for the royal visit by reason of coincident maternity. Isotta, the eldest daughter, had died in infancy ; and Medea, the youngest, died four years after the coming of the King. Both were buried in the sanctuary church of Basella, upon an eminence across the Serio.

In the very midst of his humane occupations the sands in the Condottiere's hour-glass ran down, and, fearing the approach of the "Black Buffaloes," he prepared himself for their "Triumph." On October 27, 1475, he executed his will, leaving the Castle of Malpaga and the estate to his eldest daughter Ursina and her family, on the understanding that Count Gherardo should add the patronymic Colleone to his surname. On November 3 in the same year the redoubtable warrior,— truly a noble-hearted "Lord of the Lakes,"— breathed his last in his well-beloved castle. He was buried at Bergamo, in the very beautiful Capella Colleone, by the side of the Romanesque church of Santa Maria Maggiore, which he had caused to be built. A superb monument was erected by his daughters and their husbands, and then Medea Colleone's monument was removed thither from Basella. The chapel, with its lavish adornment inside and out, is one of the architectural gems of the fifteenth century.

Many years after the Condottiere's death another

memorial of a striking character was completed within the Castle of Malpaga. Girolamo Romanino was commissioned to fresco the walls of the banqueting-room of the castle with scenes from the memorable visit of King Christian of Scandinavia. The first shows the arrival of the royal visitor at Malpaga, and it is interesting from the fact that the likeness of the Condottiere's eldest grandchild, Bartolommeo Martinengo, is introduced. The second scene is a tournament, with the city of Bergamo in the distance. The King and the Condottiere are seated in a *loggia*, apart from Madonna Thisbè and her ladies. The third fresco is a royal hunting-party in the wooded country bordering the Serio : the huntsmen are in Colleone liveries. The Banquet is, perhaps, the most striking of the series. The King presides, but the host is placed below the salt-cellar ! Colleone's seneschal, Alberto de' Quarenghi, is by his side. A lady in blue and white,—the Colleone colours,—is the Countess Ursina, with her little son. Prince Johann of Saxony wears a big plumed hat. The fifth tableau represents the Condottiere seated at table in the open *cortile* of the castle, superintending the serving out of liveries and gifts to the King's attendants. The sixth picture shows the departure of King Christian, and among the notables is Colleone's state-

KING CHRISTIAN ENTERTAINED BY CAVALIERE BARTOLOMMEO COLLEONE

GIROLAMO ROMANINO

Fresco at the Castle of Malpaga

To face page 280

trumpeter, Lorenzo della Scarperia. The last fresco depicts a wrestling match,—perhaps that between the Dacian champion and Zorzio da Spinone. The series is exceedingly valuable, as illustrative of the dress and manners, and of the scenery and architecture of the period. Romanino was not born until ten years after King Christian's visit, but tales of the gorgeous festivities were rife on the countryside for several generations. Doubtless the Counts and Countesses Martinengo-Colleone were able to give the master full particulars of the scenes, and perhaps to reconstruct them for his benefit.

The Castle of Malpaga remained in the possession of the Martinenghi family until 1888, when it was sold, with the estate, to Conte Francesco Roncalli, who most carefully restored it.

There is a little story connected with the neighbourhood of Malpaga, which characteristically illustrates the simple and unquestioning religious fervour of the men and women of the fourteenth century. It is as follows: April 7, 1356, was a dark day in the annals of Lombardy by reason of the severe belated frost which devastated the province, and was, perhaps, most destructive throughout the plain of Bergamo. Early in the morning of that day a young girl, Marina, the fifteen-year-old daughter of Pietro Leone, a peasant farmer of the Borgo di Urgnano, sallied forth to her daily task in the flax-fields. To her intense surprise she found the whole crop blackened and hopelessly withered. Knowing that this meant an irreparable loss to her father, she burst into tears, and, falling upon her knees, cried out piteously : " Holy Virgin, why is this ? Why has thy Son sent this affliction to my parents ?" Then she cast her eyes across a stubble-field hard by, and beheld an amazing vision—a lovely regal woman, gorgeously apparelled, with a little child in her arms. Marina knelt and crossed herself devoutly, and then a voice spoke to her in the sweetest accents she had ever heard :

" Do not be afraid, child ; why art thou weeping and lamenting ?"

" Do you not see, noble lady," replied the girl, " what terrible damage the cruel frost has done ? and do you not reflect how terribly poor people will suffer in consequence ?"

" Fear not, child," the sweet voice replied ; " none shall suffer want for this ; there shall be an abundant harvest."

Marina, less fearful than at first, asked the lady who she was. The lovely woman told her not, but said : " Come again to this spot in nine days, at this hour, and I will then tell thee all ;" and then she vanished.

Upon the ninth day—it was April 16, and the girl's sixteenth birthday—she was again at the hallowed spot, and the beauteous vision was again vouchsafed to her.

" Thou hast done well," the voice said, " to come here to-day. Thou art on the verge of womanhood, but I conjure thee to keep thyself a virgin, such as I am. Go, tell the men of Urgnano to dig deep here,—see, there are three flat stones to mark the spot,—and they will find a buried church, which they must excavate, repair, and re-dedicate. The priest must be newly ordained, and he must say his first Mass at the altar interceding for souls who lost their lives in the long-ago earthquake."

That was all; the vision passed away, but Marina knew it was the Blessed Virgin Mary who had so miraculously revealed herself and her wishes. Marina told her father, but he made fun of her story; nevertheless, it fascinated him and the men of the parish, and everyone lent a willing hand to lay bare the engulfed sacred edifice. Saint Mary's commands were exactly carried out, and not alone were the ruins of the ancient Christian basilica discovered and repaired, but the miracle drew thereto scores and scores of pious pilgrims. Bartolommeo Colleone caused the church to be richly decorated, and named it " Santa Maria della Basella "—the vernacular for " Earthquake."

III.

Bergamo and Brescia are twin sisters, and the Brescian Alps are own brothers of the Bergam esque. Alike, too, in number and in charm are the verdant valleys that debouch at their gates : Brembana, Seriana, and Cavallina salute Bergamo ; Brescia is embraced by Camonica, Trompia, and Sabbio. Val Brembana is famous in the history of art ; from out of it sprang a phalanx of artists to enrich mankind for good with things of beauty and renown : Bernardino Licinio (1511-1544) ; Andrea Previtale (1480-1525) ; Rocco Marconi (1472-1529) ; Antonio Donati (1502-1568) ; Andrea da Solario (1460-1515) ; Agliardo Algiardi (1592-1654) ; Lorenzo Lotto (1480-1556) ; Francesco Capodeferro (1472-1532) ; Giovanni Belli (1540-1577) ; Gian Antonio Amadeo (1421-1476) ; the brothers Santa Croce,—Girolamo (1520-1549) and Francesco Rizo (1524-1562) ; Giovanni de' Busi " Cariani " (1485-1541) ; and, last, but not least, Jacopo Palma Negretto—Palma il Vecchio, (1480-1525).

Specimens of art and craft in street, church, and gallery of every Italian town testify to the excellent handiwork of sons and daughters of the Val Brembrana. It might be an interesting occupation to inquire why in particular this lovely valley should be the cradle of art. Man's capacities are developed by his environment, and in the pursuit of healthy avocations. First of all, the scenery is exquisitely beautiful and greatly diversified. From the sun-fretted plain of Lombardy beyond Bergamo up- to the Falls of the Brembo, bursting out of the snow-fields of the Val Tellina mountains, every kind of climate may be enjoyed. The air is never stagnant, the sun makes lavish growth, and the water is impregnated with salt. The occupations of the peasants are various, but there are four industries which absorb the majority of workers—sheep-pasturing, copper-mining, charcoal-burning, and linen-weaving. All these tend to the isolation of labourers, and solitude is provocative of meditation and invention. Perhaps all the army of Brembana artists had flat stones, soft clay, and prime wood upon which to experiment, much as had Giotto of Tuscany. Anyhow, there is not a family in the whole length of the valley, and along the converging valleys, which has not exhibited in the present or the past artistic temperament. These families, by the way, are abnormally numerous, and sons and daughters drift to the art cities of the plain and beyond. Nature's best gifts are for Nature's most simple and unaffected offspring. The Brembanese display their artistic proclivities in a hundred different ways—their carriage, their dress, their household goods, their instruments of melody and labour, their love of flowers and perfumes, their skill in games, their popular festivals, and all they put their hands to proclaim them subjects of the realm of art.

Jacopo Palma Negretto is the Prince of Bergamesque painters. His natal place was the secluded village of Serina-Alta, three thousand feet above the sea, in the valley of the same name, which converges upon the Val Brembana at Zogno. He first breathed that delicious mountain air, say, in April, 1480, the son of Antonio de' Negretti. No one has painted the blue mountains of those valleys more intimately than did he. "Sacred Conversations" were much in his way—groups of finely proportioned, noble-visaged Saints in flowery meadows—ideal and sensuous. In portraiture, —for his "Saints" are living entities,—he is Bergamesque; one may even think one hears the country "burr," for they are "speaking likenesses." One grand model in particular strikes the eye and the imagination; she is the most splendid and grandiose woman in Italian art. Her verisimilitude culminates in the grand "St. Barbara" in the church of Santa Maria Formosa in Venice. Who is she? For answer we must seek again the Brembo's banks, and look among the

YOLANDA DA SERINA

PALMA VECCHIO (OR PARIS BORDONE?)

Prado Museum, Madrid

To face page 286

maidens of the hills and dales. Lithesome, graceful, with perfect figures and distinguished carriage, those damsels of the goat-herds and woollen
distaffs, bearers of heavy agrestical burdens on
their heads, breathe the free, exhilarating air of
the mountain and the forest—equal partners with
the men in toil and play. Yolanda da Serina was
such an one; and when painters of the valley
sought for models, none surpassed her in physique
and bearing. Whether she was Jacopo Palma's
daughter or not, we shall never know,—for he was
never married,—but we know she was his most
attractive model, and upon her his fame was built.
With Jacopo she went to Venice, and his studio
was her home. There Vecellio Tiziano beheld her,
and noted how she easily surpassed the drab girls
of his native Cadore in every charm of virginity.
To paint her was his strong desire; to love her,
too, need not perhaps be said. At any rate,
Yolanda's attributes were transcendent, and
henceforth the two great painter - friends made
complacent Yolanda's life a burden; they painted
no woman else. " La Bella " may be Titian's;
it may be Palma's too. She had all the personal
charms loved of Venetian painters—a distinguished
air, fair hair and skin, blue eyes, and a supple figure.
Was not Yolanda " The Virgin " of that masterpiece,
" The Assumption," in the Academy at Venice ?

19

All the painters in Venice admired and loved Yolanda, and many a suitor sought her favour—among them no less distinguished a person than Pietro Aretino. She turned a deaf ear to them all, remained true to Jacopo Palma, and, when he died, she quietly returned with her few belongings to the peace and contentment of her native valley. If the chronicler lies not, she married a good-looking countryman, a boy-lover, and lived happily. Strange, indeed, it was that " il Vecchio's " will never so much as named Yolanda ; perhaps all his was hers. Who knows ?

One other painter there was among the many who issued from that rich source of artists, Val Brembana, whose name is held in high esteem in Lombardy, not only for his artistic merit, but for his ardent patriotism—a gift, alas ! so rare nowadays among the self-seeking inhabitants of the United Kingdom. Giovanni de' Busi was born at the forest hamlet of Fiupiano, beyond San Pellegrino, in 1480. The name " Cariani," by which he is generally known, betokens that of his mother's family. She was a forest maiden, minding her goats and spinning, what time Giovanni de' Busi, a young patrician of Venice, fared to Bergamo and beyond to find pastime and fortune. An accident brought the two together. A bear had mauled the valiant sportsman and left him wounded in the woodland. As Fate would have it, a comely damsel happened on him, nursed him, and loved him—Bettina Cariani. Alas! Bettina saw no more of her lover, but Giovanni had not forgotten her, and when she died " Giovannino " joined his father in Venice—a growing lad, full of artistic sympathies and poetry.

In Venice three famous masters appealed to the budding painter, Giorgio Barbarelli (Giorgione), Jacopo Negretto (Palma il Vecchio), and Lorenzo Lotto ; the two last being natives, like himself, of the Val Brembana. With them he worked and studied till, at the age of twenty-two, love of his mother's home overpowered him, and back he went to Bergamo and Fiupiano, to paint the landscapes he remembered so well, and the people he loved, with their costumes and occupations. In all his religious compositions may be seen a lady —a Saint—of noble appearance, richly dressed and wearing abundant golden hair, her pure face fair as a blush-rose. Sometimes she holds the bridle of a white horse. Tradition has pointed her out as Yolanda da Serina : Cariani was in love with her, too !

Perhaps with Cariani should be named his contemporary of Brescia, Girolamo Romanino, of the same age as himself, a native of Romano, on the Serio, some ten miles east of Treviglio. They worked together, and among their paintings in common are the characteristic frescoes of the Castle of Malpaga. There is a certain air of romance about an altar-piece Cariani painted for the Benedictine monks of Santa Giustina at Padua. Alessandro Bonvicino (Moretto) painted a similar picture for the same complacent patrons. Whether the painting at the Imperial Museum at Vienna is Bonvicino's, or Romanino's, or Palmo Vecchio's, critics have not yet determined. Anyhow, here we have once more the striking traits of the splendid model of the " Santa Barbara," Yolanda.

One of the most picturesque and at the same time most ancient villages in Val Brembana is Botta. High above the road stands the quaint old Church of Sant' Egidio—the patron of smiths and, preferentially here, of coppersmiths and copper-miners. Bishop Guala di Bergamo, a native of the hamlet, in 1178 set up ten tableaux or groups of the Passion of Christ upon the approach to the church—one of the oldest mountain " Stations of the Cross " in Christendom. He also instituted the quasi-Jewish custom of the offering of a lamb by each sheep-owner at Easter to the high altar. Such offering gained the promise of a prosperous year, and gave rise to the common Bergamesque proverb : " *Al mior piu agnei a Pasqua che pegore en tütt l' an,*"—-He who presents a lamb at Easter

shall have food enough for a twelvemonth.
What became of the bleating baby creatures no
one has been careful to record; perhaps the
worldly wise ecclesiastics kept them for their
own larder, or perhaps,—as in the parish of Sant'
Alessandro della Croce, in the thirteenth century,
—they were distributed amongst the poor families
of the neighbourhood.

At Cornello, beyond the Electric Zinc Foundry,
is a tablet in a house wall: it records the ancestral
home of a notable Brembanese family—the Tassi.
Omedeo de' Tassi, in 1290, first made the name
famous as the forbear of the Princes of Thurn ünd
Taxis, founders of the post service of Germany.
Bernardo and Torquato Tasso,—"Lords of the
Lakes,"—greatly added to the family renown, and
made the Val Brembana a poet's Mecca. They
were not the only poetasters who came of the
valley soil. Poets, we know, are rarely town-
bred: the country is their home, and the more
beautiful the scenery, the more exquisite their
poetry. Nevertheless, it is rather singular that
the dulcet tones of song should emanate from a
district where the dialect of the inhabitants is
crude and uncouth. The Bergamesque vernacular is as remarkable for its "burr" as is, say,
the Zulu for its "cluck." Torquato's great
work, "*Gerusalemme Liberata*," was actually first

written in the dialect of the Val Brembana! Signore Bernardo Tasso, the great poet's father, had a small estate near Cornello, and was also enrolled as a citizen of Bergamo. He left home to seek his fortune elsewhere, and wandered to distant Naples, where he met and married Portia Gherardini. He lost his fortune in the disasters of the Prince of Salerno, in whose service he was, and Torquato, born at Sorrento, March 11, 1544, was the child of adversity.

> "   I am content,
> Thyrsis, to tell thee what the woods and hills
> And rivers know, but men as yet know not."

This breathes the sweet air and rhythm of the Val Brembana. Count Alessandro Tasso, the poet's cousin, of Bergamo, sent a post-chaise all the way to Mantua to fetch him home. His welcome in the city, and all the way to Cornello, was triumph; the street through which he passed is still called Via di Torquato Tasso. The " *Aminta* " was the poet's record of his Iseoan appreciation—the precursor of the sweet songs of sylvan poetry.

> " The dales for shade, the hills for beauty glow,
> Past fragrant groves the crystal rivers flow,
> All fair scenes doth Dame Nature grace,
> My heart's in my sire's native place."

Poet by heredity, he loved his ancestral soil.

The people of Bergamo,—where nobles and

traders were synonymous,—although provided
with excellent educational institutions, and famous
for artistic culture and enterprise in commerce,
affected the archaic speech of the countryfolk
beyond their gates. Daily in church, market,
meeting, and at home it was the curre nt coin of
language. This is perhaps not exceptional, for it
is a noticeable habit of all town populations. The
dialect is a curious blend of Lombardian and
Engadinese—a mixing of Latin roots with German.
Its origin may be traced to the Romansch of the
valleys and alps of the Bernina and the Örtler,
where rough medieval footpaths intersect the
well-made Roman roads. Thither valley dwellers
of the Bergamo and Brescia country, following the
employment of shepherds, lead their immense
flocks of lanky, tawny sheep and goats for
aromatic pasturage. Travellers along the Val
Bregaglia to-day are familiar with picturesque
manly figures posed on rugged rocks and under
gnarled oaks, habited in huge brown cloaks and
wide leather breeches, their legs swathed, like the
ancients, in loose, coarse woollen cloth, with black
leather thongs. On their heads of long, unkempt
hair felt sombreros ; in their hands sturdy poles or
staves; on their backs bagpipes, and in their leathern
belts pipes or horns, for they are all, men and boys,
pifferari—musicians of the mountain solitudes.

These peasants, too, can dance and grimace ; they always could, for was not the first race of Harlequins shepherds of Bergamo and Brescia ? And did not the nimble, sly and dancing Brighetta mother the whole family of the Marionettes which sprang forth from the valleys of the Lombardian Alps ? Italian masques and burlesques look to these sister valleys for their first steps into fame. The name Harlequin—" *Arlecchino* "—proclaims the child a servant of Erli, the King of the spirits of the mountain and gnomes of the cavern. The posturing measures of the mountain-valley dances, the *monfrine*, are danced to-day in the villages of Lombardy as the *tarantelle* are in Naples and the South. To see such sights in naïve perfection one must be at Bergamo on the Fiera di Sant' Alessandro, originally the annual fair of the silk trade, which has not been intermitted for a thousand years.

In and about Brescia, and particularly in the Val Trompia and the Val Sabbia, the children still keep up the traditional dance-songs of the olden time. In two divisions,—boys and girls severally, —they sing :

> " *O dansa, bella dansa,*
> *Che fa la dansa tora,*
> *O ri, o ri oltela,*
> *Chi fa la rioltà,*
> *Alto alto camerada,*
> *Lasé pasà sta mascerada.*" etc.

Then they approach and retire, one party saluting the other ·

> " *Apri, apri le porte,*
> *Logina logià,*
> *Apri, apri le porte,*
> *Logina al cavalià.*"

and the other replying :

> " *Le porte sono aperte,*
> *Logina, logià,*
> *Le porte sono aperte.*
> *Logina al cavalià.*"

The Valleys of Brembana and Cavallina have always been famous for the virtues of their thermal waters. Trescore-Balneario, within twelve miles of Bergamo, was known in Roman times. In the eighth century it yearly attracted gouty patients by the score. Then the good, far-seeing and com mercial Benedictines acquired the chief springs,— which included pungent sulphur as well as bitter saline waters,—and added to their cure of souls the cure of bodies. Warlike times were destructive of monkish investments, and the healthful streams ran to waste, until the grand old Condottiere Bartolommeo Colleone, from his new castle at Malpaga, set to work to undergo the cure for his own wounded, suffering humanity, and then to provide similar healing opportunities for his poorer neighbours. He made cisterns, basins and baths, wherein to store and use the waters ;

and whilst he made his wealthy neighbours pay high fees, the baths were free to the needy sick. The worthy old soldier, too, did excellent service to the countryside in the direction of irrigation works. He harnessed the wasteful flood of the Serio, and started saw-mills and mills for grinding corn upon the deepened and walled-in canal.

Everyone who passes by Trecore makes a point of visiting Villa Suardi, belonging to the Conte di Bergamo. There is Lorenzo Lotto's exquisite portrait of two beautiful " Ladies of the Lakes " —Madonna Orsolina and Donna Paolina, mother and sister of Signore Battista Suardi—both painted in 1524. Happily, in the restoration of the villa, 1706, these precious memorials were uninjured. They are in the villa chapel.

" Lords and Ladies of the Italian Lakes " have followed in Colleone's steps. You will not find a more agreeable health-resort anywhere than San Pellegrino, half-way up the valley. The pine-woods are good for respiration, and chestnut-groves pleasant for alfresco meals. In the Val Cavallina is a very splendid villa, the Castello di Costa di Mezzate, with lofty towers and open columned *loggie*. The original building dates from early Visconti days. Refortified by Niccolo Piccinino, it was sacked and burnt, and then rebuilt, by Otto Piccinino, and the towers were surmounted

FRATE-CAVALIERE CRISTOFORO VERTOVA

From a Painting of the Lombard School   Armoury Museum, Malta

To face page 296

315..

by Ghibelline machicolations. In the twelfth century the family of Vertova held it ; they came from the hamlet of Vertova, in the Val Seriana, where are the ruins of their ancestral castle, the most renowned member thereof being the first Consul of Bergamo in 1160—Albertoni da Vertova. Charles V. visited the castle, and in a way annexed it, but created Leonardo and Galeazzo Vertova Knights of Malta. Frate Cristoforo Vertova was the Commander of Malta what time the Piedmontese warred in Turkey and Barbary, and he fell into the hands of the infidel. In the armoury of Malta are preserved his suit of black armour, with a record of his victories at sea, and his portrait. Coming to more recent days, Giovanni Battista Vertova was appointed Regent of Lombardy under Napoleon Buonaparte, but with his daughter, Countess Elizabetta, his race ended. She married Count Camozzi de' Gherardi, and all the Vertova property passed to that family, with the name Vertova hyphened to Gherardi. All the Camozzi-Vertove were Knights of Malta, and addressed, as usual, by the affix " Frate."

Many interesting objects are carefully preserved in the villa : a cannon used by Bartolommeo Colleone ; the sabre of the Archduke Sigisimondo of Austria ; the bedstead of San Carlo Borromeo,

whereupon he laid when residing at the house of
Conte Suardi, in Rome; portraits of King
Stanislaus of Poland and the Empress Catherine
of Russia, given by Her Majesty to Cardinal
d' Archetti, whose mother was a Vertova; and
the flag of Count Giovanni Battista Camozzi-
Vertova, borne at Tonale and riddled with shot.
In a room hung with fine tapestry are exhibited
many letters of Marie Antoinette. One gruesome
object is the head of a young girl, killed in the
Revolution of 1848-49. The historian Antonio
Calvi, in his "*Cronache Bergamesche*," relates the
story of a tragedy which happened in 1703 at the
villa. A young lady, a Gritti, married into the
house, through the malignity of a rejected lover
was accused unjustly by the miscreant before her
husband, Guglielmo Vertova, of gross infidelity.
Deaf to all assertions of innocence, and probably
content to be free for other intrigues, he hurled
his young wife from one of the windows into the
moat below. She fell dead into the water. The
false friend fared no better, for the enraged husband strangled him and threw his body after
that of his wife. It must have been a dark night,
for the genial sun of that sun-kissed valley could
not have borne witness to so foul a deed !

The River Mella,—of the honey-bee and apricot,
—which tentatively waters the city of Brescia,

flows from Monte Dosso-Alto, at the head of the
Val Trompia—a valley full of iron and copper
mines, which furnish fine metal for the splendid
swords and weapons of Bresican fame. The valley
is enclosed in mountain-heights, but these are inter-
spersed with grassy alps or meads, whereupon are,
in many places, very curious circles of rough
stones whereat the traveller wonders. At Taver-
nola, perhaps, is the most perfect *rondo.* Their
purpose was to serve as meeting-places for the
headmen of the valley when gathering for
counsel and defence. The meadow enclosed by
these stone circles was regarded as common land,
but withdrawn from pasturage. Each peasant
had to give a portion of his time to dress the
grass, and the crops of hay were sold by public
auction for the benefit of the parish priest. The
district of Bagolino, which separates the Brescian
from the Trentino Alps, has the designation
" *Romanterra,*" as indicating the limits of the
Roman power, and where Italian, Greek, and
German met to watch each other. There is a
very curious story about the earliest Greek settlers
in the Val Trompia, which relates that when they
reached, with their flocks and herds, the region of
Bagolino, it began to snow. They had never seen
or heard of the like before, and when the children
asked what the white flakes were, they were told

that they were " *Nipa nipa alla marina* !"—Foam scuds from the sea !.

The young country people of the Brescian Alps seem to have been especially addicted to music and the dance. In the " *Cronaca di Brescia* " of 1400 many folklore ditties and measures are enumerated. Venus and Mars quite naturally furnished the *motifs* of those roundelays. It would seem that the young girls from the Lake of Iseo were especially sought after by amorous youths of Brescia. The chronicler Malvezzi gives at length one of these songs, called " *Le Donne Lombarda* "—

LE DONNE LOMBARDA.

Donna lombarda fammi piacere
  Ve al val con me.
Ben volentieri me vegnerìa
  Se no gavesi el mio marì.
Quel tuo marito fallo morire
  Fallo morì.

*　　*　　*　　*　　*

Donna lombarda, a che maniera
  Che questo vino l' è intorbidà ?
L' è stato el vento de l'altra sera
  Ch' el ve la fato entorbidà
Quando on bambino de sete mesi
  Che non ancora sapea parlà.

*　　*　　*　　*　　*

Tuti li goti che la beveva.
  A rivederci caro marit
A rivederci sacra corona.
  Un' altra sposa cingi per me
Così si trata donne tiranne
  Donne tiranne col so marit."

The Bresciaese have a game which old and young are never tired of playing, "*Le Poste al Paradiso*," in which they ring bells—the bells of Heaven—and strike tambourines with canes—the rattles of Hell—and sing ·

"*Öna ledo, te tre canele*
Che sonava le capanele,
Che sonava loril lorillo
Che sonava le ventitrè
Ona, do e tre."

Then all scramble for places. Unlucky is the one left out in the scrimmage. Perhaps this game has its British replica in " Musical Chairs."

In Bergamo and Brescia there is much that is Spanish in their architecture, and Spanish in their manners. Brescia is a typical Renaissance city,—her castle was called the " Falcon of Lombardy,"—and her people are less migratory than the Bergamese, and more self-reliant. She is the city of the wine-press *par excellence*, and her mood is always merry. Still, one of her most venerated heroes was a monk, Arnoldo, the leader of political and ecclesiastical reformation in Lombardy and Rome. For his intrepidity he suffered death at the hands of Pope Hadrian IV. ; but his influence survived, and the historian has placed him along with Rienzi and Savonarola in the Temple of Fame. There are three palaces of the Martinenghis : in one of them—Martinengo-Salvadego Moretto painted the walls of the *Salita* in fresco, with portraits of eight beautiful daughters of the house,—some say they were sisters, children of Count Cesare. The decorative use in the compositions of campanulas and butterflies is very beautiful and suitable—those being the emblems of the family. The backgrounds of the tableaux show a complete panorama of the city. Countess Cassandra, one of the galaxy of beauty, has about her something of the "Ariadne" of Romney's "Lady Hamilton." She seems to be almost listlessly looking for her lover; anyhow, she is a beautiful girl, and she wears a very becoming dress. She and her sisters seven are as comely as any of the countless lovely "Ladies of the Lakes."

Two noble "Lords" there were who made their residence at Brescia famous—Bayart—"*Sans peur et sans reproche*"—and Gaston de Foix, Duke of Nemours, both worthy captains of the usurping hosts of France. The former lay wounded in the head by a cannon-ball, and he was waited on by a virtuous lady of Brescia and her two young daughters. All three were smitten with devotion to their patient; but, resisting somewhat their impetuosity, the gallant chevalier embraced them in turn affectionately, and promised them their own again. On parting, the host offered his

THE COUNTESS CASSANDRA MARTINENGO

ALESSANDRO MORETTO

Martinengo Palace, Brescia

To face page 302

distinguished guest a casket filled with gold ducats, and in return begged for a voucher of security from pillage by the troops. "Take back your ducats, my good sir," replied Bayart. "Your daughters want husbands ; give half the sum to each in token of my gratitude for their care of me. . . . Fare you well !"

The Val Sabbia,—with its continuation, the Val Buona, in Southern Tirol,—is the most lengthy and the narrowest of all the valleys of the Bergamesque and Brescian Alps. Topographically and climatically, it differs considerably from the other verdant vales further west. It is less fertile, less temperate, less inhabited, and it offers fewer points of interest to the passer-by. From the great sweep of road beyond Gavardo there are captivating views of Salò, on the Lake of Garda, and of the Riviera to Gargnano. The soft breeze from over the lake wafts perfumed inhalations of oleander and lime ; but farther on the sternness of precipice, waterfall, and pine-tree overawe the traveller. Enclosed by bare and lofty mountains right away to the Bocca di Brento and the giant Adamello, the valley assumes the character of the sally-port and drawbridge of a battlemented stronghold. In truth such it is, for it is the frontier between great rival States, where Latin meets Teuton face to face ; and such it has been for more than one thousand years.

Few outposts of civilization have witnessed as many tragedies and scenes of pathos and of sanctuary as the Val Sabbia and Val Buona. Ruins crown each elevated spur of crag, hermits' cells are caverned in the rock, and the few churches are weirdly ancient and inornate. Man's work has but taken its cue from the harshness of Nature round about. Rank and sparse is the grass, gaunt and gnarled the trees ; gay butterflies and melodious nightingales of the lakeland are rare visitants ; the eerie eagle and the ravening crow are monarchs of the air, and the gusty winds blow cold from ice-fields not far away. With something akin to relief the wayfarer comes upon the mountain Lago d' Idro, a six miles round stretch of deep indigo-dyed water, clear and cold as a cheerless tarn. The eye fastens upon the Rocca d' Anfo, hanging dizzily over the gloomy waters—once a Venetian frontier fortress, a prison-house in later days, and now a ruin of the gory past. What tragedies have not eyes, peering through those iron window-slips, beheld time out of mind ! From Verona, Mantua, Cremona, Brescia, and Bergamo, many a fugitive rode through their gates and made a dash for liberty in the fastnesses of the Val Sabbia. Witches in the hands of captors were hailed to the mountains, there to expiate their crimes by the sword or by starvation. Many a luckless princeling and

many a maiden forlorn hid where the wild torrent
Caffaro splashes foam on the dank rocks. In the im-
passable gorge discovery was impossible, and there
the whitened bones of outcasts from the strife of
men were all the birds of prey left to tell the tale of
human failure. " Gurth the Swineherd," painted
by Charles Edward Johnson, was not the only
man of renown who sought safety in disguise and
distance from his foes. One other picture at the
British National Gallery points as well the moral
of the story of Anfo and Caffaro—" Found," by
Sir Hubert Herkomer. The dying fugitive is
discovered by an old hag goatherdess, his blade
broken in two, and his life-blood running out.

Dante must have had these harsh mountain
valleys in his mind,—he knew well their dismal
fame,—when he wrote in his " Inferno " ·

> "   . Risen upright,
> My eyes rested, I moved about and sought
> With fixed gaze to know what place this was
> Wherein I stood.   Suddenly upon the brink
> Of the lamentable vale I discovered
> The dread abyss that gives a thunderous sound
> Of plaints innumerable, dark and deep,
> With thick clouds overhead."

From Crossa in the Giudicaria, beyond Caffaro,
a road leads through the sequestered Val Ampola,
past the peaceful Lago di Ledro, to Riva on the
Lake of Garda—a very rapid transformation scene
indeed !

CHAPTER VI

"BENACO"

THE LAKE OF GARDA

" BENACO " is the greatest and the most seductive of all the North Italian lakes. Dante Alighieri, in his " *Inferno*," Canto XXI., sings thus of the magnificence of regal Garda :

> " Mid fair Italia's highlands, lies a lake
> Shadow'd by Alpine barriers 'gainst the Teuton foe,
> Away beyond Tirol—' Benaco ' it is called."

From ancient Roman times its charms have fascinated men and women of light and learning. Its shape,—not unlike that of a comet,—its tail to the north,—is unique, and lends itself to constant permutations of surface and reflections.

> " *Palpito il lago di Virgilio, come*
> *Velo di Sposa.*
> *Che s' apre al bacio del promesso amore !*"*

Aleardo Aleardi, the Veronese poet, likens the sweep of Garda's flood to the trail of the sunbeams across the sky :

---

* " The tremulous ripplings of Virgil's lake
Like a bridal veil
Just rais'd and lower'd a nuptial kiss to take."

" Il Sol dall' orizzante
Saettava sul piano
Purissimo del Garda." *

Garda is the lacustrine Juno of Italy. Her
history is Imperial, her influence upon mankind
is pageant-like,—the pageantry of a Royal Court,
—her affluence the most radiant and luxuriant
in the rival arenas of love and arms. Like a
capricious beauty, Garda displays all the airs and
graces of the boudoir, and all the jealousies and
tragedies of the rendezvous. Launched upon her
deep waters, the idyll of her charm changes with
the wind from the prosaic to the romantic, to the
heroic. Her shores, now low-lying, now piled in
precipices, resemble walls of storied buildings bedight with frescoes. Her hamlets and villages are
seething vessels, whence pulsate the hot Italian
blood of mortals, prone to passion, yet born to
love. No greater contrast in Nature can be
imagined than the bewitching amenities of the
Riviera,—between Salò and Gargnano,—and the
stern repulsiveness of the sheer cliffs of the
Austrian frontier. Every aspect of the realm of
Flora is presented to the ravished eye : her rarest
blooms and fruits are ready to be gathered by
the craving hand, and every prospect pleases.

* " The languishing sun
    Darts beams across the plain
    No purer than the face of Garda."

Beneath the shine and shadow of her chameleon-like waters, swim the rarest and the most toothsome fish that can engage man's skill and delight his palate. The fish of Garda,—the *trota, carpione, scarline,* and *luccio* in particular,—have been famous historically ever since Catullus and his brother epicures built their fishing-temples, their baths, and their villas upon her shores, and laid out her pristine gardens. Merliñ Cocai writes thus, after regaling on lake carp or silver trout :

> " There is a lake—and men call it Garda,
> Whose fish, none better for the larder—
> Enslave the tongue and will."

The *carpione* of Garda was regarded by the travelled Venetians as a dish for the immortals, and no banquet in the city of Venus was complete without that delicacy ; they cooked it in white wine, and strewed it with citroñ flowers. The Emperor Frederic III., in 1489, — when passing over the troubled lakes and resting upon its shores,—testified to two, at least, of Garda's excellences. " The taste," said he, " of the silver trout, and the scent of the golden lemons, are unsurpassable !'" Certainly the whole five senses of human enjoyment are superlatively gratified along and on Lake Garda.

I.

Sirmione, — the " olive-silvery Sirmio " of Tennyson,—on its narrow promontory, resembles, perhaps, a silver dagger plunged into the heart of a golden pomegranate. Its fame goes back for ages. The ruins of the castle of the Scaligeri are, in fact, the base rock of Queen Ansa's Convent. Consort of the eighth-century Desiderio,—the far-famed Lombard King,—she renounced on widow-hood quite conventionally the pleasures of the world, and withdrew to the loveliest, loneliest spot she knew. At the point of the peninsula she built a dower-house for Benedictine nuns, and dedicated her convent to St. Salvatore—the patron of the armed Longobards. Queen Ansa's founda-tions also included the three churches—St. Martin, St. Vito, and St. Peter.

The advent of the Scaligeri was of much more recent date. Martino della Scala, the Ghibelline *Podestà* of Verona, was assassinated in 1277 ; but his brother and successor, Alberto, revenged the foul deed, and raised his family's fame and banner high. For one hundred years they dominated the plain of Lombardy and all lakeland until, with Bianca, widow of Giovanni Galeazzo Visconti, their possessions in 1405 passed to the Serene Republic of Venice. The Scala male-line ended in 1392, on the death of Conte Francesco.

Sirmione was one while the scene of fanaticism. The " *Patareni*," — Manichœans, — set up their standard there to flout the frivolities and ferocities of the Della Scala Court. They were driven from place to place, until, at Sirmione, they found an ideal refuge and sanctuary. Accused of nameless atrocities, and denounced by the Pope of Rome, Martino II., Lord of Verona and the Lakes, issued a commission to inquire into their tenets and their aims. Condemned, with scarce a hearing, the deluded sectarians were ordered to recant and receive the Communion in the Church of San Pietro,—the only remnant of good Queen Ansa's munificence. Some gave way, and some stood firm, and these were ordered to be burnt. The venerable and infirm were fastened to stakes set up in the little square before the church, and there, in the midst of the sweetest sights and sounds of God's universe, the crackling flames devoured their limbs and the sickening stench of roasting human flesh contaminated the fragrance of oleanders and magnolias. One hundred and fifty younger folk were carried off to Verona, and suffered, like gladiators of old, in the arena.

For his vindication of the Catholic Religion, Pope Nicholas III. bestowed upon Martino the title of " Son of the Church," and gave him the Castle of Ilassi, some ten miles from Verona. In

CASTLE OF THE SCALIGERS AT SIRMIONE, LAKE OF GARDA

From a Print.   *Note the large Fishing-Net*

To face page 310

the sixteenth century it passed to the Conti de'
Pompei of Verona, and they built villas and laid
out gardens on the slopes of the castle hill.
Charles V.,—who, with his fair daughter Maria,
loved Sirmione, and relished well its trout and
sardines,—made the Pompei citizens of Milan.
Count Antonio was something of an archæologist,
and he had a hobby for digging up old stones and
probing ruins. Perhaps he was induced by a
weird story of the times of the Scaligeri. A fair
maiden,—a *Patarena*, be it said,—was saved from
the holocausts at Sirmione to be attached to the
signorial household. She, however, disappeared
mysteriously, and rumour had it that Martino II.
made her his mistress ; but, finding the connection injurious to his reputation for dogmatical
perfection of deportment, he had her strangled
and her body buried in an unknown spot at Ilassi.
There is, to be sure, another legend at Ilassi,—
gruesome, too,—but it affected the family of the
Pompei. Countess Ginevra, wife of Count Gior-
lamo di' Pompei, was unfaithful to her husband—
her paramour being an under-seneschal of the
castle. The Count strangled her—a ready way
then in aristocratic circles, and very popular—and
the lover was thrown into a river. The body of
the murdered Countess was buried within the
keep of the castle ; some, indeed, say she was
built alive into a hollow in the thick wall of the

dungeon and left to die—another not uncommon end for noble ladies none too true to, or outraged by, profligate spouses. Anyhow, Count Antonio de' Pompei found one day what he was looking for—the skeleton of a woman, with beautiful auburn hair. Among the remains were articles of jewellery which betokened rank and wealth. Around the ankle-bones and wrists were still the iron rings, and there were also iron chains which had chafed the breasts of the frail beauty. What a sad time must Prince Cupid have had when lovers were parted thus '

Hidden away in its exquisite bay lies the smiling and ambitious little town of Salò, its white and painted houses all smothered up deliciously in fragrant groves of oleander—the laurel of the Greeks. A coronal of sumptuous villas crowns the undulating upland. Some are of ancient origin, others of modern date, but blend wide-parted centuries of struggle and romance. Famous families have come and gone; names of some only remain to individualize traditions of the past—others are incarnate still. As pre-eminent as any stands the noble house of Martinengo,—named from the simple cradle of the family,—a little village of obscurity midway between Bergamo and Treviglio, out upon the great Lombardian plain. Many branches have issued from the parent stock, but all look to Tebaldo of that ilk as the initial figure of the race. Tebaldo was the Lieutenant of the warfaring Emperor Otto II., and the recipient of Imperial honours—fifteen castles, great and small, being held by him in chief.

Cesare Martinengo, in the sixteenth century,— the head of the Cesaresco branch,—made himself a name in war and peace alike. Father of four-, teen vigorous sons and eight most beauteous daughters, he was indeed the creator of a glorious progeny ; and, if Sansovino, the chronicler, is to be believed, he lived up to his great parental fame in the exhibition of such splendour and prodigality as carried the glory of the Martinenghi far and wide through Europe. The vigour of this famous sire is still maintained in his descendants ; the chief of the family still resides and rules at Castello Roccafranca.

The grandson of Cesare Martinengo,—" the Magnificent " Sciarra,—was educated at the Court of France, and became an eminent soldier of fortune. The same worthy historian says of him : " He was gifted with extraordinary genius ; unconquerable by fatigue or strife, a scorner of danger, he was a pillar of strength to any cause he assumed. . . ." Count Sciarra rose to high commands in the army of the King of France. When still a youth,—it has been recorded,—he heard that his father had been basely assassinated by Count Aluigi Avogardo of Brescia. Posting immediately to Lombardy, he reached that city with five stalwart comrades, sworn to secrecy and revenge. Their lying in wait was told to Avogardo, who eluded his adversaries adroitly, and at length, when they had cornered him, he very narrowly escaped Sciarra's blade, having changed clothes with one of his suite, whose life was taken for his master's. Count Sciarra had to seek safety in flight, for, by the laws of Venice, which then ruled Gardan territory, life was had for life. Back went the Count to France, resumed his prowess, and died a hero's death in the war of the Huguenots.

Count Sciarra's father, Count Giorgio Cesaresco Martinengo, scrupulously carried on the family tradition for ostentation : he is known in story as "the superb Italian." Doubtless jealousy was at the root of his murderer's ambition. It was only by cutting down men more prominent than themselves that those who envied their fame and fortune succeeded to their places. This altruism is still a force in modern socialistic circles '

Count Giorgio, as became all opulent and powerful nobles, was nothing if he was not chivalrous to boot. A story goes that the Marchioness of Mantua, making one of her famous progresses through her husband's dominions, and beyond, where they were ready to welcome her, passed through Brescia. The Count met her at the Venetian gate of the city, and offered her the hospitality of his palace. Her Highness declined the invitation, having, as she said, " already secured accommodation at the Albergo del Castello." With ready wit and consummate gallantry, the not-to-be-denied "*Magnifico*" immediately secured the hanging sign of the hostel, and hung it out triumphantly over the portal of his ancestral mansion. The Duchess, of course, entirely unaware of this excellent subterfuge, made no demur at dismounting from her litter at the palatial Albergo del Castello. The Count had played his ace of trumps upon the Queen's trick !

The chivalry of Counts Giorgio and Sciarra distinguished quite naturally their relative, Count Fortunato Cesaresco Martinengo. He was the third son of Count Cesare " the Magnificent." His fame was that of his nephew, the daring Sciarra : " Skilled in arms and knightly exercises, a compiete Courtier, he was the right-hand man of all Italian Sovereigns ; he loved to right the oppressed and to scorn the proud. To moral superiority he added charm of manner. Whatever he undertook he was enthusiastic in its prosecution. Accomplished beyond most men of his time, he was a profound Latinist, a capable musician, a worthy poet, and a fluent speaker. First President of the Brescian "*Società di Dubbiosi*,"—perhaps Englished as "Friends of impoverished nobles"—he expended his fortune as the munificent patron of struggling gentlemen and scholars. Among those who have sung Count Fortunato's praises was Pietro Aretino, who styles him "conspicuous for rare literary ability."

Married when a lad to a wife younger than himself, Donna Livia, daughter of Count d' Arco,—a famous Latinist,—she inherited her father's scholarship, and was a rare helpmeet for her accomplished husband. Alas! the Countess died young, too, leaving as pledges of her love two sons and three daughters. Count Fortunato was disconsolate; but although he never married again, he formed a platonic association with a woman more famous than any of her time—the celebrated Marchesa di Pescara, Vittoria Colonna. The Count's conduct was marked by rare courage and devotion. The world affected to look down upon the heroine, and the Pope himself tried to injure her by banning her as "unworthy of decent society." Count Fortunato would have none of it. "She was aged more by sorrow than by years. Nature had taken back her beauty; but she was erect of carriage, with a noble presence, the mirror of tranquil energy. She wore black velvet, covered with her graceful white widow's veil, and she found a delectable asylum in a Benedictine convent." Thus has she been biographed

VITTORIA COLONNA (1520)

G. MUZIACO

Colonna Gallery, Rome

To face page 316

in faithful terms. The Count himself found her
even so, and wrote sympathetically as follows :
" Certainly Vittoria is a most rare and distinguished woman ; great is her humility, as remarkable as her former pride. Her whole conduct, no
less than her character, is princely. She has an
amazing talent for conversation, and her words
are like fetters which enthral the hearer. Her
voice has reached my inmost soul, and I delight
that her influence has made me her willing but
unworthy slave—the slave of the most excellent
and most conscientious woman that the sun of
Heaven shines upon." The letter is dated from
Salò, June 7, 1546. The marchioness was then just
fifty-seven years of age, and the following year
Count Fortunato was once more struck to the
heart by the dart of death—the death of the
woman he loved and reverenced.

No juster epitaph for Count Fortunato could
be desired than those touching words of Shake-
speare :

> " The dearest friend to me, the kindest man,
> The best conditioned and unwearied spirit
> In doing kindly acts, and one in whom
> The ancient Roman's honour more appears
> Than any that draw breath in Italy."

We in England have a link with Count Fortunato
Cesaresco Martinengo in the person of his brother
Girolamo, who, entering Religion, rose from dig-

nity to dignity in the Church until he became
Papal Legate to Austria and Poland. In 1561
he was sent as an Envoy to Queen Elizabeth, to
ask her to name a representative at the Council of
Trent. He, too, maintained the family traditions
for pompous circumstance. He lived sumptuously as a Prince of the Church ; his household and
all his appointments were splendid. His income
was splendid, too, for he possessed the tempor-
alities of three bishoprics, and farmed many fat
benefices besides.

If the Martinenghi could count their heroes,
and emblazon their names in glowing colours upon
the "Libro d' Oro" of the family, they could also,
as may be naturally supposed, adorn its pages with
names and romances of heroines. A greatly revered
"Lady" of olden times was Diana Maria Maddalena Martinengo—as devout as she was beautiful,
as chaste as she was cultured. Her father was
Leopardo Martinengo, Count of Barco, a noted
warrior and a notable mathematician and astron-
omer. Gian Francesco,—the founder of the
fame of that branch of the noble family,—built
the stronghold Rocca d' Anfo,—on the Lago di
Idro, in the Brescian Valley of Sabbio,—but ceded
it to the Republic of Venice. Count Leopardo
had planned a favourable marriage for his daughter, but she refused to see her prospective husband, and told her father that she wished to follow

St. Teresa of Spain. For four years the Count,
in vain, tried to move Donna Maria's resolution,
but upon her seventeenth birthday he yielded,
and the devotee entered the Franciscan convent
upon the Isola de' Frati—Garda's most lovely
island. She gave herself not only to works of
devotion, but wrote many mystic books on
patristic teaching. Her fame for sanctity and
learning travelled far : Bishops and worldlings
sought her counsel ; and when she had attained
the age of forty, she was chosen Abbess of the
convent. For seven years she ruled her nuns
with firmness and affection, and died, bewailed
by gentle and simple, in 1684. In June, 1900,
Maria Maddalena Martinengo was beatified, and
to-day miracles are awaited to proclaim her
saintship.

Salò is rich indeed in romantic stories of " Lords
and Ladies of the Italian Lakes," but something
of the lurid fastens to the memory of one of the
most beautiful women that ever made a home
there. Vittoria Accoramboni was remarkable
alike for her extraordinary beauty and her tragic
history. Her contemporaries regarded her as the
most captivating person that had ever been seen
in Italy. She was the daughter of Messer Claudio
Accoramboni, one of the nobles of Gubbio, a scion
of an ancient but undistinguished family. Like

most of the men of his time, he was a soldier,—it
was the universal rôle,—but in periods of peace
and rest from adventure he bestowed his time and
means in studies, craftic and artistic. Vittoria
was the tenth child of her parents, and her mother,
—worthy Donna Tarquinea,—with almost Spar-
tan severity, determined that her offspring should
be placed out in the world as soon as ever they
reached reasonable ages—" to improve their
fortunes," as she quaintly expressed it. Accordingly, little Vittoria, on her twelfth birthday, was
sent off to her eldest brother, Marcello, who was
established in Rome.

The young girl grew up lovely and chaste—the
admiration and envy of her companions, and the
cynosure of many amorous eyes. At sixteen she
was affianced to young Francesco Peretti, the
favourite nephew of Frate Felice, who eventually
became Cardinal di Montalto. This aspiring
ecclesiastic had acquired great wealth in the business-like exploitation of fat livings and rich
bishoprics. The Peretti family was poor, but
the Frate encouraged the match, although he
was himself, it was hinted, smitten with the
young debutante's charms. He eventually set the
young couple well up in the world, and encouraged
them to mix with the great ones of the Pontifical
Court. Whilst every courtier and gallant raved
over Vittoria's beauty,—much to the embarrass-

ment of Francesco,—the young couple speedily found themselves heavily in debt. Dress and pleasure and consorting with richer people are concomitants of financial straits the world over, and, in spite of their early devotion to one another, temptation loosened their marital bonds. What young wife's head would not naturally be turned by such encomiums as the following lines, written in 1681 :

" Nor nymph, nor goddess thou, but woman born.
  None, fair Vittoria, doth thy grace exceed.
In utmost worth thy charms none else adorn.
  Moved by the sight of thee I stand aggriev'd
  That thou, Mistress of thy heart, may not be mine."

No child came to bless the marriage bond, but tongues of gossip were unloosed, whilst many an evil-guided finger pointed from Francesco to the admirers and lovers of his wife, and rested significantly upon no less a personage than Cardinal Farnese—the boon companion of Montalto. Matters drifted from bad to worse. Living with their uncle, Francesco and Vittoria became dependent entirely upon his benevolence, but Vittoria saw the risk she ran, and warned Francesco to be vigilant. One pair of eyes in particular fastened themselves sympathetically upon the lovely young bride. They belonged to a noble of high degree— a Prince indeed, a widower, wealthy more than most, and perfectly unscrupulous. Five years

before,—as rumour, only too correct, had it,—
he had strangled his Medici wife,—Isabella, the
lovely eldest daughter of Cosimo I., Grand
Duke of Florence,—at the Florentine villa of
Baroncelli. Whether Vittoria Peretti knew the
details of that tragedy one cannot say, but when
Paolo Giordano Orsini, Duke of Bracciano, prevailed upon her to quit the palace of Cardinal
Montalto,—where dangers unknown surrounded
her,—and take refuge under his roof, she acceded
to the temptation, but at what a terrible cost '
The night after her flight Francesco Peretti was
discovered dying—stabbed to the heart. By
whose order, or by whose hand, the deed was done
none have certainly recorded, nor has anybody
told us what effect that horror had upon the
youthful widow.

A very plausible story was rife at the time—to
the effect that Marcello Accoramboni, Vittoria's
brother, had compassed the murder. He had not
disguised his displeasure at his sister's marriage
to Francesco Peretti, a poor man, dependent upon
an unstable man of the world, the fickle Cardinal
di Montalto. As soon as he was conversant with
the Duke of Bracciano's admiration for Vittoria,
the story goes, he considered every possible means
of securing a separation. As wife of the most
splendid Prince in Rome,—with a record of heroic
deeds upon the mad battle-field,—Vittoria would

indeed be able to lift her family, and Marcello in particular, to affluence and honour. Well, late one night Marcello sent a missive secretly,—his own liberty, indeed, was at stake, for he had been outlawed for killing, perhaps accidentally, young Francesco Giovanni Pallavicino,—to Francesco Peretti, begging him to meet him at a lonely spot outside the Porta Giulia. He had, he said, an important communication to make to him. Donna Peretti and Elizabetta,—Francesco's mother and sister,—in vain dissuaded him, but he went, in spite of their tears and entreaties. The unhappy young man was attacked by *bravi*, and fell. That Bracciano had a hand in the assassination is more than likely, for Marcello Accoramboni was an assistant-chamberlain in the Ducal household, and held very especially his master's confidence.

Of course, intelligence of the foul deed was circulated everywhere, and reached at length the ears of the Pontiff, Gregory XIII., who at once intervened in the interest of his brother-Cardinal, Montalto. Vittoria Peretti was taken by Papal command out of the care of the Duke, and confined for a whole twelvemonth within the Castle of St. Angelo. She soon dried her tears, for, although her heart was sad at Francesco's terrible death, there had been no real love between them ; she had borne her husband no child, and they had

lived separate lives. Whilst in seclusion a priest,
—presumably in the pay of the Duke of Bracciano,
—paid the comely captive visits, solicitous for her
spiritual welfare. He told her how deeply the
Duke felt her present distress, and how he was
only too ready to adopt any plan which would
set her at liberty and provide for her future. Very
circumspectly this priestly visitor brought Vittoria to regard his master as personally devoted
to her, and anxious to make her his wife. Vittoria
resented the advice, adducing the inequality of
station and the uncertainty of the Duke's fidelity.
At last the adroit confessor alleged that the Duke
had made a vow, in his hearing, before Francesco
Peretti's death, to the effect that he would marry
Vittoria should she ever become a widow. Spiritual
counsels prevailed, and a secret marriage was
effected within the fortress. Then Bracciano left
Rome for a time, and Vittoria, dreading the fury
of Cardinal di Montalto, was minded to commit
suicide. News of the marriage speedily stole out:
the complacent priest was unfrocked, and Vittoria's imprisonment became more rigorous.

The death of Gregory in 1585 raised the Cardinal di Montalto to the Papal throne as Sixtus V.,
and during the engrossing ceremonies of the election, the Duke of Bracciano returned to Rome,
rescued Vittoria from her prison, and carried her
off to his estates at Bracciano. This property

SCIARRA CESARESCO-MARTINENGO

ALESSANDRO MORETTO

National Gallery, London

To face page 324

had been bestowed upon Duke Paolo Giordano's
father, Signore Girolamo d' Orsini, by Papal
favour, and was held as a Papal fief. Consequently, when the new Pope directed proceedings
to be taken against the Duke, he, like the wise
and cunning man that he was, took flight from
Civita Vecchia with his young wife,—she was
twenty-four years his junior,—and stayed not his
course until his feet trod Venetian soil,—the soil
of the shores of Lake Garda.

The Ducal refugees made their home within
the Martinengo Palazzo called " Barbarano " at
Salò—a new edifice, built in 1577 by the Marchese Sforza Pallavicini, the Generalissimo of the
armies of Venice,—filled with treasures of all kinds,
and famous for its lovely gardens. There the
Duke lived in sumptuous style, and the Duchess
became the centre of a brilliant Court,—apparently Marcello Accoramboni had received his reward ! The pageant was brief, for, in five months
after the arrival of the distinguished fugitives,
the Duke died suddenly, November 13, 1585,
leaving all he possessed to Vittoria. Overcome
with grief, she ordered his body to be embalmed
and buried in the Church of the Capuchins, at
Salò, where she erected a splendid monument to
his memory. One direction in her bequest to the
clergy was significant and touching. She for-
bad entry into the memorial chapel to everyone

except to Virginio—the Duke's only child by Isabella de' Medici.

In the name of this youth, his uncle, the Grand Duke Ferdinando I. of Tuscany, claimed the whole of the Bracciano property, and proceeded at once to depute his representatives to enter upon the palace at Salò and seize its appointments, disowning and denouncing the Duchess as an intruder and impostor. The facts of the Duke's death were never made public, but it was the universal impression that the Pope and the Grand Duke were in full accord, and greatly pleased by that tragedy. Anyhow, a course of action, prompted by them, was adopted towards the widowed Duchess, which amounted in virulence to a *vendetta*.

Very, very sadly Vittoria left Salò within a twelvemonth, and although her connection with the Lake of Garda practically ceased, it may not be uninteresting to follow her career, as one of the most beautiful and most unfortunate " Ladies of the Lake." She rejoiced in the peace and happiness, the beauty and the salubrity, of that lovely expanse of storied water. Alas ! she never saw its brilliance again, though she repeatedly spoke of the fascination which stole over her during those brief joy months in 1585. The Duchess settled at Padua, where she resided in " a sweet old palace," as she calls it, and observed

the strictest retirement, with a very limited
household. Still young and surpassingly beautiful, her life was surrounded with a halo of pathos
which found expression in poetry and song. The
sadness of her existence speaks eloquently in the
words she uttered :

> " Weep, weep, my grieving eyes,
>   Till life itself is dissolved in tears."

Very many poems of hers she made public, under
the name of " Virginia N——" In one, " *Lamentadi
di V. N.*," she deplores the unhappy death of
Francesco Peretti.

Flaminio Accoramboni, Vittoria's youngest
brother, joined her at Padua, and Marcello followed him, only once more to display his rashness
of temper and greatly embarrass his sister. It
was said that the death of poor Giovanni Balbi,—
one of the young Duchess's faithful retainers,—
was due to Marcello Accoramboni. The man
owed him a consderable sum of money, and,
being unable to pay, the irascible Cavaliere struck
him a blow, which ended fatally. Be this as it
may, still another person arrived in Padua who
was greatly interested in the concerns of Duchess
Vittoria—Lodovico Orsini,—a near kinsman of
the Duke. His presence, he pretended, was called
for to consider certain provisions of the Duke's
will, with a view to an amicable settlement with
the Duchess. He stated that the Pope,—Mon-

talto,—was about to declare the second marriage of the Duke of Bracciano void, and, further, had the intention of quashing the Duke's will. He proposed that Vittoria should carefully consider the position of affairs, and agree to some arrangement by which she would retain all her own personal property and certain properties of the Duke, but should relinquish her assumed rights to the bulk of the estate. This Orsini was a man in a high position ; he had been Governor of Corfu under the Venetian Senate, and had been just appointed to a similar position over the shores of the Lake of Garda.

Vittoria met her husband's relative with her usual charming affability, and,—whilst she acknowledged the claims of young Virginio Medici-Orsini,—she positively refused to surrender her own rights as widow of her husband. It was said that she had made up her mind to name the lad her heir before the visit of Lodovico Orsini. Orsini, on his part, made the most of Marcello's intervention, and demanded his departure from Padua. Vittoria stood by her brother, and then Orsini insisted upon the Duchess then and there rendering up to him the costly decorations the Duke had worn. Vittoria, roused to indignation, dismissed the disturber of her peace, and forbade him her presence. This was apparently just what Orsini wanted.

The next step was as unexpected as it was tragical. On December 22,—the eve of St. Vittoria,—the Duchess received the Communion, and spent the day pleasantly with a few companions at the palace. Evening came, and she sought her chamber, where, pacing to and fro, she sang *Miserere* softly to herself, and then dropped her beads before retiring for the night. Suddenly twenty masked *bravi* rushed up the stairs with flaming torches, lead by one Conte Paganello—an out-of-elbows nobleman, and anybody's tool for a liberal consideration. Flaminio, whose room adjoined his sister's, threw himself upon the first ruffian, but was promptly run through by many rapiers, and, crawling into Vittoria's room, lay dying at the foot of her couch. Vittoria herself, hearing the tumult, and ever suspicious of foul play, had risen and was kneeling before the crucifix. Paganello seized her, tore off her breastkerchief, which he wound round her neck. Vittoria raised her hands and spoke: " I freely pardon thee and these thy men, but let me die clothed decently." She had no shrift, for every villain's sword was thrust into her back and chest, whilst they uttered obscene jests. Their innocent victim fell prone, and, as her life's blood stained the carpet, she cried, dying: " Jesus, Jesus pardon ¹"

All Padua flocked to see her lying-in-state within the choir of the thirteenth-century Augustinian Church of the Eremitani,—where the Bishop of Fossombrone preached a funeral sermon, wherein he lauded Vittoria's modesty, prudence, goodness, and dignity. As for Lodovico Orsini, the Serene Republic had him strangled, Paganello was killed with the dagger he had thrust into Vittoria's heart, and all the accomplices were captured and put to death. That was a sad, sad Christmas at Salò and Padua. In the city men and women went about with bowed heads. They had learned, in the short time of Vittoria's residence in their midst, to sympathize with her sad career, and to admire her gentle virtues. To her devoted retainers at Salò, and the peasants of the country-side, with busy fishermen, her terrible end gave pangs of sorrow. Simple-hearted in their respect and love, they were true mourners of their *castellana's* death. It was winter, and the feast was that of the Nativity, and better-minded people were chastened in their joy. Such tragedies, alas ! were frequent in those wild, sensuous days ; but each one gave pause, and made for prayer for souls in purgatory. "*Requiescat in pace—Signora Vittoria—Misercordia Jesu.*"

II.

Among the famous " Lords and Ladies of the
Italian Lakes " none has graced the story of the
Lake of Garda more vividly than Isabella d' Este,
wife of Marquis Gian Francesco Gonzaga of Mantua.   The enchantment of that bewitching mirror
of the beauties of Nature and art seized on the
fair Marchioness's soul and body, and she revelled
in the charms of its buoyant waves and its fairy
riviera.   Not once, but many times, she fled from
the allurements of the gay and gossipy Mantuan
Court to find refreshment and relaxation.   One
such jaunt she took in company with her best-
loved friend, Elizabetta, Duchess of Urbino, and
she has recorded her impressions in one of her
graphic letters to her husband.   Writing on
March 18, 1492, to the Duke,—they had been
married two years before,—she says : " The
Duchess of Urbino and I, together with the
fascinating wife of Signore Tracassa, went to dine
at Desenzano, and thence to Toscolano to supper,
where we spent the night.   We greatly enjoyed
the sight of the lovely riviera.   On Friday we
returned to Sirmione by boat, and then we rode
together in the country.   Wherever we went we
were warmly received and treated with the greatest
consideration, most of all by the Captain of the
Lake, who loaded us with delicious fish and other

delicacies. The good people of Salò sent us many goodly presents. To-morrow we are going to Goito, and from there we shall return to Mantua ''

The two Princesses were ideal companions. Duchess Elizabetta was nineteen years of age, and Marchioness Isabella just seventeen. Whilst the former was somewhat delicate and grave beyond her years, sweet and good, if somewhat plain, Isabella was robust and lovely, a brilliant conversationalist, witty and talented in piquant repartee. One foiled the other : together they sang saucy French songs, and read the latest Italian romances. They were never tired of playing *Scartino*,—the card-game then most in vogue,—or of strumming well-strung guitars. They rode and walked, and rowed and swam— sometimes quite alone, or at most with a single lady of their suites. They also spent much time quite characteristically in the mysteries of the toilet, and in conning over such fashion-plates as those early days of sartorial literature afforded. One of their favourite conceits was to attire themselves in similarly cut costumes, but graded in colours to suit their dissimilar physical charms— Duchess Elizabetta, as became a brunette, in the deeper shades and more stately *passementerie*, the Marchioness in lighter tones and trimmings, to suit her blonde hair and fair complexion.

ISABELLA D' ESTÈ-GONZAGA, MARCHIONESS OF MANTUA

VECELLIO TIZIANO

Imperial Museum, Vienna

To face page 332

Writing from Cavriana,—another of the Marquis's country villas, near Mantua,—Stefano Sicco,
chamberlain to the Marchioness, records the happy
life his mistress and her devoted companion
spent in country pleasures. " These Madonnas,"
he says, " be indefatigable in making excursions
by boat and on horseback, and they have visited
all the lovely gardens on the lake with the greatest
delight. The inhabitants vie with one another in
doing them honour. One worthy gentleman,
Signore Fermo of Caravago, caused his larder to
be depleted for Her Excellency, and stripped his
lemon and pomegranate trees of all their fruit for
her behoof."

The Marchioness's second visit to her favourite
Garda was with many ladies of her suite, and she
occupied, for quite a long time, the lake-side residence of the archpriest of Toscolano. His bewitching gardens appealed to her passionate love
of the beautiful, whilst the views thence over land
and lake fascinated her spirit of romance. She
wrote frequently to her friend the Duchess, telling
her how greatly she was enjoying the delights of
her surroundings, and indulging, much to her
content, in delicious fruit and fish, ravished by
the scent of exquisite flowers and the sweet songs
of birds. Of none of the many excursions she
made to the Lake of Garda has the chatty Marchioness left more pleasant narratives than of a

visit she paid to Sirmione, Salò, and the riviera of
Gardone in 1535. She was accompanied by a
numerous suite of ladies and courtiers; indeed,
this journey partook of the circumstance of a
royal progress. The send-off of the party was from
Cavriana, and upon the box-seat of her chariot
rode, by the driver, her favourite dwarf, Morgan-
tino. The elements were unpropitious for the
course to Desenzano: a heavy downpour of rain
wetted the poor little man to the skin, and then
he was dragged inside the vehicle and sat on
Isabella's knee — "trussed up," as she laugh-
ingly said, "like a spring chicken!" Wherever
horses were changed, and many times a day, in
that lovely Garda-land, the clever little mortal
delighted the country yokels and the staider town-
folks by dancing "*morescas*" upon the greensward
or upon the sandy beach, the Marchioness and
her entourage beating time the while, and enjoying
the merriment with the merriest. The peasants
wove garlands of flowers, and decked the midget's
neck and head, and this delighted the jolly young
Marchioness exceedingly, for she invariably detached from her cincture her jewelled money-
bag, and caused its contents to be distributed by
way of scrambling. Then the fun grew fast and
furious, until the Court and its chief lady flung
themselves in convulsive laughter under the trees
or upon any ready couch or seat! Overhead

feathered songsters and gay butterflies and bees
flecked the cerulean sky with flashing cross-lights,
and all the scents of fertile Mother-Earth were
expressed by sun and breeze for the delectation of
the delighted company.

From Sirmione the Marchioness wrote to her
consort in Mantua : " I am as happy as happy can
be in this Paradise. . . . I am perfectly sure
that we ought to build a fine villa here, for this is
the most beautiful spot in all God's wide world.

I will not hide from you that I have taken
bodily possession of this charming spot, for, in
descending a flight of steps at the castle which
were wet after a shower, I lost my footing and
fell awkwardly, but, fortunately, without receiving
serious damage. I was talking to the reverend
Pievano at the time, and he made me laugh, after
he had assisted me to regain my feet, by a ridicu-
lously flowery speech, in which he said that perhaps my fall was due to my excessive admiration
for the beauty of the view ! The situation of the
castle is splendid, but the rooms are so small and
dark that I have taken up my quarters in the
priest's house, where I have one large, lofty room,
wherein I sleep and eat. So really, you see, there
is need for you to make haste and build a goodly
suite of apartments. . . . One of my maidens
has also followed my example and come in contact

roughly with Mother-Earth. She has taken possession of Lonato, a very lovely spot near Desenzano ; for the mule which Livia was riding on the
way to Morgusano ran away, and the poor girl
fell off, one foot remaining in the stirrup. She
was dragged some distance, and presented a
ridiculous appearance ; but, had it not been for
some worthy peasants who stopped the animal,
she must have come to great hurt. Travelling
would be, as you will readily understand, very
dull if such absurd accidents did not occur to vary
the tedium occasionally. . . . My headache and
sore throat have almost gone, and so I hope to
enjoy this lovely land thoroughly once more."

Then the fair traveller urges the Marquis to
join her, and let affairs of State take their own
course, and she continues her eulogies. " Yesterday," she writes, " I climbed the hill to see the
Roman ruins, and entered the grottos, and fully
examined all of them. They are indeed marvellous and very striking for one who, like myself,
has never been to Rome. I do not in the least
wonder that the Romans loved this place and
chose it for their villas. . . . If God gives your
Excellency good health, and we are able to come
here together and enjoy fully the peace and
pleasure, then we shall certainly build a Casino for
social delights and domestic pleasures."

This most interesting and lengthy epistle goes

on still—a prolific record of human enjoyment!
" To-day I have been," the Marchioness writes,
" to Peschiera, stopping by the way to visit the
Madonna della Pergolana, who graciously works
many miracles. I saw many images and *ex votos*,
and the beginnings of a fine church, wherein I
prayed for your Excellency's health. Afterwards
I rode through the town, and met the Spanish
castellano, who most courteously escorted me into
the castle. He had only twelve men-at-arms,
and they were of such small stature that I verily
believe I, with my ladies, could most easily have
taken them all prisoners and made myself mistress
of the place! To-morrow I propose to pay
a visit to the island monastery of the Minor Friars,
and then go on to Salò to sleep. "

The next letter to the Marquis describes Isabella's visit to the Franciscan brethren on the
Isola di Garda,—or, as she calls it after the common use,—" *Isola de' Frati.*" " The Friars," she
writes, " welcomed me very warmly, and the
Spanish Captain of Salò, Guglielmo de Castiglio,—
a chamberlain and creature of the Viceroy,—came
there to greet me, accompanied by many soldiers
and civilians in boats. He made me most courteous offers of service. I took him and another
Spanish officer off in my barge, whilst more than
twenty boats, heavily laden, followed in our wake.
There was an extraordinary beating of drums and

blowing of horns, and piercing shouts of ' *Turco !*
Gonzaga ! Isabella !' Thus escorted, I rowed to
Salò under the shore to see the enchanting view.
I landed at the Town Hall steps, where I was
saluted ceremoniously by the Captain of the
town, and vociferously by the immense crowd of
people who had gathered there—so much so that
I felt completely bewildered. Both at the Town
Hall and under the open *loggia* by the lake-side
we were overwhelmed with gifts from the kindly
townspeople of baskets of apples, pears, and
grapes, boxes of sweetmeats, marzipan, wax, and
confetti, and large dishes of every kind of fish.
The *Sindaco* made me a long and eloquent speech,
to which I cordially replied, with my compliments,
on behalf of your Excellency, in whose name, of
course, these honours were paid me : perhaps we
may see the day when it will be very useful to
have these well-disposed people for our friends !
To-day I am staying here to see the place and
visit the monastery. To-morrow I have determined to drive to Gardone and on to Toscolano
to behold once more the lovely gardens. If it is
fine, I shall return to the monastery by water.
On Saturday, being the Feast of the Annuncia-
tion, I shall attend Mass with the nuns. On
Sunday I mean to row across the lake, and sleep,
if possible, at Laciso, in order to see that side ;
and on Monday I shall be at Peschiera, and on

my way back to you and Mantua. I will say no more, only that each time I see another lovely spot I wish most heartily that you may be in sound health, and some day soon come here with me."

At Salò, on that very Lady Day, the Marchioness received a gift she greatly prized from Giangiorgio Trissino, a Vicenzaese poet-friend of Cardinal Bembo. The gift in question was his " *Ritratti delle Donne d' Italia,*" in which he pays Isabella ecstatic homage. He had first been presented to her seven years before, in 1507, at her Court in Mantua, and she had stood his friend when his fellow-townsmen outlawed him and drove him from his home.

This mention of Trissino recalls a romance in which he figures—a romance of the Lake of Garda. Among fair and frail travellers by boat and road was Donna Margherita Pia, sister of Emilia Pia da Carpi and of Alda Pia—the mother of Veronica Gambara. After the death of her first husband— Antonio di Sanseverino—Trissino wooed her for many weary years, all to no purpose. She professed to return his devotion, and in his absence bewailed herself as " *La Margherita la Infelicissima.*" She refused to exchange a state of platonic love for the blessed bond of matrimony. Trissino died at last, and then Margherita buried herself in a convent near Salò, dead to the world and all save Giangiorgio's memory. It is but true to say, however, Trissino was an inconstant fellow, for he had all the time another *innamorata* —the widowed Duchess of Sora—Margherita Cantelina, who was in the suite of Marchioness Isabella during her romantic visits to the Lake of Garda. She it was who first told her mistress of Trissino's "*Ritratti*," as they were rowed across the lake one day. It was just the sort of book to delight a woman of the Marchioness's temperament : it set forth in glowing colours a symposium of fair women and true—much after the manner of Count Baldassare Castiglione's "*Il Cortigiano*." The "Lady" of Trissino's imagination was, of course, none other than his gracious patroness,— the Marchioness of Mantua,—in the description of whose charms of mind and body he quoted Petrarca's apt metaphor :

"*Una Donna piu bella—assai che 'l sole.*"*

Among the sententious speakers in the symposia was Pietro Bembo, in fancy, and he thus extols Isabella : "I know her very well indeed— Isabella, Marchioness of Mantua. I know all her charms. Truly the gods have bestowed upon her all the storied gifts of the sacred Muses. She is a profound lover of poetry, as becomes the ruler of Virgil's own country" Then the speaker goes

* "A Lady as fascinating as the Sun !"

on to describe the person of his heroine, and the glories of her palace, with its " dear little rooms full of rare books, pictures, sculptures, cameos, and gems. . . . She is a woman to see once, maybe, but to love for ever. . . ."

Isabella wrote to Trissino that happy Lady Day her best thanks, and called him " *Il mio magnifico amico.*" " Your letter and verses and the delightful little book could not have found me in a fairer or more suitable spot than the riviera of Garda, where we now are, and free to give up ourselves unreservedly to the delights of meditation and poetasting."

The same day—March 28th, 1514—Isabella also wrote to the Marquis—still in Mantua : " Yesterday I was at Grignone, where the inhabitants entertained me with delightful gifts of fish and fruit, but where I had also to listen in the best fashion I could to a very tiresome oration by a pedant in most stilted language. All along the riviera they have received me with regal honours, and have addressed me as ' *Magnifica Signora.*' . . . To-morrow we go back to Sirmione. I have given up Laciso because it was impossible to find suitable accommodation for my ladies." It was at Sirmione that the Marchioness addressed her last letter from Garda to her consort : " The Governor of the Commune," she says, " accompanied me to Salò with two well-found boats, and

very handsomely treated the members of my
suite. To-day has not been without happenings;
for example, my good-looking page Rodolfo attempted to jump from the castle bridge across
the sunken moat, when a wooden post suddenly
gave way, and he fell into the water. Luckily, I
saw him fall, and gave the alarm. A stout pole
was thrown down, upon which he might keep himself afloat until a rope could be obtained, by which
he was ultimately drawn up. Happily, he was
not in the least hurt, but what would have happened to the poor youth had I not witnessed his
fall your Excellency can well imagine."

Elizabetta Gonzaga, the Duchess of Urbino,—
who was often the companion of her sister-in-law
in jaunts on and by the delicious waters of Lake
Garda,—recalls, in letters addressed to the Marchioness, the happy days they spent together in
that romantic paradise of mirrored waters and
echoing woodlands. She rallies her for her success
in playing *Scartino*,—it was a forbear of *Ecarté*,—
to her purse's disadvantage. Women and men
played for high stakes then as now; but *Flusso*,
a game after Isabella's own heart,—where, for her,
all the cards were trumps, and all the tricks her
own,—led its votaries not infrequently into serious
financial difficulties. Duchess Elizabetta had a
confidential chamberlain, one Francesco da Bagni-
cavallo, who had charge of her private accounts,

ELIZABETTA GONZAGA, DUCHESS OF URBINO

G. CAROTO

Uffizi, Florence

To face page 342

and wielded his influence to his mistress's advantage by doling out no more than two packs of cards for a sitting. If more were demanded, the Signore was equal to the occasion with plausible apologies for the meagreness of the supply! Marchioness Isabella never lost her love of gaming; but when she was past her zenith, and her physical charms were surpassed by those of her mental culture and reserve, *Flusso* gave way to *La Primiera* — a less reckless way of dissipating ducats.

Among the family papers of the Gonzagas has been preserved a characteristic little missive written to Federigo Giovanni, Marquis of Mantua. It is dated August 4, 1471, and bears the signature of Yolanda de Predis, a sister of Ambrogio de Predis, the Milanese painter, who is most intimately remembered by his Portrait of " Bona of Savoy." Yolanda was governess to the two daughters of the Marquis—Elizabetta and Maddalena. " They are," she writes, " very well in health, and in the very highest spirits, quite amenable and obedient. I have formed an excellent opinion of the two *Signorine*. They are studious and enthusiastic in their lessons, but are out and about everywhere, and best pleased when they can gallop off together on horseback, one on the saddle, and one on the crupper." The letter would appear to have been written from the villa of Cavriana to the Marquis in Mantua.

To return to the fair Marchioness : her favourite pastime when she visited the borders of her beloved lake took the form of journeys by boat to some beauty-spot or other. These expeditions were quite remarkable, for the number of her guests wellnigh exhausted, not only the energies of her caterers and chefs, but those of the lake fishermen to furnish craft sufficient. Every boatload had its musicians, preferably guitarists. Landed, the merrymakers betook themselves to shady boskets, where dance and song alternated with repast and flirtation. Perhaps the Marchioness's *Festas* inspired literally the brush of Giorgione and Watteau—painters of gallantries ! One very excellent and most popular item of the day's festivity was singing to the guitar, wherein Isabella was easily *prima cantatrice.* Her sweet and melodious voice and her extremely clear enunciation rendered her a dangerous rival for all competitors. Can anything be conceived more delightful than those alfresco pleasure picnics ? Sometimes held in lovely gardens, where the perfumes of roses and oleanders, carnations and acacias, mingled in the sweet fresh air : sometimes on some breezy woodside, where limes and lilacs, horse-chestnut and honeysuckles, screened the amorous sun—green velvet to the feet, cerulean

satin overhead, and gay songsters and gayer
butterflies darting in and out of the crystal spray
of ornamental fountains and the soothing rush of
rivulets ! Very much of the success of the entertainment depended upon the skill and gallantry
of the guitarists. The measures which they
strummed suggested bold love-passages : no dismal
dirges or sorrowful swirls were admissible. The
musician who most effectively touched human
chords was adjudged the laureate, and forthwith
crowned with bays, fresh-gathered, and twisted
wreathwise for his brow by Beauty's hand.

These gatherings of the fair and brave on sweet
Lake Garda's banks, where hand clasped hand
and hearts beat in sympathy, were responsible also
for many bewitching delights—the true kiss of
love—lips to lips. Time out of mind, to kiss the
hand signified dependence and loyalty ; the kissed
cheek displayed equality and ceremony ; the fore-
head touched by the lips told of parental affection ; but none of these was quite in Love's consummate way. It was Isabella of Mantua who
taught her courtiers how to kiss as Cupid wills !
Betrothed couples meeting for the first time after
that ceremony embraced each other's mouths, and
this became a canon of etiquette. Certainly it
had its inconveniences, which sometimes touched
the ludicrous, as exemplified at the first meeting of
Duke Giovanni Galeazzo Sforza of Milan and

Princess Isabella of Aragon. The royal pair advanced towards one another attended by numerous and distinguished suites mounted on horseback ! To kiss the lips was of course impossible, so, after much ado, they dismounted and embraced, whilst grooms held their steeds, despite the mud and dirt, and then loftily reascended to the saddles, and so rode on !

The mention of Emilia Pia,—who was the wife of the Marquis's brother, Antonio di Montefeltro,—a few pages back, recalls intimate touches of feminine civilities which passed between the sister of " *Margherita la Infelicissima* " and the Marchioness of Mantua. Isabella was a devotée of the toilet and all its accessories, and no fair damsel or dame who revelled in the charms of Garda was a more subtle priestess of the cult than Emilia, her sister-in-law. She had many secret nostrums for the preservation and development of personal attributes. To the Marchioness once she sent, with an apologetic letter, a piece of ebon wood shining like most brilliant lacquer, to be used for polishing the nails. " You should," she wrote, " *Magnifica Signora,* rub and rub until you feel a sort of heat. This you may find a somewhat fatiguing business, but you must persevere, and you will be pleased by your exercise !" Beauty-culturist Emilia Pia had other patronesses too, for to the Queen of Naples she despatched a

special wash for the teeth, which she was directed
" to hold in your mouth until you can retain it no
longer, moving it about with the tongue the while."
These recipes bear date March 10, 1505. Donna
Emilia became a widow in 1500, and died in 1528.

Marchioness Isabella, on her part, responded
cordially to all such welcome hints and notions by
returning to their donors delightful little silver
coffrets, exquisitely chiselled and embossed, full
of delicious perfumes, which she had herself con-
cocted. The gardens which she so loved at Toscolano and along the riviera of Lake Garda furnished
ever so many odoriferous blooms, whence sweet
scents could be expressed ; and numberless sweet
herbs, too, were hers for her laboratory. Her
favourite nuns,—Franciscans of the *Isola*,—were,
as is their general wont, past mistresses in the art
of distilling and expressing fragrant perfumes.
Possibly Isabella was quite as much drawn to
their sweet manipulations as she was to their
melodious voices in their convent chapel. Oleander,—single, not double, and both pink and
white,—was the foundation of her functions, and
in its delicate aroma she blended many a wise
admixture of secret artistry. Maybe that which
we now know as " Ess. Bouquet " should be writ
" Este Bouquet," for scents are older than the century in which we live—indeed, the pomegranate was
Mother Eve's pomander, if romancists flatter not !

A very favourite pastime of the Marchioness,
and one "which she indulged in to her heart's
content" under the greenwood tree by Garda's
sparkling ripples, was dancing—not, indeed, as
we understand that delectation, where men and
women romp and perspire together, and think
themselves quite smart ! At the Castle of Ferrara
her mother saw to it that her three pretty
daughters should excel in the cult of Terpsichore.
Isabella, Beatrice, and Lucrezia had for master
the famous professor Lorenzo Lavagnolo. No
captivating step, no bewitching pose, escaped his
acute attention, and his Sovereign's daughters
excelled all damsels at that cultured Court for
graceful carriage and emotional posture. Isabella
held dancing revels in the archpriest's garden
with her many maids of honour. Vivid memories
of such pastoral plays have been preserved to us
in the romantic paintings of Andrea Mantegna,
Pietro Perugino, and Lorenzo Costa, which
adorned the "Paradiso" of Isabella d' Este-
Gonzaga at Mantua. The musical and literary
tastes of the accomplished Marchioness sought
environment suggestive of poetry and beauty.
The grim, dingy old castle was well enough for
State ceremonials, but the gallantries of sympathetic companionship were quite out of place in
those solemn chambers. Within the area of the
Castella Vecchia she created what she called " *La*

Grotta," where she placed her many art treasures, her sweet singing birds, and other captivating pets. The " Grotta " was a series of rooms, loggie, and parterres on the ground-floor of the old castle, which Bonnacolsi and Bartolino da Novara built for the d' Esti. The central apartment was Isabella's Studiolo — her library and workroom. Opening out of it were several small closets,— camerini, they were called,—arranged for quiet tête-à-têtes with poets, philosophers, linguists, and lovers. To her favourite camerino the Marchioness gave the name " Il Paradiso," as marking a serene retreat, wherein, undisturbed by conventions of the Court, she could recline in meditation or converse with such favourite visitors as Battista Guarino and Jacopo Gallino,—her early teachers, —and Pietro Bembo, Baldassare Castiglione, Giovanni Aldomanuco, and Galeazzo Bentivoglio. She loved to lie there at ease and listen to tales of romance and chivalry. Small in size and low in height, with two doors and a balconied window, there was just room for the divan couch, two chairs, a table, and a stool or two. Upon the walls she had painted her own ideas, conveyed by way of compliment to the most realistic painters of the day. To the three already named she added Giovanni Bellini, the Venetian, but he declined the honour, much to Isabella's annoyance. To Mantegna she assigned " Parnassus," and,—when

Bellini refused,—" Minerva Triumphant "; Perugino did the " Combat of Love and Chastity,"—which she disliked immensely, and placed behind her couch. " I do not like it at all—it is too stiff and artificial," she said. " Salò is more beautiful than that, and my ballets were very much more animated and amusing." To Lorenzo Costa, the Marchioness assigned the most captivating subject of them all—" The Court of Isabella." The scene, of course, is the riviera of Lake Garda, where her revels were held, and she was the floral Queen of the Orchard. Costa has very characteristically painted his patroness, and he has represented her as being crowned by the god of Love ! She is the most prominent figure on his panel, beautifully dressed, with her lovely hair artistically coiffured. The martial personage leaning on a halberd in the foreground is Count Castiglione. Donna Paride Ceresara, — the Marchioness's favourite lady of honour,—herself a poetess, an incantatrice, and a brilliant conversationalist,—is standing beside her mistress. Isabella's favourite slave-girl is there, too—a Moorish maiden, seventeen years old, very lovely, but with thick lips—" Niella," she called her. It is a delightful composition, thoroughly descriptive of the fascinating amusements which had for their theatre one of earth's chief beauty-spots. Isabella greatly admired Costa's work, and arranged it between

COURT OF ISABELLA D ESTÈ-GONZAGA

Mantegna's panels in the place of honour. These happy compositions are now in the Louvre ; for, though the " Paradiso " escaped the wholesale destruction of the Lansquenets in 1630, when the castle was reduced to ruins, they have, alas! not been allowed to remain *in situ*. However, a reproduction of half the " Paradiso " has been placed in the Victoria and Albert Museum, with excellent copies of the three pictures, and the name " Isabella " and her motto " *Nec Spe nec metu* " are recorded underneath.

One only *envoi* of Isabella d' Este-Gonzaga is required to complete her story, and it is in the very words of her doting, indulgent husband, Gian Francesco, Marquis of Mantua. In his last will he speaks of his dear wife as possessing " a wonderful mind capable of any undertaking however exalted its nature." The Marquis, who died in 1519, was himself a soldier by profession, of course, but a man also of highly cultured tastes, and a high-toned poet besides. His delicacy of health, to which the Marchioness frequently alludes in her letters, precluded his sharing her pastoral pleasures by the enchanting Lake of Garda. They were married in 1490, and Isabella spent twenty years in widowhood and retirement.

III.

The Palazzo Barbarano at Salò has sheltered, on and off, many a notable visitor. In one of its lofty chambers was born, in 1640, Cammillo Martinengo Cesaresco, whose grandfather purchased the estate from the Marquis Alfiero Pallavicini. As a youth he early entered the military service of the Serene Republic, but, after doing many doughty deeds, he was banished on suspicion of treacherous dealings with the Genoese. Taking arms under the Duke of Parma, the ally of the Grand Duke of Tuscany against Papal aggressions, he attracted the attention of Ferdinando, who, in return for successful strategy, obtained the cancellation of his outlawry. Returning to his home on Lake Garda, laden with riches and honours, he set about the reparation and decoration of the palace, and once more took up his residence there. Like other noted Condottieri, Count Cammillo retained a numerous guard of armed retainers, and entertained many a knight-errant and many a tired warrior. Venus, as is her wont, followed in the wake of Mars, and the sheen of silken skirts made harmony with the glitter of steely swords. In 1668 a very gallant company made rendezvous at Barbarano. The Prince of Florence,—Cosimo, —later Cosimo III., Grand Duke,—returning from a lengthy tour through Europe, spent a consider-

able time on the Lake of Garda as Count Cammillo's guest—ever greatly in his father's confidence.

Some interesting records of that visit have been
preserved in the form of a diary. On Tuesday,
April 30, the princely party embarked at Riva
upon stately barges sent from Salò by Count
Cammillo. Enchanted with the beauty of the
lake, and intoxicated by the sweetness of the air,
they landed at Maderno for a *siesta*, and thence
made way to the marble steps of the palace
landing-place.

" Wednesday, May 2 : Tempted by the serenity
of the weather and the beauty of the lake, abundantly full of delicate fish, with several fishermen's
boats we went to Gargnano, where, when we had
dined, we fished for quite a long time, but caught
very little ; yet what there was, was excellent
eating. Following us all the way were many
boats from Salò, full of musicians and singers,
who discoursed sweetest music all the afternoon
till eventide, when we returned to the palace and
spent the night right merrily. .

" Thursday, May 3 : We went to Maderno to
look over a villa belonging to the Duke of Parma,
with exquisite gardens and some interesting ruins,
and then back to Salò

" Friday, May 4 : We made an excursion to
Isola de' Frati, where the monks provided us with

some delicious fish. We hurried back to the palace to receive an important embassy which had come from Florence to greet his Highness upon his return to Italy. . . .''

Accompanied by the members of the embassy and a great following of Count Cammillo's retainers, the Prince embarked at Salò for Desenzano. The Count went on with his guest as far as Bologna, and even then Cosimo was unwilling to allow him to return home, so great a regard had he for him. The friendship so auspiciously inaugurated never ceased between the Prince and the Count. After he attained the throne, Cosimo III. constantly employed Count Cammillo upon important secret embassies, but he could never prevail upon him to quit Salò and take up his abode in Florence, where the freehold of a palace was conveyed to him. The Count died in December, 1690, at Brescia, upon his way to his beloved palace at Salò. His will, made at Venice, November 3, 1690, directed that his body should be buried at Brescia at the Church of St. Barnabas, where he founded three hundred Masses for the repose of his soul. His estates at Salò, Sirmione, and Rivolletta he entailed, in the Martinengo family, to his next of kin,—he had no child of his own,—but required his heirs to add Cammillo to the family name. The widowed Countess Bianca adopted a young niece, Virginia Corner, to whom

she left what her husband had willed as heiress for
life, and married her to Count Giuseppe Foscarini.
Count Cammillo's renown was that of an intrepid
soldier, a considerate master, and the patron of all
good works; nevertheless, his memory is preserved as the tyrant of a weird legend—" The
Mysteries of the Palace of Count Cammillo "—
still played by local artists.   Therein he is represented as a villain of the deepest dye; he levies
tolls on every passer-by, and no man's life or
land was safe when Count Cammillo sallied forth.
It was said he had a mistress who perverted the
morals of all the youths and damsels of the neighbourhood by her wild example.   They styled her
" *La Violenta Signoretta !*"   How such tales are
brewed and how they mature is well known in
the science of the black art which the Comtessa
professed.   Her incantations, it was said, were conducted in a cave in the gloomy Barbarino ravine
near Gardone, the gem of the riviera.   The region
bears still an uncanny reputation.

Maderno, which so greatly charmed Prince
Cosimo de' Medici, has thus been eulogized:
" *Maderno il Paradiso del Benaco !*"   It was,
perhaps, Marino Sanuto, the historian of Venice,
who first so called that Elysium, where he spent
many hours and days serenely enjoying the fascinations of the lake, ever famous for its gem-
feathered songsters and its pearly-silver fishes, all

" possessed," so said the quaint old story, " with
the intelligence of man and the grace of God."
St. Ercolano, Bishop of Brescia, in the tenth century, was the first herald of the fame of Maderno.
After a life of tempest-tossed devotion, he retired
from the graceless world, and sought repose upon
the lake shore, under the shade of the solemn
cypresses. There he prayed and fasted, and the
fame of his sanctity attracted troubled souls by
scores to seek the secret of his tranquillity. " So
full was the holy hermit of piety and holiness, of
grace and divinity, that not only men and women,
but birds on wing, and fish on fin, and beasts of
the field,—wild and tame,—stopped,—silent at his
voice,—to yield themselves to his will and pleasure,
and with him praise their God." Well beyond the
space of ordinary human life the good Bishop
lived and testified, and then he died. Alas '
peace was not to be for his dead body : Brescia
claimed it, and the lake-dwellers claimed it ;
living creatures came by to hold their Saint. The
contention waxed fierce, but at last the sacred
corpse,—fully vested,—was placed upon a festal-
decorated and candle-lighted barge, with neither
oars nor rudder, and none on board to guide a
course. Drifting hither and thither at the mercy
of the gentle swell, the strange barque now crossed
the lake, but touched no bottom, and back it
pointed, first to Gardone, and then, perhaps in

answer to the prayers of men and other creatures, it came to rest between Maderno and Toscolano, and holy men and humble fisherfolk joined hands to lay the venerated relics in holy ground.

A thousand years later,— when devotion to St. Ercolano still survived,—came champions of his master, the great St. Mark, and planted a winged lion of gold upon a marble column before the shrine; but then the Marquis of Mantua worsted the Venetians, and where had been the recreation cloister of the Saint he built a palace, and laid out glorious gardens and picturesque grottos. It was Marquis Carlo who put up the Casino in 1660, and made it the scene of his orgies. Simple-hearted men and women had erstwhile gathered, with beast and bird and fish, to listen to St. Ercolano ; now there was no place for them, for repro-bates and prostitutes, ruffians and satellites from every corrupt Court, settled on those pleasant shores. They cared not for the natural beauties there spread out : they minded only their own unnatural lusts. Upon the dissolute Prince they preyed, vampire-like, they sucked him dry, and then dropped off, like leeches full of blood, into dishonoured graves, leaving their master—their slave—miserably to die alone.

The Plazzo Martinengo at Salò, with its beautiful environment, drew forth the hearty encomiums of a very notable but eccentric " Lady "—none

other than the celebrated Lady Mary Wortley
Montagu. " I have been pressed," she wrote to
her daughter, the Countess of Bute, " to make a
sojourn at a palace at Salò, on the vast Lake of
Garda. It is altogether the finest place I ever saw.
There are sweet gardens diversified with splashing
fountains, cascades, and statues—many covered
walks, where one is quite sheltered in the hottest
part of the day by the shade of orange-trees as
large as lime-trees in England. A magnificent
open-air bath there is, with statues ; and in the
adjacent fish-ponds the water is so clear that it
causes the fish which are therein to come daily to
eat out of my hand. It is a veritable paradise for
human beings worn and torn in this crazy world."
Lady Mary revelled in the delights of that " corner
of the enchanted lake," as she called it, and recovered much of her natural taste for the beautiful
and the cleanly. Truly, it was a great contrast
for her when she found herself once more in London, and lodged in George Street, Hanover Square.
" I am," she wrote, " handsomely lodged in truth :
I have two very decent closets and a cupboard on
each floor." Horace Walpole's description of this
remarkable woman, only six months before her
sad, sad death, is interesting, if pathetic · " Lady
Mary Montagu is arrived in town ; I have just seen
her. Her avarice, her dirt, and her vivacity have
all enlarged. Her dress, like her language, is a

mixture of many countries—the groundwork rags and the embroidery nastiness '" To such a pass had she come. The squalid environment of London in the uncouth days of Dr. Johnson had blotted out the sweetness of the life she had gloried in at Salò by Garda's healthful waters. But perhaps Walpole exaggerated—men and women did so one hundred years ago, much as they do now, and nothing is so elastic as personal gossip !

The fourth year before the end of the century, in 1796, a French *corps d'armée*, under Saurat, Rusca, and Guyeux, occupied Salò, and the day following the Austrian flotilla appeared off Gargnano. The riviera was devastated—earth's finest garden ravaged. The democratic movement swept over Brescia and the cities of the plain, and Buonaparte was acclaimed by the Martinenghi, Lecchi, Ferraroli, Alessandri, and other noble families. Then came a counterblast, and Marshal Wurmser occupied the shores of Garda with thirty thousand men. Salò was attacked and sacked and the French were cut to pieces. Guyeux pillaged the flour-mills at Barbarano, and then entrenched himself in the grounds of the Palazzo Martinengo—"*un vieux château,*" as Las Cases called it ; "*espèce de forteresse à l'abri d'un coup de main.*" The palace was bombarded from land and lake, and then delivered over to the fury of the peasantry, who sacked and burnt it. Seventy vears later again the palace, which had been restored by Count Lodovico Cammillo, was occupied by a military force : six hundred Garibaldians —patriots of all Italy. So Salò and her suburbs witnessed martial deeds as well as romantic episodes, and her " Lords and Ladies " wept for the brave as well as laughed with the fair !

Gargnano is the northern limit of the Riviera di Garda ; it is still dominated by the thirteenth-century buildings of the famous Franciscan monastery, with their splendid cloisters. Here dwelt, meditated, and worked the pioneers of industry. Their devotion to religion and their enthusiasm for craftsmanship yielded great results. Like the "*Umiliati*" of Tuscany,—mostly Lombardians too, —the friars changed man's heart and altered the forces of Nature. Swords and staves they turned to ploughs and looms. The cloth of Gargnano, the paper of Toscolano, and the cordage of Salò, with the leather work of Riva, commanded every European market. Then came along the warring Scaligers, and, whilst their ladies hunted deer with them in the forests of Mustone, their lordships built fortresses upon the heights, and a chain of Martello towers along the shores right on to Riva. " Riva di Trento," it is called by some, to indicate dependence upon that noted Tyrolean city ; but patriotic Rivese will have none of it. Riva expands like a "Lady's" fan widespread beneath the shadow of Monte d' Oro. One suburb lies right under the precipitous Rocchetta, whence stony trouble often comes in avalanches. The ruined *Bastione,*—watch-tower,—recalls the iron rule of Venice and the exploits of her Condottieri. Those castle walls take one back to still earlier days, for Romans had here a *castrum.* The Church led the way to more modern things at Riva, as elsewhere, and Prince-Archbishop Allemanne of Trent, in 1124, erected a huge episcopal palace fortress. The Scaligers cut off the mitre blazonments, and carved up their " ladders," and then the " Lion of St. Mark," in turn, pulled them down. Thereafter the historic stones became a quarry for ill-conditioned modern builders.

Riva has a patriotic story anent the unhappy " *Patareni.*" The edict of the Pope and the onslaught of the Lord of Verona caused very many fugitives to escape from Sirmione before the vengeance fell. Almost everywhere along the shores of the lake, in twos and threes, and in families, the poor people hid themselves. At Riva and Arco,—farther on towards the mountains,—some rallied, under the leadership of men devoted to the heresy. One such was Frate Dolcino, who in 1303 renounced his vow, and took for his companion, in the propagation of the heresy, a beautiful and high-spirited peasant-girl Margherita. She was born in the wild Val di Ledro, away above the noble falls of Ponale, not many miles from Riva. Attracted one market-day,—as she touted for customers by her mother's side,—by the eloquent words of Dolcino, she ran impetuously up to him, gave him her silver earrings and locket, and asked to be there and then added to his flock. She refused her mother's endearments to win her home, and, broken-hearted, the good Madonna went painfully back to her village to rouse the menfolk for the rescue of the misguided girl. The morrow of her flight found once more the terrors of the Church launched against the sectaries, and Frate Dolcino hurried off, nor stayed his steps till he trod Vercelli's streets. Margherita remained concealed at Riva, and when the wave of persecution had expended its fury, she and some seven simple women established themselves as "*Amice de' Patareni*," and sheltered sufferers for mistaken conscience. She became famous as an advocate of the persecuted opinions, but, when news came to Riva, in 1317, that Frate Dolcino had been burnt to death at Vercelli, Margherita elected to share his crown. She gave herself up to the seculars of the Archbishop of Trent, made open profession of her errors, and with scant ceremony and not any pity, she and five of her associates were imprisoned, tortured, and done to death in the dungeons of the castle ; some say, indeed, that they were burnt alive.

Riva is the parent of the national game of

"*Palla.*" As long ago as 1555 one Antonio Scaino, of Salò, published at Riva the earliest treatise on the pastime. The youth of Riva was athletic ever, and the annals of the town have entries of notable games, which attracted strong men and agile youths, and beautiful women and lovable girls to Riva. For example, upon his election as Prince, in 1535, Marchese Alessandro Sforza-Pallavicini welcomed the brave and fair to an octave of pageantry. In 1548 a regatta was added to the list of sports by the *Provveditore* Giulio Donato ; and when the Archduchess Maria of Austria passed through Riva in a gorgeous progress, in 1582, the whole lake-world flocked to pay her homage and to display their champions' prowess and their ladies' charms. The classic *Palla* ground is the town square, where, Sunday in and Sunday out, iron netting covers every pane of glass against volleys of the scudding ball. This is as characteristic a scene as any to be beheld up and down the gracious shores of Garda.

It was Goethe who, speaking of Lake Garda, exclaimed passionately : " No words can express the beauty of this richly dowered spot." He had, in 1786, entered lakeland at Torbole, and he beheld what Countess Lunthieu had spoken of—" little white figs most delicious." He remarked that the doors had no locks, and in place of glass the windows of the houses had oiled paper. " I have

never," he said, "seen an idle woman." He
rowed past Limone, and noted the terraced
gardens, and orchards, with great square white
pergola pillars, bearing beams for the vines to
run along. At Malcesine he met with a weird
adventure. Sitting quietly sketching the ruined
castle, a crowd assembled, and one of the men
demanded roughly why he was drawing. Not
waiting for an answer, he seized the paper and
tore it to pieces ! A peasant woman ran to the
Podestà, and that dignitary came, attended by
his javelin-men. He told the stranger that Malcesine was the frontier town of the territory of
Venice, and that the inhabitants were very suspicious of strangers. He asked Goethe whether
he came from Rome or Milan. " I am," said the
poet, " a native of Frankfort." " Of Frankfort !"
cried a pretty woman in the crush ; " now, Signore
Podestà, we can test this man's veracity, for my
Gregorio lived at Frankfort a long time, and knows
it and its people well." The good Gregorio was
sent for, and said he had heard the name of Goethe
in Frankfort, and he knew it was much respected.
With that he embraced the stranger, and peace
came to Malcesine and its irascible people !
Goethe names all the beauty-spots upon the lake
—Gargnano, Bojaco, Cecina, Toscolano, Maderno,
and Salò, and adds that " the mere mention of
these places raises in my mind the most delightful

memories, but no words can sufficiently express
their charms."

To Malcesine he gives the palm. " It is," he
says, " a garden of olives and myrtles, fit only
for the abode of the gods." It appears, from his
" Diary," that he came upon Garda somewhat
unexpectedly, as though he had not planned to
visit what was, in his day, very much out of the
range of travellers from Germany to Italy. " This
evening," he notes down, " I should have gone
straight on to Verona, but one of the most wonderful works of Nature lay almost at my feet—the
exquisite Lake of Garda—which I would not have
missed, and I have been richly rewarded for going
out of my way."

The *Rocca di Garda*—the Castle of Garda—which
shares with the *Isola di Garda* (*Isola de' Frati*),
by the opposite shore of the lake, the distinction
of giving its modern name to classic " Benaco,"
has a stirring story.

The castle was considered a very proper place
for the confinement of a distinguished princess—
Adelheïd of Burgundy, Queen of Italy. At fifteen
she had been married to the Emperor Lothair,
but, widowed when still a girl, the new Emperor,
Berengario III., determined to marry her to his
son Adelbert, whom, in 950, he proclaimed and
crowned King of Italy. Adelheïd refused to join
her hands with those of the young King. Beren-

gario was furious, and his bad humour was fomented by the Empress-Queen, Willa, who hated
Adelheïd with a right mediæval hatred. Willa,
indeed, sought opportunity to slay her rival, but
Berengario chose another way of bringing the re-
calcitrant Princess to do his will—a way they had
in those strenuous days. He would clap the girl in
prison, and starve her into obedience to his wishes!
She was taken to the Castle of Garda, thrown into
a dark dungeon, with no more than a crust of
bread and a can of water for her daily fare. Willa
hoped the girl would die there, but that she refused
to do, and set about a very worthy task, befriended
by her faithful old nurse, who had been permitted
to follow her to prison. Moza brought her flax
and wool, a spinning-wheel, and its accessories,
and the captive Queen spent her time usefully in
making cloth and garments for poor men and
women. For years she lived upon the fruit of her
industry, subsisting on coarse food, and lying
upon a hard, hard bed. At length a hero came
forth to rescue the Princess. He wore not the
gay uniform of a cavalier, but the sombre habit
of a monk—Frate Martino. By some means or
other he put the sentries off their guard, and bore
his royal burden to a place of safety hard by.
Then, favoured by a moonless night, he rowed with
her across the lake. The pair hid themselves in
the forest above Peschiera, and thence they made

their way to Mantua. There the Frate left his
Queen, and hied him off to Reggio, and confessed
to the Bishop what he had done. The prelate
at once sought out the royal fugitive, and he came
upon her quite unexpectedly in a meadow outside
the city, where she was resting peacefully and
listening to the nightingales. With the utmost
courtesy and gentleness he led her to the Castle
of Canossa in the Emilia.

The story of her escape and her fortitude in
captivity travelled far and wide, and greatly
affected rich and poor—all hearts were touched.
The Emperor Otto—Otto the Great—heard it,
and, inflamed with admiration of Adelheïd's
courage and the story of her beauty and noble
character, he came with an imposing retinue to
Canossa, and there laid his heart and his crown at
the feet of the heroine. The Empress soon became
the lady paragon of all Italy and of folks across
the border. Men and women in distress, in death's
danger, and in need of sovereign aid, sought the
precincts of her palace. She held her Court at
Verona, and none who sought her aid went away
disappointed. When her son mounted the Imperial throne, Adelheïd still held sway in Courts
of equity and chivalry. The romantic abduction
of her lovely daughter Adelazia, by the gallant
young officer Aleramo,—the forsaken baby boy of

24

Acqui,—whilst full of disquietude on account of the unknown perils in their way, appealed to the Empress, now well past her zenith. She had been run away with too, it was true,—but her fairy Prince was by his sacred vows forbidden to taste the joys of his adventure,—and sympathetically she succeeded in softening the Emperor's heart towards the fugitives. Her joy was great when she folded to her bosom her beloved daughter, and fondled the dear children—hers and Aleramo's. The Emperor created Aleramo Marquis of Monferrato, and endowed him with a princely income.

In grateful memory of joys and sorrows shared at Brescia and Cremona, Aleramo and Adelazia bestowed munificent endowments in both cities, whilst the Empress Adelheïd's name is still associated with noble works at Peschiera and Verona.

The *Isola di Garda* (*Isola de' Frati*),—with its sister islets of Olivo, Sogno, and Trunclone,—was bestowed in 879, by Charlemagne, upon the monks of St. Zeno of Verona; but the Religious were not long left in peaceful possession of their fief. It changed hands many a time,—the prey of warring lords,—and years swiftfooted masked man's work and God's with vicissitudes. Seasons, too, of peaceful ownership encouraged art and craft, and fisherfolk and toilers in the soil laboured zealously for home and common good. In 1220 the Emperor Frederic II. made over the rights of proprietorship for faithful services in the field to Condottiere Biemo di Manerbo, on the mainland. After a while the new lord sold a portion of his possessions to St. Francis d' Assisi for a monastery of "*Observanti Minori*"—the first of the Order in the Province of Brescia. Once more pious visions and sonorous " Hours " were wafted on the lemon-scented air, but how short was that religious episode ! Lakeland became again the battle arena of envenomed enemies—the Scaligeri, the Visconti, and the Sforze held in turn the upper hand. Brescians, Veronese, and Mantuans fought out to a finish their harsh disputes, till 1426, when Venice laid all rivals low, and absorbed all Garda and her gracious shores into the integrity of the Serene Republic. When peace reigned again upon that fair riviera,—too lovely for the disfigurements of war,—a man of prayer, a holy hermit, found his way to the little island,—known to him best and many more by the name of *Isola de' Frati*,—and ensconced himself in his solitary cell—sweet-faced San Bernardo di Siena. A century of years, some good, some bad, passed on, and then the joys of the homestead were added to the religious delights of the Isola, for a noted family from Brescia obtained possession—the Lecchi. They dwelt in security, and laid the foundation of the island's literary fame, making it, too, the delightful sanctuary of distinguished refugees. Cesare Arici, Giovito Salvini, Filippo Ugoni, Antonio Giovanni Arrivabene, with the two Camilli, and many others, foregathered under Lecchian auspices, and there, too, Alessandro Fregoso and his son Giacomo, from Genoa, sought asylum. The beneficent rule of the Lecchi gained still another name for the island—*L' Isola Lecchi.* The last hundred years have seen many changes of ownership and interest—Benedetto di Portese, Giovanni Fiorentino di Milano, Barone Scotti di Bergamo, Duca Raffele de' Ferrari di Genova, and, last of all, in 1870, Prince Scipione Borghese. All of these placed their arms and ensigns on the castle walls. They, and members of their families, their guests, retainers, and tenants, all paced the shingle of the beach ; all sought the shelter of the trees, all fished the lake for carp, whilst ladies fair and ladies frail trailed skirts of silk and stuff in storied hall and secret bower—" Lords and Ladies " of Lake Garda.

> " Then, bending back her head,
> With those sweet lips so rosy-red
> Upon his eyes she dropped a kiss,
> Intoxicating him with bliss."
>
> *Sir Theodore Martin, after Catullus.*

BIBLIOGRAPHY

I. ITALIAN AUTHORITIES CONSULTED.

" Ville e Castelli d' Italia." Lombardia e Laghi. Milano, 1909.
"I Tre Laghi." F. Taramelli Pallanza, 1907.
"Viaggio da Milano ai Tre Laghi." Milano, 1764.
"Villa di Delizia di Milano." Dal Rè. Milano, 1763.
"Il Lago di Garda." G. Solitro. Bergamo, 1904.
"Pallanza antica e Pallanza Nuovo " A. Viani. Pallanza, 1891.
"Italia Artistica—Milano." F. Malaguzzi-Valeri. Bergamo, 1905
"Italia Artistica—Bergamo." P. Pescati Bergamo, 1906.
"Italia Artistica—Brescia." A. Ugoletti." Bergamo, 1907.
"Mantova e Urbino." A. Luzio. Torino, 1904.
"Varese vel 1901." A. Godara. Varese, 1901.
"Angera e Arona." L. Beltrami. Milano, 1904.
"Tradizioni e Costumi Lombardi " G. Rosa. Bergamo, 1891.
"Tradizioni Popolari Ticinesi " V Pellandini. Lugano, 1911
"Famiglie Celebré Italiana." P G. Litta. Roma, 1880.
"Della Famiglia Sforza " 2 vols. N. Ratti. Milano, 1901.
"La Vita vel Castello di Milano al tempio digli Sforza." L. Beltrami.
    Milano, 1900.
"Caterina Sforza " 3 vols. G. Pasolini. Roma 1893.
"Illustrate Bergamerchi." P. Locatelli. Bergamo, 1900.
"Il Giorno." G. Parini. Milano, 1624.
"I Promessi Sposi." A. Manzone. Milano, 1818.

Many articles in Serial Publications :
    "Archivio Storico Lombardo." Milano, 1874, etc.
    "Bollittino Storico della Svizzera-Italiana." Locarno, 1878, etc.
    "Arte." Bergamo. "Emporium." Bergamo. "Verbania." Pallanza-
    Intra. "Rassegna d' Arte." Roma.

II ENGLISH AND FRENCH AUTHORITIES CONSULTED.

"Lombard Studies " Countess Martinengo Cesaresco. London, 1902.
"History of Milan under the Sforzas." C. M. Ady. London, 1907.
"Italy, 1494-1790." H M. Vernon. London, 1909.
"The Lake of Como." T. W. M. Lund. London, 1910
"Life of Bartolommeo Colleone." O. Browning. London, 1878.
"Isabella d' Este." 2 vols. J. Cartwright. London, 1903.
"Beatrice d' Este." J. Cartwright London, 1899.
"Milan." E. Noyes. London, 1908.
"Verona." A. Wiel London, 1902.
"The Journal: Letters of Madame de Mont (Queen Caroline's Court)."
    London, 1814-1816.
"Autumn Rambles." Finetta Staley. Rochdale, 1863
"King René and his Seven Queens." E. Staley. London, 1911.
"La Femme Italienne." E. Rodocarnachi. Paris, 1906.
"Historie de Chevalier Bayart." Jacques des Mailles. Paris, 1524.
"L'Univers et ses Peuples." J. Arlaud. Paris, 1885.

Articles in Serial Publications :
    "Gazette des Beaux Arts " Vols. 1888, 1890, 1897.
    "L'Art." Vols. 1877, 1892, 1893.

INDEX

CPSIA information can be obtained
at www.ICGtesting.com
Printed in the USA
LVOW01s1603111115

462082LV00021B/1318/P